CONTENTS

For My Parents
Paul E. Martin
and Dorothy M. Martin

PREFACE

Since the end of the Second World War, there has been a veritable flood of valuable studies on nearly every aspect of the American Revolution. No topic, it seems, has been left untouched, whether ideology, poorer citizens, military engagements, elites, women, loyalists, crowd violence, or constitution making. The Bicentennial celebration, likewise, served to intensify the outpouring of materials, with new essays, pamphlets, monographs, biographies, and general studies appearing with enthusiastic regularity. Even before the national Bicentennial celebration had reached its zenith, it had become obvious that some synthesis would be very helpful, if not intrinsically valuable, for individuals interested in comprehending major issues of the American Revolution. The study that follows, then, is unabashedly intended not only to be a synthesis, but also an interpretive exploration of causes and consequences.

Over the past two hundred years, the American Revolution has been etched in almost every shade of interpretive hue imaginable. Most recently—and in a mood perhaps befitting a national Bicentennial celebration—the era of the Revolution has most often been pictured as a united quest among provincial Americans to protect their liberties, a quest resulting in the creation of the first republican polity in the New World, all of which meant the beginning of the end for feudal, monarchist influences upon mankind.

There can be no doubt that such patterns were at play, most certainly in the minds of the participants, but the human interaction making for revolution and nation making was much more complex than might first appear. Indeed, the push and shove of human relationships form the essential core of the materials that follow. As the story unfolds, the record reveals a rebellion against British authority less committed to the implications of change than once was suspected, but in the end a revolution productive of more profound alterations in human institutions and ideals than the bulk of leaders actually wanted. It was a revolution more sweeping in its implications for a long-term uplifting of humanity than in its immediate accomplishments. More than any other sequence of events in the American experience (and through inadvertence as much as by planning) the American Revolution, despite its narrow and cantankerous beginnings, truly became an agency of lasting change.

In shaping this volume of synthesis and interpretation, the author has benefited from innumerable insights, the vast bulk of which reflect directly upon the work of so many other chroniclers of the Revolutionary period. Beyond these generations of dedicated authors, there has been a committed group of scholars who have accepted with good fellowship the pleas of the author for what must have seemed like unending instruction and guidance. Robert A. Becker, H. James Henderson, Herbert Lasky, and John M. Murrin read early drafts of the first portions of the final manuscript. Their suggestions strengthened immeasurably the later drafts, full portions of which have been given careful scrutiny by Richard H. Kohn, Arthur S. Link, and Carl E. Prince. Messrs. Kohn and Prince not only provided superb commentary, but they forced the author to think with exacting care about the full implications of the text. Professor Link was unfailing in his devotion to the task of making the volume as worthy of its audience as possible. Likewise, David Syrett and Richard H. Kohn provided an education in military history for which the author is most grateful. Errors in fact or substance are of course the responsibility of the author.

No other person has been any more fortunate in having supportive professional colleagues, or in having the opportunity to work for a university with so many helpful associates and friends. At Rutgers University, graduate students Robert J. Babbitz, Carol Petillo, Jill Schumann, Karen Stubaus, and David Szatmary were of unfailing assistance. My good friends, Edward J. Bloustein and Paul G. Pearson, lightened my administrative duties at a critical point that made completion of the manuscript possible. Ellen Hall, Gail Heseltine, Lynn Michalski, Shirley Meinkoth, and Betsy Woodward typed various drafts with extraordinary care and good cheer. All of these as-sociates, along with my wife, Karen, and my parents, Paul E. and Dorothy M. Martin, who constantly encouraged their son not only to be interested in but committed to life—past, present, and future—have made the completion of this volume a pleasure.

James Kirby Martin
Bridgewater, New Jersey

LIST OF
MAPS AND ILLUSTRATIONS

History is entertaining and instructive; but if admired chiefly for amusement, it may yield little profit. If read for improvement, it is apprehended, a slight attention only will be paid to the vast variety of particular incidents, unless they be such as may meliorate the heart.

—John Dickinson,
"Letters of Fabius," 1788

1

The Conspiracy
from Above

Has not his Honor the Lieutenant Governor
discovered to the People in innumerable Instances, a very ambitious and avaricious Disposition? Has he not grasped . . . the most
important offices in the Province into his own
Hands? . . . Is not this amazing ascendancy of
one Family, Foundation on which to erect a
Tyranny?

—John Adams of Massachusetts,
referring to Thomas Hutchinson
and his family, August 15, 1765

NORTH AMERICA
after Treaty of Paris, 1763

— Proclamation Line, 1763

Spanish Possessions

Thirteen Colonies

British Possessions

St. Lawrence R.

NOVA SCOTIA

MAINE DISTRICT (MASS.)

NEW HAMPSHIRE

LAKE SUPERIOR

CANADA

Connecticut R.

Boston

LAKE HURON

LAKE ONTARIO

LAKE MICHIGAN

LAKE ERIE

NEW YORK

Hudson R.

Providence

RHODE ISLAND

CONNECTICUT

New York

PENNSYLVANIA

Philadelphia

NEW JERSEY

DELAWARE

Wabash R.

Ohio R.

Baltimore

Potomac R.

MARYLAND

VIRGINIA

RESERVED FOR INDIANS

Ohio R.

James R.

Cumberland R.

N

NORTH CAROLINA

Tennessee R.

SOUTH CAROLINA

Savannah R.

Alabama R.

ATLANTIC OCEAN

Charleston

GEORGIA

Tombigbee R.

Savannah

Mississippi R.

Chattahoochee R.

0   100   200   300 Miles

WEST FLORIDA

EAST FLORIDA

GULF OF MEXICO

I

Day of Defiance:
August 14, 1765

Dawn came peacefully to Boston on August 14, 1765. For most of the 15,000 inhabitants residing in that bustling provincial capital and northern seaport, the waking hours seemed like those of any other hot summer day. But on this particular morning there was an electric feeling in the air, an expectation that something of great significance was about to happen. Earlier in the year, King and Parliament had approved a plan of uniform, direct taxation for the American colonies. The Stamp Act, as that legislation came to be known, was unprecedented; for the first time in the history of Britain's North American provinces, King and Parliament were about to take money directly out of colonial pocketbooks. Ministers in England thought that Parliament had that right: the vast bulk of Americans disagreed. Only their local representative assemblies, such as the General Court in Massachusetts, they claimed, possessed the power of direct taxation.

Provincial citizens at first seemed confused about how to respond to what they called taxation without representation. Some Bostonians were about to clear up the confusion. On the morning of August 14 the first sign of organized resistance appeared when effigies of Andrew Oliver, Massachusetts' stamp distributor-designate, and Lord Bute, former head of the King's cabinet and close friend of George III, were found dangling from what became known as the Liberty Tree. The enraged royal governor, Francis Bernard, ordered local magis-

trates to remove the effigies, but to Bernard's dismay not even the
sheriff dared to take them down. The climate was that of intimidating
defiance. To touch the two effigies was to invite the retributive wrath
of Boston's newly formed "Sons of Liberty"—artisans, mechanics,
apprentices, day laborers, merchant seamen, and other "street
people"—who were willing to employ physical coercion against
those who defied their will.

The Boston Sons of Liberty organization, a model for similar groups
springing up throughout the American provinces, had taken its name
from a phrase uttered during the Stamp Act debates in Parliament.
One vehement opponent of the tax plan, supporting the American
position before the House of Commons, asked with rhetorical
flourish: "They nourished by *your* indulgence?" Of course not. "They
grew by your neglect of them. As soon as you began to care about
them, that care was exercised in sending persons to rule over them, in
one department and another . . . sent to spy out their liberty, to mis-
represent their actions and to prey upon them; men whose behavior
on many occasions has caused the blood of those *sons of liberty* to
recoil within them. . . . And believe me, remember I this day told
you so, that same spirit of freedom which actuated that people at first,
will accompany them still."[1]

The phrase stuck. To Andrew Oliver and other royal officials in
Massachusetts, the Sons of Liberty were a terrifying, brutal, and destructive mob. From a less jaundiced perspective, the Sons, in Boston
and elsewhere, represented one important weapon in the arsenal of
American resistance. They were the indispensable artillery in what
many persons were coming to believe was a righteous battle against
Englishmen who would enslave Americans by usurping their political
liberties.

The Boston Sons of Liberty came largely from the class of skilled
and unskilled laborers. Prior to 1765, two workingmen's groups—the
North End and South End associations—dominated in the streets and
mainly fought among themselves. The two groups enjoyed making
mayhem on each November 5, known as Guy Fawkes's or Pope's Day
(referring to an alleged Catholic plot in 1605 to blow up Parliament).
The two Boston associations annually paraded through the streets on
that date, their leaders carrying before them stuffed effigies of the
devil, the pope, and the Roman Catholic (Stuart) pretender to the
British throne. Winding through the streets, the crowds eventually
moved toward each other. Mostly they were giving vent to widespread anti-Catholic feelings while acknowledging fears of satanic
forces in the world. But the associations were also building toward

the day's climax, oftentimes a bloody fist fight—Northenders against Southenders. The Pope's Day street fighting was so brutal in 1764 that at least one participant died.[2]

Boston's popular political leaders, led in 1765 by the brilliant but erratic James Otis, Jr., and the pugnacious Samuel Adams, wanted to turn these warring associators away from street fighting toward the defense of broader community interests. Although no one knows under what circumstances, the popular leaders met with representatives of the two associations sometime after passage of the Stamp Act, but before August 14. The representatives agreed that everyone's energy could be more judiciously spent in resisting imperial threats to American rights; the two groups thus melded into one as the Sons of Liberty. Whenever necessary, the popular leaders intended to tap the Sons' threatening force and to employ it against all those who compromised American rights. August 14 proved to be the first of many such days.

Typical of such alleged subverters of American liberty were Governor Bernard and Andrew Oliver (the latter was also the province's secretary); Oliver's brother, Peter, an associate judge of the superior court; and their brother-in-law, Thomas Hutchinson, lieutenant governor under Bernard, as well as chief judge of the superior court. They seemed to be endangering American rights by their execution of imperial policies in Massachusetts. To make matters worse, they were longstanding political enemies of Otis, Adams, and other popular leaders—men who represented local interests in factionalized provincial politics. To Adams, Bernard's "royalist" supporters were power-hungry sycophants, eager for the rewards of high office and unwilling to suppress their political greed even for the sake of long-established liberties. Andrew Oliver's willingness to administer the "enslaving" Stamp Act seemingly proved that point. These men, Adams and his cohorts believed, had to be stopped. And so August 14 became a moment of confrontation.

It was an anxious day for the hundreds of citizens who viewed the effigies. Toward nightfall, the Liberty Boys and interested onlookers gathered about the Liberty Tree, awaiting the signal for further action. It came when the street leaders tore down the effigies. Oliver's likeness no doubt replaced the devil's countenance, while Bute's related directly to England's tyrannical Stuart kings. Bute's surname was Stuart, and he was distantly related to that Scottish royal family. Symbolically, the effigies meshed Guy Fawkes's day themes with those portending more immediate acts of imperial tyranny.

With the effigies held high before them, the crowd moved forward toward Boston's docks, where a new warehouse belonging to Andrew Oliver was under construction. Rumor had it that the dreaded stamped paper was to be stored in the warehouse. The crowd leveled the building within a matter of minutes. It was only a short distance to Oliver's gracious home. Moving quickly, the Liberty Boys reassembled on a hill overlooking Oliver's property and celebrated around a large bonfire which in time consumed the effigies. A few participants broke into Oliver's home, ransacking the first floor while enjoying his excellent wine collection in the cellar. Oliver and his family had wisely fled the premises.

The demonstration ended at about midnight. Oliver obviously understood the message. Although only his property had been victimized this time, the threat of personal harm was clear. Early the next morning, Oliver, "despairing of protection, and finding his family in terror and great distress . . . came to the sudden resolution to resign his office before another night."[3] His resignation made it virtually impossible for the Stamp Act to be administered in Massachusetts when it was to go into effect on November 1. No one was foolish enough to offer to take Oliver's place. And none of the Sons of Liberty ever had to defend himself in court for participation in the riot. If it had not been known before, the "popular" faction and the Liberty Boys had demonstrated how feeble royal authority was in the face of organized violent intimidation. Perhaps that is why Samuel Adams later wrote that August 14, 1765, was a day which "divert[ed] the impending stroke of ruin aimed at ourselves and our posterity. . . . A day which ought to be forever remembered in America. . . . The people shouted; and their shout was heard to the distant end of this Continent."[4]

Boston had set the tone of violent resistance, as it would do time and time again during the deepening imperial crisis after 1765. Equally important, a clear fusion had occurred between working people and popular party leaders, resulting in a powerful alliance for resisting British authority. Sons of Liberty in other provinces quickly expanded upon Boston's example, bringing other stamp distributors to their knees. All of the protesting seemed to pay off when Parliament revoked the Stamp Act in March 1766. Americans cheered mightily, but the celebrating stopped once new parliamentary plans received the King's approval—again and again.

Notes

1. Colonel Isaac Barré spoke these words, as recorded in Jared Ingersoll to Thomas Fitch, London, February 11, 1765, Connecticut Historical Society *Collections*, XVIII (Hartford, Conn., 1920), 322–330. Spelling in all quotations has been changed to conform to modern usage.

2. Dirk Hoerder, "Boston Leaders and Boston Crowds, 1765–1775," *The American Revolution: Explorations in the History of American Radicalism* (ed. A. F. Young, DeKalb, Ill., 1976), 233–271, and *Crowd Action in Revolutionary Massachusetts, 1765–1780* (New York, 1977), 1–118. For a discussion of Fawkes's day themes and oral traditions among people who left few if any written records, see Alfred F. Young, *The Crowd and the Coming of the American Revolution: From Ritual to Rebellion in America, 1745–1776* (New York, forthcoming).

3. Thomas Hutchinson, *The History of the Colony and Province of Massachusetts-Bay* (3 vols., ed. L. S. Mayo, Cambridge, Mass., 1936), III, 88.

4. Adams as "Candidus," *Boston Gazette*, August 19, 1771, *The Writings of Samuel Adams* (4 vols., ed. H. A. Cushing, New York, 1904–1908), II, 201.

II

Tensions and Frustrations: The Anglo-American World Nearing Rebellion

The rioting in Boston did not end on August 14. New rumors began to spread. Citizens were whispering it about that tall, angular Thomas Hutchinson had secretly helped London ministers to draft the Stamp Act. And there was no way for Hutchinson to rebut the rumormongers. On the evening of August 26, 1765, Liberty Boys, turned out by their street leader, South End cobbler Ebenezer Mackintosh, made two threatening forays before finally descending on Hutchinson's home, considered Boston's most palatial residence. The anguished Lieutenant Governor later summarized the scene: "They continued their possession until daylight; destroyed, carried away, or cast into the street, everything that was in the house; demolished every part of it, except the walls, as far as lay in their power."[1]

Ostensibly, Hutchinson had been the victim of a vicious, unfounded rumor. He had had nothing to do with the writing of the Stamp Act. The destruction of his property, in fact, can only be comprehended within the broader setting of the tensions and frustrations characterizing political life within the British Empire during the years immediately preceding the War for American Independence—years in which that Empire was at one of the peaks of its power and grandeur.

One source of tension was ministerial favoritism shown toward men like Hutchinson. Hutchinson came from distinguished old New

England stock and grew up in Boston surrounded by family and friends of wealth, education, and political distinction. He attended Harvard College and was a diligent student. He then entered the family's prospering mercantile firm, demonstrating a high aptitude for business. Before his twenty-sixth birthday, Bostonians confirmed Thomas as the successful son of a distinguished family by naming him to the Boston Board of Selectmen; a few months later they elected him to the lower house of the Bay Colony's General Court. That was the beginning of a burgeoning political career. As royal governor of Massachusetts during the early 1770s, Hutchinson tried desperately to preserve the world that had been so good to him and to others of his favored standing.

Thomas Hutchinson was from one of a small number of "older" families in the late colonial period with strong imperial ties stretching back for as many as five or six generations. Not all older families were prospering, but those that were made up an important element in an identifiable provincial-imperial socioeconomic and political elite. Families such as the Hutchinsons and Olivers in Massachusetts and their counterparts elsewhere may have represented 2 to 5 percent of the population, but they had come to control a much larger proportion of the available wealth. A fair over-all estimate is that 10 percent of the late provincial population held at least 50 percent of the measurable wealth.

The data now available suggest a progressive concentration of property holdings into fewer and fewer provincial hands during the eighteenth century. For the decade 1690 to 1699 in the northern Chesapeake area, for example, only 1.6 percent of the population possessed estates inventoried at over £1,000 sterling. The figure jumped to 3.9 percent for the decade 1750–1759, but 90.4 percent still held less than £500 sterling (1730–1739), as compared to 96.3 percent in the 1690–1699 decade. Given over-all increases in the standard of living as well as in the value of property, the northern Chesapeake region probably contained more poor families in 1740 than in 1690. In Chester County, a commercial farming area near Philadelphia, the distribution of wealth increasingly favored the population's top decile. In 1693 that group held 23.8 percent of the taxable wealth, as compared to 38.3 percent in 1800. At the same time, the poorest 30 percent was losing significant ground (17.4 percent of taxables in 1693 as compared to 3.9 percent in 1800). Greatest stratification in wealth by comparison, existed in the cities. Boston's 1687 tax list reveals that the wealthiest 10 percent owned 46.3 percent of the taxable property; by 1771 the figure for the same group had climbed to 63.4 percent, with families like the Hutchinsons and Olivers (the top 5 percent) controlling 48.7 percent of the total taxable wealth. Similarly, the wealthiest 10 percent of Philadelphians held 46 percent of the taxable wealth in 1693 and 72.3 percent in 1774. In both cases, the bottom 30 percent had infinitesimal property holdings.[2]

A widening gap between rich and poor, most notably in the cities, had come to denote the distribution of provincial property on the eve of rebellion. The numbers of working-class propertyless poor and struggling day laborers were rising steadily, so rapidly that public relief subscriptions seemed to be getting out of hand. The "poorer sort," the "rabble," or the "meaner sort," as the "better sort" often referred to them, usually formed the backbone of urban street associations. Many of those rioters in Boston who joined in the destruction of Thomas Hutchinson's home were venting their anger over straitened economic circumstances, aggravated by a short but sharp downturn in the imperial economy after 1763. The gap between expectation (the dream of prosperity and opportunity) and reality (inexplicable poverty) was vividly real for the poor. It was an important tension-producing gap, finding one outlet of dissatisfaction in the urban, anti-imperial popular faction-Liberty Boy alliances which developed as part of the Stamp Act crisis.[3]

Figures on wealth distribution, scattered as they are, also indicate the existence of a relatively large, modestly prosperous provincial middle class. Over-all, 50 percent of the late colonial citizenry may have fallen into this category. Many such citizens lived among the very wealthy and the poor in older seaboard settlements and the cities—in 1760 the five most populous urban areas included Philadelphia (23,750), New York (18,000), Boston (15,631), Charleston (8,000), and Newport (7,500). There they practiced their skills as craftsmen and artisans, doing everything from making furniture to getting out newspapers. By far the greatest number of middle-class citizens inhabited the countryside, where they worked the land for respectable, although in many cases spartan, livelihoods. Freehold and tenant farmers normally produced for the market, hoping for some profit for their labors. Quite rare were self-sufficient, self-contained farming households producing exclusively for the family unit. With 80 percent or more of the provincial population engaged directly or indirectly in agriculture, normal in a preindustrial economy, the late provincial landscape had a bucolic cast, becoming more roughhewn as one traveled westward toward the great wall of the Appalachians.

The presence of so many freehold farms created among some contemporaries a sense that the yeomen were universally prospering.

Contemporary commentators often stressed the theme of abundance. "It does not seem difficult to find out the reasons why the people multiply faster here than in Europe," wrote one mid-century observer. "As soon as a person is old enough he may marry in these provinces without any fear of poverty. There is such an amount of good land yet uncultivated that a newly married man can, without difficulty, get a spot of ground where he may comfortably subsist with his wife and children."[4] Because of the abundance of cheap, arable land and the shortage of laborers, commentators often assumed that anyone willing to work could get ahead.

In reality, "getting ahead" in eighteenth-century America was quite difficult for those lacking family advantages. Moreover, the process was often accompanied by upsetting psychological experiences. The fact that the population in the thirteen provinces exploded between 1700 and 1760 exacerbated conditions. In the former year, a modest number of 250,000 people inhabited the vast open space, but that number had multiplied to nearly 1,600,000, including black slaves, by 1760. Population was doubling every twenty years, both from natural increase and from heavy immigration from the Old World. The phenomenon of "overcrowding" became a disrupting source of psychological strain for maturing adults in older seaboard farming communities (primarily in New England and the middle colonies). Children of second- and third-generation families were reaching adulthood only to find that family landholdings had been so subdivided through the generations that not enough acreage existed to support their own families. The practice of partible inheritance, or dividing property evenly among heirs, intensified overcrowded conditions. Lacking enough land from the family patrimony to sustain themselves in the communities of their youth, maturing adults had to accept the psychologically bleak prospect of leaving behind all that was familiar and stable and to face the task of beginning life anew somewhere else. Thousands pushed out to the frontier; many also drifted into the cities, where they swelled the numbers of unskilled, unemployed day laborers.[5]

A booming population growth rate thus abetted rather heavy horizontal and vertical (largely downward) mobility rates among mid-century provincials. The dream of opportunity and abundance was fading for countless individuals in the decades immediately preceding the 1760s. On an individual level, this meant that thousands of "historically silent" citizens were descending into a state of economic peonage. It was of little comfort to them that the European socioeconomic structure, with its fixed class lines, gave the more fluid provincial system the aura of unbounded opportunity. Rather, all that they could hope for was that, with luck and good fortune, they could reenter the middle-class realm of property holders within their own generation. Only because of this hope did the statement that "this is one of the best poor man's Countries in the World" have any meaning.[6]

Luck and good fortune were rare, however; and the reality on the eve of the Revolution was that the ranks of poor were expanding rapidly. Personal poverty in turn predisposed many suffering citizens to lash out against new imperial policies. The poor, by striking back at policies which threatened to bury them even deeper in oblivion, were protecting their interests while venting frustrations over personal degradation.

The bulk of uprooted eastern provincials pushed westward rather than into the cities, exterminating Indians in search of a living. By the 1760s, the frontier line of settlement neared the Appalachian barrier, which stretched in a wide southwestward arc from northern New England to the newest mainland colony of Georgia. People would soon be spilling over into present-day Kentucky and Tennessee. The westward rush was caused not only by overcrowded conditions in the East, but also by the influx of thousands of Germans and Scots-Irish fleeing degraded economic and political conditions in the Old World. These migrants, along with representatives from many other European stocks, poured into the Middle Colonies, normally debarking in Philadelphia before first pushing westward, then moving as far south as western South Carolina and Georgia. In the South they took to freehold farming, forming a barrier between coastal plain plantation operators, on the one hand, and western Indian nations, on the other hand. The Scots-Irish in particular earned a deserved reputation as Indian fighters.

Population in the South grew rapidly, not only because of natural increase and frontier settlements, but also because of the forced introduction of black Africans into the North American labor pool. In 1700, there were approximately 27,000 blacks in the provinces, and Virginia held 60 percent of them. By 1760, an estimated black population of 325,000, most of whom were caught in the dehumanizing web of chattel slavery, dotted the American landscape. The bulk of the slave population lived south of Pennsylvania, although slavery existed in the North. In 1760, 30 percent of Maryland's population was black; in Virginia, 40 percent; in North Carolina, 30 percent; in South Carolina, 60 percent; and in Georgia, 33 percent. The total

Afro-American population for New England and the Middle Colonies was under 4 percent. Africans were the most numerous non-English immigrants entering the American provinces during the eighteenth century.

Black labor in tobacco production did not become an important element in the Chesapeake Bay area until late in the seventeenth century. For one reason, England had adequate labor supplies. From the founding of the first settlements until about 1660, England's economy was sputtering along at best. Starving, unemployed Englishmen entered the system of indentured servitude by the thousands, selling their labor for fixed terms in return for passage to the New World. (Many Germans employed a similar system in the eighteenth century, signing redemptioner contracts, to assure passage to America and the opportunity of someday acquiring land for themselves and their families.) Mortality rates among early indentured servants were high; individuals succumbed to excessive labor demands in tobacco cultivation and to rampant disease. Those who survived their terms of bondage gained their "freedom dues," which included clothing, agricultural tools, and often even small parcels of land. After 1660 and a sharp upturn in the English economy, fewer Britons found themselves facing debtors' prison or sturdy beggar status; the New World was no longer attractive. But the insatiable demand for labor of any kind in order to reap profits from America's abundant land remained. Africans became the substitute source of muscle power; consequently, black human cargoes were increasing precipitately by the turn of the century.

In the early years of the struggling Chesapeake Bay settlements, Englishmen did not clearly define African laboring status as both a permanent and inheritable badge. The concept of chattel slavery in North America developed only through time. By 1700, whatever legal rights Afro-Americans in the tobacco-planting colonies had once enjoyed had been lost. They could neither sue nor testify in court; they could not own weapons; they could not intermarry with whites. They were becoming human property, dependent for just treatment upon the whims of planters or plantation overseers.

Planters at first bought primarily young black males, who seemed to be more physically prepared than women for arduous field work. With an initial sex ratio heavily favoring men, natural population increase among first-generation Afro-Americans was negligible. Disease also heightened mortality rates among first-generation slaves, as compared to native-born blacks, as it had done earlier with whites.

Since occupational stratification (skilled labor or housework as compared to field work) developed very slowly, there was no way to avoid the debilitating drudgery of tobacco production.

In addition, blacks were at first widely spread out among hundreds of white owners. In Maryland before 1710, more than 50 percent of the Africans labored on plantations with ten or fewer slaves; nearly one third were on plantations with five or fewer slaves. This wide geographic dispersion made it difficult for blacks to communicate with one another and to maintain their African cultural traditions, which caused feelings of isolation and loneliness. Only in the eighteenth century did Chesapeake Bay Afro-Americans begin to enjoy more stable family lives and expanded opportunities for relief from field work. The sex ratio began to balance, and the increased size of some plantations necessitated a greater degree of job differentiation. As more blacks became concentrated on fewer plantations, the strength of comradeship alleviated the despair of cultural isolation.[7]

It is ironic that these "positive" trends (making life in the provinces a bit more tolerable for chattel slaves) reflected directly the pattern of increased stratification in provincial wealth which was making life less comfortable for so many white inhabitants. Yet blacks still faced the process of legal dehumanization, which varied from region to region but had common motivating factors everywhere. White provincials defined blacks as being outside the pale of English liberties. They thought that Africans were "heathenish," "savage," and uncultured, reflecting their pejorative attitudes toward darker skin colors.

The process of legal dehumanization may be traced by using South Carolina as an example. There, the formation of racial attitudes paralleled other developments. The first Carolina Afro-Americans contributed immeasurably to local knowledge about rice production, which, along with indigo, became important sources of income for white Carolina planters. But that knowledge went unrewarded; in a certain sense, in fact, it backfired. Huge profits from the production of rice, which required enormous amounts of labor, encouraged turn of the century Carolinians to demand more and more slave laborers from Africa. By 1710, there were as many black as white Carolinians; by 1740, there were twice as many blacks as whites. Planters drove their slaves, caring little about human needs or life itself, because they could replenish the supply so easily, thanks to profit-hungry slave traders, many of whom were New Englanders. Blacks in Carolina resisted in a variety of ways: they broke tools, burned valuable buildings, stole goods, and ran away. Nevertheless, the system of slave labor took firmer hold as the years passed.

Denigrating white racial attitudes, the demands of rice production, and individual incidents of black resistance culminated in the Stono Uprising in September 1739, when a small band of recently imported Angolan Africans rose up near the Stono River and began a bloody march toward Florida. To clear their path, the slaves killed at least twenty whites before the militia trapped them, inflicting death on all rebels as a warning to other slaves. The South Carolina assembly, in reaction, did legislate penalties for planters who pushed their slaves too hard; but those penalties were designed to protect the numerically smaller white community, not the blacks. Moreover, the assembly passed a comprehensive Negro Act, strictly circumscribing the ability of slaves to gather freely, acquire any education, earn extra money, or maintain any rights of privacy. Fear, above all else, influenced the development of these slave codes, which had completed the process of legal dehumanization for Afro-Americans in South Carolina by the mid-eighteenth century.[8]

While blacks were falling into abject slavery, the Byrds, Carters, Fitzhughs, and Lees were emerging as representatives of the great white families of the Chesapeake Bay area and joining other aggrandizing family units like the Pinckneys and Rutledges in South Carolina, the DeLanceys and Livingstons in New York, and the Hutchinsons and Olivers in Massachusetts. They were at the pinnacle of the provincial socioeconomic pyramid. Their scions were gentlemen of landed, planter, mercantile, and professional wealth. Some of them had strong imperial connections and were enjoying the Crown's favor as royal officeholders in America. Slightly below them in the socioeconomic structure were other prospering individuals (merchants and lawyers in smaller communities, skilled artisans, large-scale commercial farmers, and land speculators) who could aspire to and occasionally did earn enough wealth to be included in the late provincial socioeconomic elite, although they rarely earned free access to the social world of the great families. Often these "lesser" men in the elite served in colonial assemblies, and it was from their ranks that a number of popular leaders emerged during the imperial crisis.[9] Then came the freehold farming and skilled laboring middle class, numerically dominant among whites, but losing ground in the years surrounding 1760 to the growing "poorer sort" category. Below everyone else were the small numbers of free blacks (perhaps 2 percent of the Afro-American population) and black slaves, for whom everyday conditions seemed to be improving, except in the psychologically vital area of human rights.

Afro-Americans were not the only provincial Americans who held little claim to John Locke's vaunted trilogy of "life, liberty, and property." The many persons of indentured redemptioner status, women, and minors also had to depend upon the patriarchal goodwill of the white male population. And unpropertied white males could not vote or otherwise participate in normal channels of political decision making. If they voted, theorists argued, they would become the tools of willful demagogues who would manipulate their votes to build excessive personal power, presumably against the higher interests of the state. Thus unpropertied men and women in general who wanted to express themselves politically had few alternatives beyond controlled violence and rioting. Crowds gathered with some regularity in prerevolutionary America to voice their fury against such varied targets as advocates of smallpox inoculation, whorehouse operators, and British naval press gangs, which swept the streets looking for manpower to use and abuse on royal naval vessels. What was unique in 1765 was that popular leaders were beginning to guide crowds toward definite anti-imperial acts of intimidation.

Poorer women did participate in crowd activity. They were actively involved when the remains of Andrew Oliver's warehouse fueled the August 14 bonfire. And because they did participate, they enjoyed some freedom of expression that women of higher socioeconomic status did not.

By law, women in general, especially married women, were dependent upon men. According to Blackstone's *Commentaries*, the great legal reference work after the mid 1760s, "By marriage the husband and wife are one person in law; that is, the very being or legal existence of the woman is suspended during the marriage, or at least is incorporated and consolidated into that of her husband."[10] If a woman brought property to her marriage, she no longer retained control over it. If the husband wasted that property, she had little recourse in the courts. The assumption was that a wife should respect the husband's "superior" acumen, no matter how wrongheaded he might actually be.

Only widows and unmarried women retained some semblance of legal personalities; although they could not vote, they could in restricted circumstances engage in business pursuits, keeping profits for themselves or their heirs. By law, every widow was to receive one third of her husband's property as a life dowry, but the property would automatically pass to children when the widow died. In older seaboard settlements, where sex ratios had evened out, widows remarried with decreasing frequency, but in newer communities where men normally far outnumbered women, widows tended to remarry at much faster rates. Indigent widows who lacked inheritances or who used up their inheritances to keep themselves alive, normally became wards of their communities, and as such they were expected to work for their keep. At least one eastern New England community solved the problem by auctioning off its widows, apparently to men from western communities where marriage partners were scarce. No one seemed to think that such activities were degrading, since the dominant assumption was that marriage represented the normal state for eligible women because it kept the vast majority of them in subservient, domestic roles.[11]

By the mid-eighteenth century the general configuration of provincial values had hardened in many ways, especially with respect to notions about wealth, social standing, and access to political power. Since a rigid family bloodline class structure had not developed in the provinces, personal and family wealth had become the great desideratum in determining a citizen's social status. While men of modest family economic standing could dream of joining other "Gentlemen of the first Rank and Fortune," the reality was that families of great wealth preferred to live within their own orbits and intermarry among themselves.[12] Increasing concentration of property in the elite's hands helped to harden class lines; it also effected a tighter relationship between socioeconomic standing and the privilege of holding political office.

The provinces were maturing into *deferential* societies. The long-standing feudal assumption that there was an indivisible relationship between leadership in state and leadership in society had become pervasive, at least in the minds of the "better sort." The best families were dominating the highest political offices to which they had access, including elective seats in the lower houses of assemblies, appointive seats on governors' councils, and the highest provincial judicial offices. The Crown insisted that only persons "well affected to our government and of good estates and abilities and not necessitous persons or much in debt" be nominated by royal governors.[13] As a result, a closer congruence had emerged between the possession of an established family name and full access to important provincial offices, except in the three southernmost colonies, where the home government practice of appointing nonnative "placemen" to high provincial posts caused consternation among elite planters, merchants, and lawyers.

The elite families wanted their full share of offices, preferably at the highest levels of the three tiers of provincial government. Governors like the harassed Francis Bernard of Massachusetts occupied the highest tier. In theory, royal and proprietary governors had extensive prerogatives. Commissions and instructions, issued to each new governor, stressed that all colonists must conform to the rules and laws governing the Empire. As petty potentates, governors could issue election writs, convene assemblies, and then in turn prorogue (or dissolve) them if assembly actions were at variance with defined imperial needs. They could also veto legislation and nominate or appoint a vast array of colony-wide or local officials. Moreover, governors had the power to name the highest ranking officers in the provincial militia, of which royal governors were the commanders in chief. Outside New England, they could distribute provincial lands to aggrandizing colonists. All told, their prerogatives held the theoretical potential of building and supporting large and favored "royal" or "court" party followings.

But much of the power of royal governors was on paper, for they had suffered a steady deterioration of their prerogatives before the 1760s. The London government had not given them much support between 1700 and 1760, the so-called "era of salutary neglect." In many provinces, governors depended upon elective lower houses for their annual salaries, and many had to concede legislative points in return for a regular income. The governors, receiving scant backing from superiors in England, generally had failed to fend off aggressive assemblymen, led by those provincial gentlemen who did not have broad enough connections to obtain higher appointive offices. By attacking royal prerogatives, assembly leaders were building authority at the level of government to which they could realistically aspire. They were establishing the *de facto* claim that American provincial assemblies were "little parliaments," possessing the same legislative rights over particular provinces that Parliament exercised over the British Isles. The question of the full range of legislative authority, especially in matters of taxation, was to become a vital issue after 1760.

Assemblies in full meeting represented the second and third tiers of provincial governments. Governors had the right to nominate councilors, as appointees to the upper houses were called. Crown officials sustained nominations. Sometimes shrewd governors were able to build royalist support by making judicious nominations, thereby aiding their cause in contending with elected assemblymen in lower houses. Councilors not only served as gubernatorial advisers; they also had legislative functions as members of the upper house. Sometimes, too, they had judicial responsibilities. In Virginia, planter gentry councilors served as the highest provincial court in civil and criminal cases. Popularly elected assemblymen initiated the bulk of legislation, which ranged from currency and taxation bills to acts providing for local militia defense. When provincial politics became particularly intense, lower houses normally were the bases of operations for "country" or "popular" faction leaders and their allies in combating governors and their royalist supporters.

The tripartite structure provided an arena for provincial political decision making. Of equal importance was what each branch signified in traditional political terminology. The eighteenth century lay at the end of an epoch of hierarchical thinking, stretching back into ancient times. Political theorists assumed that there were three sociopolitical orders: the monarchy, the aristocracy, and the democracy. "Democracy" referred to the common order of people. It also could refer to a system or style of politics in which direct, popular decision making occurred. But the most learned minds knew from their historical studies that democracies rarely worked. These minds, taking their cue from Aristotle and other ancients, assumed that the *demos,* or the general mass of citizens, lacked a sufficient stake in society to be anything but self-interested and destructive of the public good if in power. Eighteenth-century gentlemen used the term "democracy" interchangeably with such epithets as "lower sort" and "rabble."

Indeed, well-educated Englishmen believed that too much authority in the hands of any order was dangerous to liberty. In the British government, the King represented the monarchy; the House of Lords, the aristocracy; and the House of Commons, the democracy. Every inquiry into ancient and modern history showed that balance among the orders in government was essential to the commonweal's continued health and stability, as well as to the preservation of the known rights, privileges, and liberties of all Englishmen.

Good eighteenth-century English Whigs, vividly recalling the previous century of Stuart absolutism, focused their concerns upon keeping the Crown in check. When the last Stuart king, James II, fled the realm in 1688 during the "Glorious Revolution," lords and commoners in Parliament rededicated themselves to constraining any future king or queen who would become a tyrant. Whigs cheered as Parliament gained much greater authority in political decision making. The constitutional balance had been restored; the British lion had been declawed. No longer, if carefully checked, would it threaten such liberties as taxation only by elected representatives or trial by jury.

Ordered, mechanistic reasoning in political theory was one characteristic of the Age of Reason in Europe and America. Educated citizens sought out the laws governing the universe; balancing the social orders in government so that liberties would be preserved for all had become an important maxim. Maintaining balance among the socio-political orders avoided the extremes of potential tyranny from above or "democratic licentiousness" from below and provided for enlightened, evenhanded decision making.

Prerevolutionary provincial Americans accepted this construct of ideas as synonymous with good government. As communications improved and colonists moved beyond the initial struggle by conquering their environment, they seemed to enter upon a phase of "Anglicization," becoming more rather than less English in outlook during the eighteenth century.[14] In dress, manners, life-styles, and architectural preferences, they often looked to the metropolitan capital of London for models. Wealthy southern planters used their slave gangs not only to produce rice, tobacco, or naval stores, but also to provide themselves with money to re-create the leisured life-styles of English country gentry. Merchants of wealth and distinction in provincial cities constructed lavish townhouses modeled after favored Georgian designs, and filled their homes with the latest Chippendale furniture. The "better sort" turned with greater frequency to the comfortable, ritualized liturgy of the Anglican fold. More and more children of provincial elite families attended schools and colleges in England or on the Continent, rather than settling for rawboned provincial colleges like Harvard, William and Mary, or Yale. Future lawyers from the great families studied more often at England's inns of court, where the best legal training could be found. Mid-eighteenth-century families, especially among the more leisured elite, were not growing so much apart from English ways as they were attempting to live up to them.

The process of Anglicization was also evident in provincial politics. There were obvious analogies with English structures and practices. Governors represented and substituted for the monarchy; councilors in upper houses for the aristocracy; delegates in lower houses for the democracy. Like their counterparts in England, provincial socioeconomic leaders assumed that all offices were theirs by right of breeding, education, and proved standing. They believed in and acted upon assumptions about the "stewardship" of the elite, only natural in a society which feared democratic excesses and maintained distinctions through deferential attitudes. Even though middle-class white males had the vote (eligible voters formed a far greater proportion of the male population in the provinces than in England at this time), their appearances at polling places tended to be perfunctory.

They usually chose only among socioeconomic elite leaders to represent them in lower houses or in the few elective local offices of any authority. One late colonial Virginian conveniently summarized the impact of deferential, hierarchical attitudes when he wrote: "It is right that men of *birth* and *fortune,* in every government that is free, should be invested with power, and enjoy higher honors than the people. If it were otherwise, their privileges would be less, and they would not enjoy an equal degree of liberty with the people."[15]

Provincial Americans were constructing a world of strange and haunting contrasts: extremes of wealth and poverty, but with a large, relatively free middle class; commitments to the maintenance of civil liberties when at least one fifth of the population wore the chains of slavery; widespread voting rights, based on low property-holding requirements, but with little actual decision-making influence even for the middle class; and mounting fascination with all facets of English culture, ideas, and values (especially among the best families) at the very time when people and events were forging resistance to British supremacy in America.

But no matter how much certain provincials aped the English, fundamental differences remained that could not be easily eradicated. Above all else, and epitomized by the presence of royal governors, all provincials—high and low, male and female, white and black—were subordinate subjects of the Empire. Their theoretical calling remained that of serving the parent state. That was the fundamental fact of provincial life, regardless of anyone's pretensions to higher status. And some Americans were beginning to resent this situation. To employ a popular metaphor of the times, the provincial children were growing up and wanted acceptance as adults. The bulk of home government leaders, however, still thought of them as children who had been spoiled by too much parental indulgence. Perhaps it was high time for the children to learn obedience and respect.

Ministerial officials in England saw the thirteen provinces as but a portion of the thirty-odd British possessions in the New World. To the north there was Nova Scotia; soon there would be all of Canada. To the south there were the valuable West Indian sugar islands, such as Barbados or the slave-trading entrepot of Jamaica, scattered throughout the Caribbean area and into the Atlantic Ocean. The Floridas soon would be added.

During the 1750s, Great Britain and its worldwide possessions became locked in mortal combat with France and Spain and their possessions. William Pitt, the elder, also known as the "Great Commoner," guided the over-all British strategy that would see Englishmen emerge triumphant over their hated imperial rivals. Since 1689, Britain and France (and also Spain, normally as a French ally) had engaged in a series of indecisive wars. Each of these European nations was afraid that the other would gain too much territory and authority, tipping the delicate balance of power in the enemy's direction. Even though England made some gains, such as humiliating Spain by wresting the Rock of Gibraltar from Spanish control, the first three wars basically maintained the status quo. But the fourth contest—the Seven Years' War (known in the colonies as the French and Indian War)—turned into an overwhelming British triumph as the great war for the Empire. In America, Quebec fell to General James Wolfe's forces in 1759; in 1762, an Anglo-American army took Cuba, returning it the next year to Spain in exchange for the Floridas.

Indeed, the Treaty of Paris in 1763 affirmed Britain's ascendancy over the other European nations. France gave up its claim to virtually all of its North American possessions, including Canada and the territory between the Appalachians and the Mississippi River. Spain licked its wounds. Englishmen throughout the world celebrated the ending of the war. It had been a long, costly, but staggeringly successful effort.

The great triumph also portended serious problems. Home ministers, having silenced England's enemies, could now concentrate more fully upon bringing errant provincial children to a greater appreciation of the parent state's authority. Provincial Americans, however, were feeling a new exhilaration of freedom. The French and the Spanish were no longer at their backs, hounding settlers on borders and threatening to bloody the provinces with their armies and Indian allies. In 1763, Americans felt more secure and more able to stand on their own feet than at any previous time. The need for imperial support did not seem as pressing now that France and Spain had been so reduced in stature. Without these two enemies to distract them, Britons and Americans began staring ominously at each other.

Feelings on both sides of the Atlantic may be captured in the postwar debate over who had contributed the most to the martial effort. "It is evident that the general exertion of the colonies in North America," declared the wealthy Maryland lawyer, Daniel Dulany, "not only facilitated, but was indispensably requisite to the success of those operations by which so many glorious conquests were achieved, and that those conquests have put it in the power of the present illustrious Ministers to make peace upon terms of so much glory and advantage." "Pure generosity" motivated American involvement, claimed Dulany, but it had "not prompt[ed] the *British*

Nation to engage in the defense of the colonies." By aiding provincials, Dulany boasted, England was doing what was "necessary for the defense of . . . herself." Enlightened citizens understood that England "could not long subsist as an independent kingdom after the loss of her colonies" to France and Spain.[16]

Determined ministerial leader George Grenville, who was about to do much to damage Anglo-American relations, perceived the situation very differently. "Great Britain protects America: America is bound to yield obedience. If not, tell me when the Americans were emancipated," shouted Grenville before Parliament. Then he added the punchline: "The [parent] nation has run itself into an immense debt to give them protection." It was time that Americans contributed more to the cost of running the world's greatest empire.[17] Thomas Whately, an influential minor official, perhaps best summarized the home government's position when he wrote: "The colonies . . . have been of late the darling object of their mother country's care: We are not yet recovered from a war undertaken solely for their protection."[18]

Each side was taking full credit but giving little to the other. To provincial elite leaders like Dulany, England's glorious future depended upon American goodwill. But to Grenville and other troubled home ministers, protecting the colonies had cost Britons dearly. By the end of the Seven Years' War, the English national debt had skyrocketed from £75,000,000 to about £130,000,000 sterling. Something had to be done to get that debt—an immense figure for its time—under control. Holding down on the daily expenses of imperial administration by shifting some ongoing operating costs to the Americans seemed a reasonable course, at least to Grenville and other ministers in London.

In reality, Americans through their commercial ties with Britain, had been stimulating the imperial economy as much as Britain had been aiding the provinces by absorbing most of the costs of imperial administration and warfare. For over a century it had been a relatively harmonious relationship, based on the concept of mercantilism which had taken hold in the second half of the seventeenth century. Mercantilism as a system of economic thought had national self-sufficiency as its primary goal. The wise nation sought to maintain a favorable balance of trade with all other powers. With gold flowing into national coffers to balance trading ledgers, countries would not be caught short of precious metals, considered the most reliable source of national solvency and wealth. Moreover, specie would be available to purchase needed military goods in case of war.

Colonies were to abet economic self-sufficiency by producing raw materials not otherwise available to the parent state. If these goods could be used to sustain national defense, that would enhance Britain's political independence. For example, tall, straight white pine trees, used as masts for naval ships (the key to England's defense), had become quite scarce in seventeenth-century England. Other national suppliers could undermine any war effort by cutting England's navy off from wood products. Thus the colonies came to be viewed as a source of vital raw materials as well as a market for the finished goods from the parent state.

To bring imperial coherence to chaotic economic development in the early settlements (which had blissfully traded with any European power), England after 1650 promulgated the Navigation System through a series of parliamentary trading acts. England was to be the superior economic authority, and the colonies were to operate for the benefit of the parent state. The acts barred foreign ships from the colonial trade; "enumerated" certain vital colonial goods which could be shipped only to other colonies or to England; and legislated that all European goods destined for America had to pass through England. The first enumerated commodities included Chesapeake Bay tobacco, which enhanced the Crown's fixed income enormously through a trade duty specifically earmarked for royal coffers. Over time the enumerated list grew, including not only tobacco, but rice, indigo, wood products, and raw wool, among many other commodities. If these materials flowed to England in greater quantity than the home market demanded, English merchants then reshipped them to the European continent and elsewhere, making profits as middlemen. In turn, European goods shipped through England to America bore various costs of unloading, wharfage, storage, and reloading. This all stimulated the English economy. Through the Navigation System, England became the economic hub of the Empire; its economy boomed accordingly.

Sometimes the home government went too far in writing trade acts. In 1733, Parliament, responding to pressures from the British West Indian planter lobby, passed the Molasses Act. Molasses was a basic ingredient in the production of rum, which had become a thriving New England industry. The 1733 Act put a 6 pence per gallon duty on all foreign molasses, most of which came from the French West Indies, whose planters sold their molasses more cheaply to North American traders. With the 6 pence duty, British planters, who did not produce enough molasses for the market, had the lowest prices. American rum producers feared the impact of the price increase on their trading activities. They predicted destruction of a burgeoning New England industry that not only warmed American stomachs, but also provided a commodity that could be exchanged in the "triangular route" for slaves in Africa or for more molasses or other products in the West Indies. (Provincial traders rarely plied this infamous but somewhat mythical route as rigorously as modern descriptions have implied.) Canny New England merchants simply ignored the duty on foreign molasses. British customs collectors in American ports also looked the other way. The duty went largely uncollected, and everyone, except for a few exasperated British West Indian planters, accepted this unwritten understanding, so characteristic of the accommodative spirit of salutary neglect.

All in all, the structure of the imperial economy supported all of its limbs somewhat evenly. Americans had a ready market in England for their raw materials and cash crops. With respect to enumerated goods, provincials held a monopoly on the English market, since Parliament prohibited Britons from producing such crops as tobacco in direct competition with American goods. Since the British market could absorb only a small portion of tobacco, most of it would be reshipped to the Continent, where an expanding buyer's market lent stability to the prices ultimately paid provincial producers. The Crown earned its duties, and the British mercantile community (including Scottish traders) gained handsome profits as functioning middlemen. Long-term per capita income growth for the thirteen provinces, allowing for short-term business downturns, averaged out to a net gain of 0.5 percent a year for the period 1720–1775.[19] Even if the increased monetary power behind that growth largely benefited the wealthiest provincial citizens, the American economy itself was stable and buoyant. It is unlikely that the Navigation System was constraining Americans unduly, despite the severe limitations which imperial laws placed on the development of American manufactures. Cash crops (the five leading American exports in market value for the period 1768–1772 were tobacco, bread and flour from the Middle Colonies and the Chesapeake area, rice and indigo from South Carolina, and New England dried fish) were booming in sales. If there was a serious long-term economic problem arising from the imperial economy, it reflected the widening gap between the value of American exports to Britain as opposed to British exports to the provinces. The specific trade deficit faced by Americans for the year 1760 alone was £1,600,000 sterling, and it was not easy to close that gap with virtually nonexistent provincial specie or with services such as shipping.[20]

The mounting provincial trade deficit with England was exacerbated at the end of the Seven Years' War by a short, biting postwar depression. This economic setback signified the beginning of a short-term downward swing in the provincial per capita income growth rate, making it difficult for colonists to appreciate more constraining laws governing the flow of commerce or the payment of increased taxes, especially in view of imperial trade imbalances. The postwar business slump and the psychology of chronic trade indebtedness undermined provincial sympathy for those home ministers trying to stabilize England's national debt, which many Americans believed had been accumulated primarily because of England's imperial ambitions in the first place.

Both sides, it seemed, were beginning to misconstrue the other's intentions. One failure of vision between the Treaty of Paris in 1763 and the Stamp Act in 1765 lay in the home ministry's unwillingness to acknowledge the multiplicity of ways that Americans contributed, either directly or indirectly, to Britain's economic health. If the colonies cost money in one area, they paid for themselves over and over again in other areas. When ministerial leaders denied the over-all balance in the imperial ledger sheet by focusing exclusively on the national debt and by insisting that colonists contribute yet more to imperial needs, they were inviting trouble.

Too often imperial administration, even during the years of neglect, had been myopic, largely because of the bureaucratic confusion, inefficiency, and lassitude that characterized responsible officials. The Board of Trade and Plantations, created by the Crown in 1696 as a permanent advisory and coordinating agency on colonial affairs, was the central agency of information and policy making. Normally, the Board played an advisory role in the selection of royal governors and other provincial-bound administrators. (The Board actually controlled appointments from 1752 to 1761.) It collected information, drafted commissions and instructions, and made recommendations regarding the allowance or disapproval of provincial legislation. Its goal was to assure that the provinces conformed to the requirements of the Empire, even though the Board rarely had members who thought it necessary to know much of anything about overseas possessions.

In making its recommendations, the Board of Trade reported to the King's Privy Council, a body whose numbers had become unwieldy and whose functions had become increasingly ceremonial during the eighteenth century. By the 1760s, real administrative authority now lay with the heads—they were also privy councilors—of the vital agencies of government (the treasury, the admiralty, the state department, and others) who worked not only as policy directors of the King's business but who also operated as managers in Parliament seeking passage of legislation affecting the good of the realm. One of these chief ministers, the Secretary of State for the Southern department, controlled general policy making for the American provinces while watchdogging relations with France and Spain. It was from this office during the late 1750s that independent-minded William Pitt constructed the grand design that would humiliate France and Spain on New World battlefields.

The King's ministers in reality represented politically sagacious, wellborn gentlemen, whose task it was to give coherence to the creation and maintenance of governmental policies. One of their number, normally the First Lord of the Treasury, headed the group as the King's chief minister in this institutional precursor of the modern cabinet system. Prior to 1760, the most durable and powerful eighteenth-century First Minister had been Sir Robert Walpole (1721–1742), who built his loyal following in and out of Parliament through electoral manipulation, bribery, and the use of patronage, sinecures, titles, and other forms of political preferment. Corrupt practices for Walpole and those who emulated him after 1742 were the tools of constructing Parliamentary majorities and getting legislation passed —the key to maintaining their high offices.

After the Glorious Revolution of 1688–1689, the preponderance of English gentlemen-politicians thought of themselves as loyal Whigs, men constantly guarding against possible royal encroachments upon Parliament's bitterly won ascendancy. Most Whigs fretted about those few lurking Tories who still advocated a powerful monarchy, a strong state-supported Anglican clergy, and such antilibertarian institutions as an independent standing army, subject primarily to the King's will. But by the 1720s, groups of Whigs and Tories had begun to blend together into pro- and anti-Walpolean coalitions. "Country" party leaders complained about Walpole's corrupting influence, while "court" party followers (correlating significantly with those who benefited from Walpolean-related patronage) defended the rising power of ministers as essential to balanced government and beneficial legislation. Thus there were no formal political parties as such. Leading theorists then believed that organized national parties promoted pure self-interest in government at the expense of an enlightened resolution of issues, a somewhat ironic view given the constant jostling over offices and preferment to the general detriment of major public policy concerns among England's powerful gentlemen-politicians during the period.

The "country" faction maintained itself upon one overarching theme in its ideological orientation—that of a plot to destroy liberties. At the center was the hated Walpolean influence. Henry St. John, Viscount Bolingbroke, a country party Tory, described that influence as follows: "The *Robinarch*, or chief ruler . . . in reality . . . is a sovereign, as despotic, arbitrary a sovereign as this part of the world affords. . . . The *Robinarch* . . . has unjustly engrossed the whole power of a nation into his own hands. . . . [He] admits no person to any considerable post of trust and power under him who is not either a *relation*, a *creature*, or a *thorough-paced tool* whom he can lead in pleasure into any dirty work."[21] The axiom was that power corrupts the actions of men. Country leaders and writers, in circulating their dire warnings, were telling Englishmen everywhere that it was no longer the monarchs, but now rather power hungry ministers, who were conspiring to upset the constitutional balance among the social orders in government and crush liberties in the process.

Walpole survived a long term as chief minister despite his critics, but his "Robinarchal" system of influence and patronage contained characteristics which added to political disequilibrium in the Empire (after 1760). For one thing, the pursuit of offices and the construction of workable coalitions, in the absence of formal political parties, tended to consume the time of the gentlemen-politicians. Their knowledge or concern about the provinces, including American attitudes and feelings, suffered as a consequence. Perhaps even more important, England in 1760 was about to enter a ten-year period when no cabinet head would be strong enough to maintain the goodwill of both King and Parliament. Chief ministers leading weak coalitions rose and fell at so rapid a pace that it proved impossible to refurbish or strengthen imperial controls over the provinces with sensitivity, evenhandedness, or wisdom.

It was while England's gentlemen-politicians were maneuvering for favor, position, and power that the youthful George III acceded to the throne in October 1760, replacing his grandfather, George II (1727–1760). George II's less than popular but lengthy reign had seen a further eclipse of the Crown's prerogatives in the face of a rising, Whig-dominated ministry and Parliament. Britons seemed pleased with their twenty-two-year-old monarch. "One hears nothing of the King," penned one admirer, "but what gives one the best opinion of him imaginable." To a female courtier, George III projected "mildness and firmness mixed; religious sentiments and a moral court unblemished." Another courtier wrote: "The King seems resolved to stop the torrent of corruption and laziness. He rises every morning at six to do business, rides out at eight to a minute, returns at nine to give himself up to his people."[22] How nice it was to have, at long last, an amiable and gracious person on the throne who spoke impeccable English without a German accent.

George III's first days went smoothly, but there were tensions just beneath the surface which portended grave problems ahead. George's childhood had been lonely and unhappy before Lord Bute, a dashingly handsome Scottish courtier, became his mentor. As a child, George suffered from his domineering mother, Princess Augusta; the early death of his father; and an overwhelming sense of inadequacy in knowing that one day he would be king. Bute, a professional courtier, changed all that. First, the Scot won the enduring affection of George's mother. The relationship became so close that scandalmongers whispered to everyone that Bute and Princess Augusta were torrid lovers. No one knows whether the rumors were true; what is important is that Augusta in 1755 named Bute to be George's personal tutor. The prince's friendship (indeed adoration and respect) for Bute ripened quickly. In many ways, George placed his full faith and trust in his mentor. He wrote such overly sentimental notes to Bute as "Let my dear friend be assured of this that in all events I will keep most steadily to the part so often talked of between us, and will with the greatest affection and tenderness be yours till death separates us."[23] George resented the vicious rumors about his mother and Bute. He swore to avenge their honor, and he also made up his mind that Bute should someday head his government. Personally ambitious, Bute did not dissuade George from such thinking.

Like the country faction, Lord Bute believed that England's political system was intolerably corrupt, and that the problem stemmed directly from ambitious, self-serving ministers. For Bute, however, the potential for bringing the ministers under control lay in the monarch's reassertion of claims to legitimate royal prerogatives. The "part so often talked of between us" referred to that very matter. Well-trained by his tutor, the young King committed himself to turning the realm back toward his vision of the path of virtue. George would be a king who would get the ministers back into line by controlling their corruption. For instance, upon his accession he demanded that patronage jobs and sinecures heretofore under the Crown's control be returned to his authority. Moreover, he began angling to make Bute head of the cabinet. George intended to build his own coalition government, which he believed would be in the best interests of all

British subjects. But to many country and court Whigs, the new King was beginning to act the part of the tyrant. The ministers saw Bute's Scottish hand everywhere. Everyone knew that the tyrannical Stuarts were Scots; the symbolic carry-over could not be missed.

By 1762, George was losing his early glamor. He never really had much with the politicians in the first place. They bowed in his presence but swore privately that they would never fall into line behind Bute. But George persisted, and Bute became cabinet head. To his credit, the Scottish courtier soon gave up. He could see that his presence in the government was seriously inhibiting decision making of any kind. In April 1763 a disappointed George III named an eager George Grenville to be First Lord of the Treasury. Grenville knew and resented the fact that he did not have the King's favor and that it remained with Bute, who by this time was contemptuously known as *"the* minister behind the curtain." On the defensive when he took office, Grenville maneuvered immediately to assume an offensive posture. One strategy was to take up many unanswered questions relating to the American provinces, dangling as they were at the end of the Seven Years' War. Proof of Grenville's political strength would come easily by getting Members of Parliament to vote for a general tightening of imperial regulations. It was an ominous moment, one that suggested the eventual collapse of Anglo-American relations, when the humorless and ambitious George Grenville took office.

Grenville was not an extremist looking for a fight. He was, rather, a gentleman-politician who felt that his own power base could be strengthened by pulling together the loose threads of provincial administration. He was aware that, even before the Seven Years' War, the ministers had worked on plans to ensnare Americans more securely in the imperial net. The immense national debt, calling for £5 million a year in interest payments alone, was his first excuse. He would not ask Americans to help pay the principal and interest on that debt, but he would demand that they bear more of the day-to-day costs of imperial administration. Grenville believed that a small tax burden would work, in light of the fact that the per capita public debt figure was £18 in England, as compared to a per capita debt and trade deficit figure of 18 shillings in the colonies.

The bulk of daily imperial revenue shortages evidenced the startling inefficiency which the Empire had tolerated in times past. Grenville was aghast to discover that it cost £7,600 a year in salaries paid to customs collectors to gain £1,900 in revenue. Hence the cabinet in the fall of 1763 ordered that all English customs agents carry out their official functions in the provinces, rather than treat their posts as sinecures and use hired hands to collect duties. The ministry, with good evidence, felt that the actual presence of appointed agents would result in more effective collections. Hired subordinates willingly accepted bribes in lieu of duties, since they received only a small portion of the regular salaries assigned customs posts, while the real officeholders luxuriated in England, doing nothing for the money that they gained. With the real agents in America earning full salaries, there would be less reason for taking bribes and more accountability for malfeasance in office.

Indeed, the ministry was striking out against the amount of illicit trade, in violation of the Navigation System, being conducted by provincial merchants. Although illegal trading represented a small portion of the total volume of American commerce, it did exist and, in fact, bordered on treason at times. During the Seven Years' War, the British navy blockaded French and Spanish West Indian islands. But shrewd American merchants, sailing under the guise of neutrality—and in the name of humanity—used the pretext of prisoner exchange to trade covertly with the enemy. Some New England traders carried more goods than prisoners; these supplies, most often food products, helped to sustain the French and Spanish war efforts. When William Pitt in 1760 discovered that some one hundred provincial ships were in the Spanish port of Montecristi, he ordered customs agents to search inbound American vessels with greater diligence. Pitt, one of the few good friends of America among the cabinet heads, was furious; he had worked for the crackdown in customs collection that was now finally taking place under Grenville.

In early October 1763, Grenville took another step by issuing a cabinet order stationing British naval vessels in American waters—and during peacetime. Naval captains were authorized to act as customs officials on the high seas; they could seize any vessel suspected of smuggling and send it to port so that its case could be heard before a vice admiralty court judge. If the ship was condemned for illegal trading, the naval captain and his crew would share in profits from the condemned vessel's sale. With such an attractive incentive plan, the ministry sought to create another line of defense against smuggling and illicit trading and further to entice American merchants to trade legally and pay appropriate duties.

The naval decision made good sense insofar as the strengthening of imperial authority was concerned. But the British navy in American waters, in peacetime above all else, smacked of tyranny by implying that military force was more important to home ministers in settling issues than civilian authority. Those who dabbled in smuggling, like priggish John Hancock of Boston, made it known among their friends that the ministry was going too far.

Just a few days after the naval instructions became public, the cabinet added another order, since known as the Proclamation of 1763. The Proclamation outlined governmental organization for newly won British territories, including Canada; it also called for a North-to-South line to be drawn along "the heads or sources of any of the rivers which fall into the Atlantic Ocean from the west and northwest." British lands beyond the rivers were to be "reserved to the Indians." The idea, in part, was to stop white encroachments into tribal hunting grounds in order to avoid further financial drains that would fall on the home government in snuffing out the costly fires of local white-Indian wars.

White-Indian relations never had been very good. They added up to a gory story of human butchery and the ultimate annihilation of several eastern Woodlands, Algonkian-speaking peoples. Some Indian groups, like the Iroquoisian-speaking Confederacy of Six Nations in New York, or the Creek and Cherokee nations west of sprawling white settlements in South Carolina and Georgia, had been able to preserve themselves and their cultures. Effective tribal organization, stable trading relationships with whites who had an insatiable appetite for furs, and diplomatic skill in refusing to become permanent allies of European powers in North America sustained these nations as independent powers.

The numerically weaker tribes did not enjoy such security. Some of them felt very threatened by the destruction of French power. In the late spring of 1763, Pontiac, an Ottawa chief, "conspired" with other northwestern Indians who feared what the English might do to them without French support. They unleashed a massive assault on British forts and scattered white settlements running north from the Virginia backcountry through the eastern Great Lakes region. No doubt Pontiac's war was one important stimulant that produced the Proclamation policy. Keeping whites away from Indians was a cost-saving decision, hardly a policy of humanitarian concern.

There were also other reasons for the Proclamation. Some ministerial heads feared the westward drift of provincial population. Settlements lying beyond the Appalachians would be too far removed from the established routes of imperial commerce. In time, western settlements might even compete with British commercial interests for seaboard provincial goods, in turn encouraging the East to become their manufacturing region in direct competition with Britain. Bottling up white settlers east of the Proclamation line could avert economic developments which, in time, would undermine the traditional dependency of Americans on the parent state.

Bute's ministry had agreed to maintain several thousand British regular troops in North America as a stabilizing force during peacetime. Pontiac's uprising seemed to settle the issue of where to locate the redcoats. Many would reside in frontier forts, where they could regulate white-Indian relations, especially friction-laden trading activities, and assure that venturesome white settlers did not squat on designated Indian lands. The various elements seemed to fit perfectly, at least from the cabinet's point of view.

But provincial reactions, although calm, were nonetheless negative. The presence of troops in the provinces, together with imperial naval vessels patrolling American waters, appeared as overt militarism (a definite sign of impending tyranny) and total lack of respect for the liberties of provincial citizens. Never before had England stationed thousands of regulars in the provinces during peacetime, not even to defend the colonists against French and Spanish incursions. It did not take much deliberation for some popular party leaders to suggest that the real purpose was to unleash the troops against recalcitrant citizens if they dared to defy the new imperial programs.

Cutting the burgeoning provincial population off from western land, too, caused dismay and alarm. To those downwardly mobile young adults crowded out of eastern farming communities, western land represented the hope of future prosperity. Now, constraining restrictions were to be placed on this road to opportunity. For some provincial leaders, especially those who dabbled in land speculation, the Proclamation suggested limitations on easy profits. They suspected that the ministry, fearing that imminent westward expansion would someday make the provinces so powerful that citizens would have no desire to maintain imperial ties, intended to stifle American claims to the West completely.

It was the matter of paying for the 10,000 troops which led Grenville to go to Parliament for legislation. Ministry estimates were that the redcoats would cost at least £250,000 sterling a year. Grenville wanted the colonists to contribute at least £100,000 each year. They certainly could meet that figure, thought cabinet officials, since the per capita debt was so much lower for the provincials than for Britons. The time had come to think in terms of refined customs duties—even direct taxes.

The year 1764 saw Parliament warming to its task. One important piece of legislation was the Currency Act, making it illegal for colonial paper currencies to be used as legal tender in the payment of debts.

Because of the trade deficit, hard money was always scarce in the provinces. Provincial currencies had no real backing except the willingness of governments to tax these fiat monies out of existence as a guard against depreciation, but they served to facilitate local commercial activity. The Currency Act dictated economic orthodoxy and protected large merchants and creditors from having to accept inflated currency in payment of debts. Its immediate impact was to depress the provincial economy further, which was already suffering from the postwar economic slump.

The other parliamentary legislation of 1764 affecting America—the Sugar Act—supplanted the old, unenforced molasses duty. Grenville decided that there was no reason for not collecting the duty if it were set at a reasonable level. Besides outlining new procedures for loading and unloading vessels to aid customs officers in ferreting out smugglers, the Sugar Act reduced the duty on foreign molasses from six to three pence per gallon. Customs agents and the navy would see to it that Americans paid the duty. The receipts—an estimated £40,000 per annum—would in turn defray some of the costs of maintaining the defense establishment in America.

More to the point of raising substantial revenue was the Stamp Act, passed by Parliament during March 1765 with the Grenville ministry's sponsorship. Grenville had held off on this scheme through 1764, ostensibly in order to give provincial assemblies the opportunity to come forward with their own plans for contributing to the costs of imperial administration. But general silence was the provincial response. The Stamp Act required that Americans pay for their own protection and defense out of revenues from the sale of stamped papers to be used on some fifty items, including newspapers, pamphlets, playing cards, wills, land deeds and other court documents, marriage licenses, college diplomas, bills of sale, bills of lading, and port clearance papers for trading vessels. The price of the stamps varied according to the article in question, but none of these items could be bought, sold, or used after November 1, 1765, without stamped paper. Estimates were that this tax would bring in at least £60,000 a year, perhaps much more. Americans would have to pay for stamped paper with hard money (which in itself made the act virtually unworkable), and violators could be tried in vice admiralty courts (where the law did not require trial by jury) as well as in regular civil courts. There was something undesirable in the provisions of the Stamp Act for nearly every provincial citizen.[24]

Grenville foresaw the prospect of significant American opposition to the Stamp duties. He realized that the colonists had never before been taxed directly by Parliament, and that they would consider it an enslaving precedent. But he reasoned that sovereignty was indivisible, and that some official agency in the Empire—clearly Parliament—had to have ultimate authority in all matters of state. The first part of Blackstone's *Commentaries*, published in 1765, confirmed the point: "There is and must be in every state a supreme, irresistible, absolute, and uncontrolled authority, in which the . . . rights of sovereignty, reside. . . . This supreme power is by the constitution of Great Britain vested in the King, Lords, and Commons."[25] The sovereign Parliament had the right to legislate in all areas, even if it had never exercised its full powers in the past.

If Americans argued that they were not represented in Parliament, then Grenville invoked the doctrine of "virtual representation." That conception, really an argument of convenience, held that all Englishmen, by virtue of their citizenship, had a voice in parliamentary deliberations. Not even in England could all citizens vote for members of Parliament, but each M.P., once in office, accepted all citizens throughout the Empire as his constituents, not just those in his immediate district.

The home ministry's arguments were logical, in fact too logical to be convincing to provincial leaders. It was more important, in the spring of 1765, how the colonists and their emerging popular leaders would perceive the flurry of ministerial orders and parliamentary acts. It was peacetime, but the royal navy was in American waters; redcoated troops instead of the French were on all sides; there was a line which barred westward expansion for the uprooted and the propertyless poor; customs agents were working with new vigor, collecting heretofore uncollectable or undesirable duties; provincial currencies had been outlawed as legal tender; a direct tax had been imposed, even though not one provincial representative sat in Parliament; and citizens who violated the terms of the Stamp Act could be tried and penalized without ever seeing a jury.

It was too much to take in such a short period of time. Grenville, while trying to prove that he was capable of heading the ministry, had erred egregiously. He had not considered the newly felt postwar provincial self-confidence. He had not considered the various ways in which Americans contributed to the imperial economy and to England's political international ascendancy. For the sake of order, efficiency, and a few thousand pounds in customs duties and direct taxes, as well as for the sake of maintaining themselves at the head of government, Grenville and his coalition had ruined what should have been postwar feelings of mutual reliance, harmony, and respect. His ministry, by ending the era of salutary neglect, stimulated, as never before, perceptions among Americans (in the tradition of England's country ideology) that a conspiracy was being carried out by high placed ministers to destroy their liberties. Images of political slavery had become more real. The timing for such a sharp change in policy was bad; the dynamics were all wrong.

But it would be misleading to blame the coming crisis in Anglo-American relations exclusively on Grenville and his followers. Indeed, they were bending to trends and attitudes in England, not resisting them. The Board of Trade had been urging a reinvigorated American policy for years. Parliamentarians seemed eager to prove their vaunted sovereignty over all possessions. To aggravate matters, George III, who desperately wanted to be a wise, beneficent ruler, never gave his trust to Grenville, mostly out of pique over Bute's fall, but also out of the desire to take power from the gentlemen-politicians so that the monarchy itself could control more directly the scope and quality of parliamentary legislation. Grenville was never in a comfortable position with his King; the best that George III could say about his Chief Minister was that his opinions were "seldom formed from any other motives than such as may be expected to originate in the mind of a clerk in a counting house."[26] Grenville fell from power in July 1765, only to be followed by yet a more weakly based and short-lived ministry. He died in 1770, never knowing the startling long-range impact of the American protest movement that his ministry helped to set in motion. Grenville, King, and Parliament had provided the matches which popular leaders in America would use to ignite their alliance of protest and resistance among those citizens who had definite reasons to fear the impact of the new restrictions and new taxes.

Notes

1. Hutchinson, *History of Massachusetts-Bay*, III, 90.
2. Aubrey C. Land, "Economic Base and Social Structure: The Northern Chesapeake in the Eighteenth Century," *Journal of Economic History*, 25 (1965), 639–654; James T. Lemon and Gary B. Nash, "The Distribution of Wealth in Eighteenth-Century America: A Century of Change in Chester County, Pennsylvania, 1693–1802," *Journal of Social History*, 2 (1968), 1–24; Gary B. Nash, "Urban Wealth and Poverty in Pre-Revolutionary America," *Journal of Interdisciplinary History*, 6 (1976), 545–584. Nash's work on Boston represents a slight revision of data presented in James A. Henretta, "Economic De-

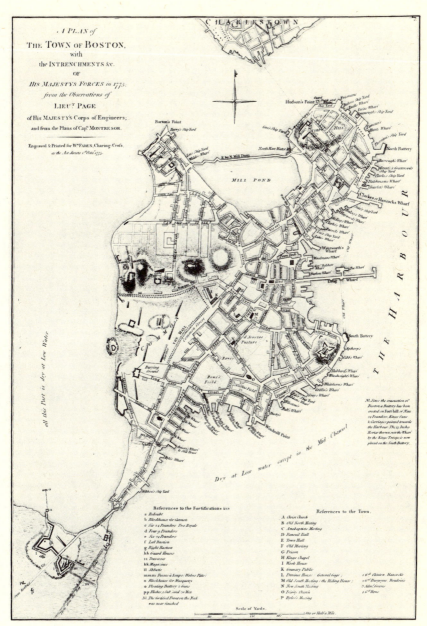

A Plan of the Town of Boston, 1775, engraved by William Faden.
(Courtesy of The New-York Historical Society, New York City.)

A View of the House of Commons, c.1741–1742.
(*Courtesy of the Trustees of the British Museum.*)

William Pitt, engraving by J. E. Nilson from a painting by William Hoare. *(Courtesy of the American Philosophical Society.)*

John Stuart, 3rd Earl of Bute, by Sir Joshua Reynolds. *(Courtesy of the National Portrait Gallery, London.)*

George Grenville, engraving by James Wilson from a painting by William Hoare. *(Courtesy of the Yale University Library, Benjamin Franklin Collection.)*

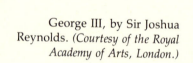

George III, by Sir Joshua
Reynolds. *(Courtesy of the Royal
Academy of Arts, London.)*

New York Harbor, as it appeared in drawing of the late 1750s. *(Courtesy of
The New-York Historical Society, New York City.)*

The Old Plantation, c.1777–1794, anonymous. *(Courtesy of the Abby Aldrich Rockefeller Folk Art Center, Williamsburg, Virginia.)*

Andrew Oliver, by John Singleton Copley. *(Courtesy of Hirschl and Adler Galleries, New York City.)*

Thomas Hutchinson, by Edward Truman. *(Courtesy of the Massachusetts Historical Society.)*

Samuel Adams, by John Singleton Copley. *(Courtesy of the Museum of Fine Arts, Boston.)*

Joseph Warren, by John Singleton Copley. *(Courtesy of the Museum of Fine Arts, Boston.)*

Abigail Adams, by Benjamin Blyth. *(Courtesy of the Massachusetts Historical Society.)*

John Adams, by Benjamin Blyth. *(Courtesy of the Massachusetts Historical Society.)*

Die Americaner wiedersetzen sich der
Stempel-Acte, und verbrennen das aus
England nach America gesandte Stempel-
Papier zu Boston. im August 1764.

Resistance to the Stamp Act, engraved by Daniel-Nicholas Chodowiecki,
1784. (Courtesy of the Library Company of Philadelphia.)

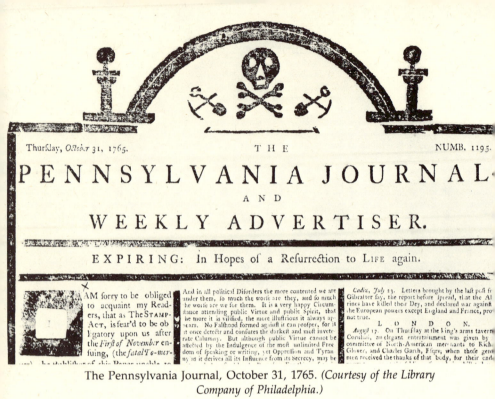

The Pennsylvania Journal, October 31, 1765. (*Courtesy of the Library Company of Philadelphia.*)

The Repeal, or the Funeral of Miss Ame = Stamp, as depicted in a British cartoon, London, 1766. (*Courtesy of the Library Company of Philadelphia.*)

Charles Townshend. *(Courtesy of the Duke of Buccleuch and Queensberry and the Scottish National Portrait Gallery.)*

John Dickinson, by Charles Willson Peale. *(Courtesy of The Historical Society of Pennsylvania.)*

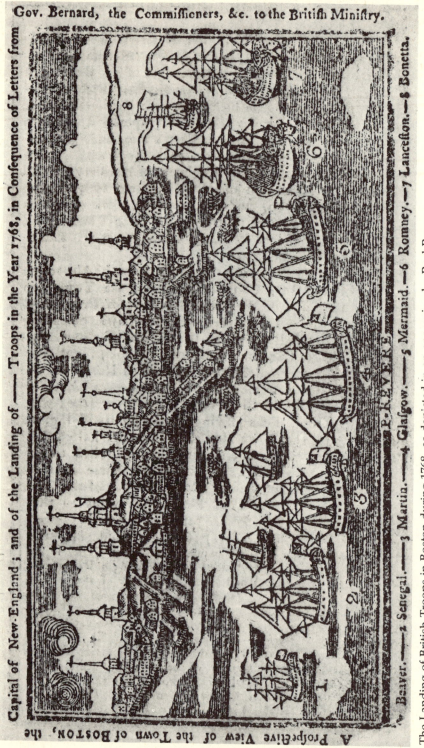

The Landing of British Troops in Boston during 1768, as depicted in an engraving by Paul Revere. (Courtesy of the Library of Congress.)

The Boston Massacre, engraving by Paul Revere after Henry Pelham.
(Courtesy of The Metropolitan Museum of Art, Gift of Mrs. Russell Sage, 1910.)

Lord Frederick North, by Rinke,
after George Dance. *(Courtesy of
the William L. Clements Library,
University of Michigan.)*

Alexander McDougall,
from a miniature by
John Ramage. *(Courtesy
of The New-York
Historical Society, New
York City.)*

Patrick Henry, by
Thomas Sully.
*(Courtesy of Culver
Pictures.)*

Richard Henry Lee, by
Charles Willson Peale.
*(Courtesy of the
Independence National
Historical Park.)*

A New Method of Macarony Making, as Practiced at Boston in North America, printed for Ca.rington Bowles, London, 1774. *(Courtesy of the Trustees of the British Museum.)*

Carpenter's Hall, Philadelphia, site of the First Continental Congress. *(Courtesy of The Historical Society of Pennsylvania.)*

Meeting of a Society of Patriot Ladies at Edonton, North Carolina, during 1775, by Philip Dawe. *(Courtesy of the Library of Congress.)*

General Thomas Gage, by John
Singleton Copley. *(Courtesy of the
Governor of Massachusetts.)*

A Contemporary sketch of British troops firing on colonial militia on
Lexington Green, by Amos Doolittle. *(Courtesy of the Library of Congress.)*

George Nelson

COMMON SENSE;

ADDRESSED TO THE

INHABITANTS

O F

A M E R I C A,

On the following interesting

S U B J E C T S.

I. Of the Origin and Design of Government in general,
with concise Remarks on the English Constitution.

II. Of Monarchy and Hereditary Succession.

III. Thoughts on the present State of American Affairs.

IV. Of the present Ability of America, with some mis-
cellaneous Reflections.

Man knows no Master save creating HEAVEN,
Or those whom choice and common good ordain.
THOMSON.

PHILADELPHIA;
Printed, and Sold, by R. BELL, in Third-Street.
MDCCLXXVI.

Common Sense:
Addressed to the
Inhabitants of
America, 1776, by
Thomas Paine.
*(Courtesy of the Library
Company of
Philadelphia.)*

Thomas Paine, engraved by William Sharp
after a painting by George Romney. *(Courtesy
of the American Philosophical Society.)*

velopment and Social Structure in Colonial Boston," *William and Mary Quarterly*, 3rd Ser., 22 (1965), 75–92. G. B. Warden, "Inequality and Instability in Eighteenth-Century Boston: A Reappraisal," *Journal of Interdisciplinary History*, 6 (1976), 585–620, questions the findings of Nash and Henretta. In the same vein, see Warden's "The Distribution of Property in Boston, 1692–1775," *Perspectives in American History*, 10 (1976), 81–128. For a generalized statement transcending particular quantitative nuances, see Kenneth A. Lockridge, "Social Change and the Meaning of the American Revolution," *Journal of Social History*, 6 (1973), 403–439. An excellent case study of growing poverty relief roles and their significance is Gary B. Nash, "Poverty and Poor Relief in Pre-Revolutionary Philadelphia," *William and Mary Quarterly*, 3rd Ser., 33 (1976), 3–30.

3. Today historians agree that early American mobs were not mindless, hysterical collections of people, but rather well-organized groups who used violence selectively, carefully, and intelligently. The most significant general statement is E. P. Thompson, "The Moral Economy of the Crowd in the Eighteenth Century," *Past & Present*, 50 (1971), 76–136. Most recent works also reflect heavily upon George Rudé, *The Crowd in History* (New York, 1964). Disagreements largely rest upon questions of fundamental crowd motivation in property destruction and related violent acts. For example, Jesse Lemisch, "Jack Tar in the Streets: Merchant Seamen in the Politics of Revolutionary America," *William and Mary Quarterly*, 3rd Ser., 25 (1968), 371–407, stresses the discontent of the poor and downtrodden as a motivating factor, while Pauline Maier, *From Resistance to Revolution: Colonial Radicals and the Development of American Opposition to Britain, 1765–1776* (New York, 1972), claims that crowds had a fundamental middle-class character and that they worked to serve the community's interests when normal political channels did not produce desired political ends. For an important comparative analysis, consult John Phillip Reid, *In a Defiant Stance: The Conditions of Law in Massachusetts Bay, the Irish Comparison, and the Coming of the American Revolution* (University Park, Pa., 1977), whose conclusions amplify those of Maier. By comparison, Hoerder, *Crowd Action in Revolutionary Massachusetts*, is more supportive of Lemisch.

4. Peter Kalm, *Travels in North America*, I (ed. A. B. Benson, New York, 1937), 211.

5. The problem of overcrowding has been analyzed in a number of studies on towns in New England. See Charles S. Grant, *Democracy in the Connecticut Frontier Town of Kent* (New York, 1961), 83–103; Philip J. Greven, Jr., *Four Generations: Population, Land, and Family in Colonial Andover, Massachusetts* (Ithaca, N.Y., 1970), 175–258; and Kenneth A. Lockridge, "Land, Population, and the Evolution of New England Society, 1630–1790," *Past & Present*, 39 (1968), 62–80.

6. This widely used phrase appeared in a number of eighteenth-century sources. See James T. Lemon, *The Best Poor Man's Country: A Geographical Study of Early Southeastern Pennsylvania* (Baltimore, Md., 1972), xiii, 229, footnote one.

7. Russell R. Menard, "The Maryland Slave Population, 1658 to 1730: A Demographic Profile of Blacks in Four Counties," *William and Mary Quarterly*, 3rd Ser., 32 (1975), 29–54, and Allan Kulikoff, "The Beginnings of the Afro-

American Family in Maryland," *Law, Society, and Politics in Early Maryland* (ed. A. C. Land *et al.*, Baltimore, Md., 1977), 171–196.

8. On the formation of stereotypes, see Winthrop D. Jordan, *White Over Black: American Attitudes Toward the Negro, 1550–1812* (Chapel Hill, N.C., 1968). On South Carolina, see Peter H. Wood, *Black Majority: Negroes in Colonial South Carolina from 1670 through the Stono Rebellion* (New York, 1974).

9. James Kirby Martin, *Men in Rebellion: Higher Governmental Leaders and the Coming of the American Revolution* (New Brunswick, N.J., 1973), *passim*.

10. Quoted in Max Savelle, *Seeds of Liberty: The Genesis of the American Mind* (Seattle, Wash., 1948), 251.

11. Linda Grant DePauw, "Land of the Unfree: Legal Limitations on Liberty in Pre-Revolutionary America," *Maryland Historical Magazine*, 67 (1973), 355–368, estimates that up to 85 percent of the late colonial population was dependent upon white adult males, in varying degrees of subordination. See also Alexander Keyssar, "Widowhood in Eighteenth-Century Massachusetts: A Problem in the History of the Family," *Perspectives in American History*, 8 (1974), 83–119.

12. Jackson T. Main, *The Social Structure of Revolutionary America* (Princeton, N.J., 1965), 221–239, offers a full discussion of thinking about classes on the eve of the Revolution.

13. *Royal Instructions to British Colonial Governors, 1670–1776*, I (ed. L. W. Labaree, New York, 1935), 55–56.

14. Many scholars have been working toward an understanding of the important phenomenon of provincials trying to recreate English society in America, especially in the context of England's post-1760 rejection of American aspirations. See John M. Murrin, "The Legal Transformation: The Bench and Bar of Eighteenth-Century Massachusetts," *Essays in Politics and Social Development: Colonial America* (ed. S. N. Katz, Boston, 1971), 415–449; Jack P. Greene, "Search for Identity: An Interpretation of the Meaning of Selected Patterns of Social Response in Eighteenth-Century America," *Journal of Social History*, 3 (1970), 189–220; Jack P. Greene, "An Uneasy Connection: An Analysis of the Preconditions of the American Revolution," *Essays on the American Revolution* (ed. S. G. Kurtz and J. H. Hutson, Chapel Hill, N.C., 1973), 32–80; Rowland Berthoff and John M. Murrin, "Feudalism, Communalism, and the Yeoman Freeholder: The American Revolution Considered as a Social Accident," *ibid.*, 256–288; and Robert M. Weir, "Who Shall Rule at Home: The American Revolution as a Crisis of Legitimacy for the Colonial Elite," *Journal of Interdisciplinary History*, 6 (1976), 679–700.

15. "Fabricus," Rind's *Virginia Gazette*, June 9, 1768. See also J. G. A. Pocock, "The Classical Theory of Deference," *American Historical Review*, 81 (1976), 516–523.

16. *Considerations on the Propriety of Imposing Taxes in the British Colonies for the Purpose of Raising a Revenue by Act of Parliament* (New York, 1765), 17–18.

17. Quoted in Stanley Ayling, *George the Third* (London, 1972), 137.

18. *Considerations on the Trade and Finances of this Kingdom, and on the Measures of Administration . . . since the Conclusion of the Peace* (London, 1766), 144.

19. Marc Egnal, "The Economic Development of the Thirteen Continental Colonies, 1720 to 1775," *William and Mary Quarterly*, 3rd Ser., 32 (1975), 191–222. Egnal notes that the per capita income growth rate in the United States averaged 1.6 percent between 1840 and 1960, fundamentally the period of the

Industrial Revolution. By comparison, the 0.5 percent figure suggests healthy growth for a preindustrial, primarily agricultural order. For an important statement on relationships between the economy and the Revolution, see Marc Egnal and Joseph A. Ernst, "An Economic Interpretation of the American Revolution," *ibid.*, 29 (1972), 3–32.

20. Jacob M. Price, "New Time Series for Scotland's and Britain's Trade with the Thirteen Colonies and States, 1740–1791," *ibid.*, 32 (1975), 307–325; John J. McCusker, "The Current Value of English Exports, 1697 to 1800," *ibid.*, 28 (1971), 607–628; and Jacob M. Price, "Economic Function and the Growth of American Port Towns in the Eighteenth Century," *Perspectives in American History*, 8 (1974), 123–186.

21. From *The Craftsman*, October 18, 1729, quoted in Bernard Bailyn, *The Ideological Origins of the American Revolution* (Cambridge, Mass., 1967), 50. For further information on radical Whiggism and its ideological variants, consult Caroline Robbins, *The Eighteenth-Century Commonwealthman* (Cambridge, Mass., 1959); Bernard Bailyn, *The Origins of American Politics* (New York, 1968); and J. G. A. Pocock, *The Machiavellian Moment: Florentine Political Thought and the Atlantic Republican Tradition* (Princeton, N.J., 1975), 333–552.

22. Quoted in Ayling, *George the Third*, 67. Another suggestive biography about the new king is John Brooke, *King George III* (New York, 1972).

23. George, Prince of Wales, to John Stuart, Earl of Bute, June 10, 1757, *Letters from George III to Lord Bute, 1756–1766* (ed. Romney Sedgwick, London, 1939), 6–7.

24. The acts of Parliament and Orders in Council for the 1763–1765 period have been reprinted in *English Historical Documents, Vol. IX: American Colonial Documents to 1776* (ed. Merrill Jensen, New York, 1955), 635–658.

25. Quoted in Esmond Wright, *Fabric of Freedom, 1763–1800* (New York, 1961), 33.

26. Quoted in I. R. Christie, *Crisis of Empire: Great Britain and the American Colonies, 1754–1783* (New York, 1966), 39.

III

Colonial Protest and
Resistance, 1765-1773

In the spring of 1765, Patrick Henry was an ambitious twenty-nine-year-old who desperately wanted to make his mark in the world. His roots were humble, although respectable. Henry's father had migrated from Scotland and eventually established his family on the Virginia frontier. Young Patrick knew that if he was going to have real wealth and distinction in life, he would have to earn it. Only great personal success could make a man of such common stock acceptable in the circles of Virginia's great tobacco-planting families. At sixteen, Henry opened a general store; it failed. Two years later he took up farming; that failed. Again he tried to succeed with a general store; again it failed. Disillusioned, he turned to the law, read quickly through a few legal manuals, and gained the pettifogger's right to represent friends and neighbors in court. At last, Henry had found his calling. He was an overnight success, instantly on his way to wealth and distinction. Local juries became the first of many groups to swoon over his amazing oratorical abilities.

By 1765, Patrick Henry had developed into much more than just another backcountry commoner. Through local court cases, he had earned a widespread reputation by defending the right of Virginians to adjust the value of tobacco as currency, especially when crops were lean, so that the community-supported salaries of clerics and others could be adjusted downward when tobacco possessed greater market value. In the most famous trial of these Parson's Cause cases, Henry attacked the practice of sending all provincial laws to England for Privy Council approval. The pugnacious lawyer feared that laws affecting the value of tobacco, adopted in the interest of the community, would be struck down for not serving the personal interests of royal officials and state-supported Anglican clergymen. Any law benefiting the community, Henry insisted, but which the King's ministers vetoed, effectively broke the political compact between the people and their English rulers. His statements seemed tainted with treason, or rang with the defense of constitutional liberties. It depended upon one's point of view.

As Henry jangled the chains of despotism and political slavery, his oratory stirred the backcountry populace. In May 1765, his neighbors endorsed his bold statements by electing him to a seat in the House of Burgesses. As he rode later that month toward Williamsburg, Virginia's small but architecturally grand, provincial capital, Henry was ready to stand up against any person or legislative act threatening him in his upwardly mobile track. He was not going to accept second-rate treatment, even from a strong-minded King in Parliament.

The burgesses, largely planter elite leaders unaccustomed to dealing with upstarts like Henry, were winding down from their spring session when the new representative arrived in Williamsburg. Only 39 of 116 burgesses were present in the capitol when Henry made his speaking debut. It was a memorable event. Chiding his colleagues, the backcountry leader noted that he "had read that in former times . . . Julius had . . . Brutus, Charles had his Cromwell, and he Did not Doubt but some good American would stand up, in favor of his Country." The startled Speaker quickly silenced him, warning everyone that this new member "had spoken treason, and was sorry to see that not one of the members of the house was loyal Enough to stop him." Henry apologized. He explained that his seeming rashness reflected upon "his Country's Dying liberty," the fatal blow having been dealt through the Stamp Act. Action of some type was necessary, he thought. He then asked for permission to present several resolutions for the burgesses' approval.[1]

Ultimately the few burgesses still in attendance adopted four of Henry's proposed seven resolutions. If his words had been bold, these resolutions were not. Legalistic in tone, they were ambivalent and confused about how far to push when committing outraged feelings to paper and in petitioning for relief through normal political channels. The four approved resolutions stressed that Virginians as Englishmen had "all the Liberties, Privileges, Franchises, and Immunities . . . possessed, by the people of *Great Britain*"; that "royal Charters" guaranteed the extension of English liberties to America; that "Taxation of the People by themselves, or by Persons chosen by themselves to represent them" was "the distinguishing Characteristic of *British* freedom, without which the ancient Constitution cannot exist"; and that Virginians had not "forfeited or yielded up" their basic rights in recent years. The Stamp Act, in short, directly violated English liberty. Parliament had to rescind this legislation or stand in violation of the British Constitution.[2]

Henry's first four resolutions epitomized what prominent provincial leaders had been saying, even before official news of Parliament's adoption of Grenville's plan of direct taxation had reached them. In 1764, for example, aging Governor Stephen Hopkins of Rhode Island, a popularly elected official, pointed out that "British subjects are governed only agreeable to laws to which [they] themselves have some way consented; and are not to be compelled to part with their property, but as it is called for by the authority of such laws." But, the disturbed Hopkins warned: "Those who are governed at the will of another, or of others, and whose property may be taken from them by taxes, or otherwise, without their own consent, and against their will, are in the miserable condition of slaves."[3] Through pamphlets, newspaper essays, and official assembly petitions directed at Parliament, American leaders were making one constitutional point: NO TAXATION WITHOUT REPRESENTATION!

In fact, the colonial assemblies, in preparing formal petitions based on words similar to Henry's and in directing them to Parliament, were exercising one wholly legitimate form of protest—the most ineffective means of protest, as it turned out. Sending petitions through legitimate channels did not have the impact upon British leaders that other types of protest, especially informal, extralegal acts, were to have—either positively or negatively in forcing Parliament's hand. It was the controlled violence accompanying crowd action, the economic coercion implicit in trading boycotts, and the outright defiance of Parliament's will after legislation had gone into effect that succeeded tactically when legitimate protest failed. But the employment of intimidation and coercion as political weapons suggested the dangerous possibility of an absolute breakdown in communications between adversaries. That could lead to an act of overt rebellion, the most extreme form of extralegal resistance. And the concept of re-bellion carried with it the implication of complete separation from the sovereign authority—and independence.

During the Stamp Act crisis, many cautious American leaders in-sisted that every means of legal protest had to be fully exhausted, despite Parliament's recalcitrance in recognizing American griev-ances. It was in that spirit that nine provinces (excluding New Hamp-shire, Virginia, North Carolina, and Georgia) sent delegates to the Stamp Act Congress, which met for two weeks in New York City during October 1765. Under the urging of James Otis, Jr., the Mas-sachusetts General Court had written all other assemblies, calling for an intercolonial gathering to prepare a "united front" statement of grievances. The delegates were not a group of extremists; their "Dec-larations" pledged "all due subordination to that August Body, the Parliament of *Great Britain*." Since it was not feasible for Americans, "from their local Circumstances," to be represented directly in Par-liament, the only way to protect "all the inherent Rights and Liber-ties" of English subjects in America was for the sovereign Parliament to concede that only elected provincial assemblies could tax their own constituents. The Congress also rejected notions about virtual rep-resentation, as had other provincial petitioners.

In essence, the Declarations argued that, even though Parliament was supreme, it could not tax the colonies. That implied divisible sovereignty within the Empire, a position that no reasonable ministe-rial leader or M.P. was willing to accept in 1765 as a solution of the constitutional dilemma. Begging for Parliament's understanding and indulgence, the Stamp Act Congress disbanded. Although its words were harmless, its meetings demonstrated that intercolonial coopera-tion was possible in the face of a common threat. The Congress clearly set a portentous precedent for future united resistance through inter-colonial bodies of deliberation and action.[4]

The Stamp Act Congress and its carefully worded constitutional arguments represented only one manifestation of American temer-ity—and the most cautious of alternatives. It did not express the emotional distress felt by many colonists and expressed in their ve-hement reactions to the Stamp Act (and other Grenville-related pro-grams) during the summer and fall of 1765. This was the sustained anger which arose out of feelings of deprivation, loss of status, rejec-tion, and declining importance within the British imperial world—and at the very time when the colonists were developing a new self-confidence. The words and further deeds of Patrick Henry may be instructive in this context.

The lingering burgesses rejected three of Henry's resolutions, much as the Speaker had previously halted his "treasonous" words. Henry had urged his colleagues to state that they, "with the Consent of his Majesty . . . HAVE the Sole Right and Authority to lay Taxes and Impositions"; that citizens "are not bound to yield Obedience to any Law or Ordinance whatsoever, designed to impose any Taxation upon them, other than the Laws or Ordinances of the General Assembly"; and that any Virginian who asserted otherwise "shall be Deemed, an ENEMY TO THIS HIS MAJESTY'S COLONY."[5] By implication, these proposed resolutions condoned more militant forms of defiance of Parliament's sovereign will.

Henry, similar to many other emerging popular leaders, was behaving like a person who was tired of being put in a subordinate position by British officials. He did not like what he perceived to be increasing restraints imposed from above upon his ability to maximize his upwardly mobile posture. From his position as a new assemblyman, the home ministry seemed to be cutting him off by threatening the burgesses with an absolute reduction in the range of their authority, specifically in matters of taxation. If Henry wanted to make money from speculating in western lands (and he certainly did), it appeared to him that the home government intended, once again, to shut the door to opportunity. It was all very aggravating for Henry, as it was for many others. The gap between expectations and the possible range of personal achievements was taking on an ominous meaning. Like others who were coming to the fore as popular leaders, Henry had expectations in common with vast numbers of provincials who were experiencing anything but universal prosperity under the British Crown. Because he was upwardly mobile, the gap between expectations and reality in his case was relative, whereas for many others, such as the downtrodden poor, it was absolute. Through his powerful oratory, Henry explained to hundreds of Virginians in the months ahead why willful ministers had plotted to take away what rightfully belonged to them all, whether property, opportunity, or political rights. As he spoke out with vehement passion, the people listened. And in time they would act together boldly in defense of what they felt was being lost.[6]

In Virginia, for the sake of social stability, elite tobacco planters in 1765 did not allow events to take a sharp and violent extralegal turn; and hotheads like Patrick Henry had little short-run impact. For one thing, the planters had developed nearly paranoid fears about slave insurrections; they did not want to provide suggestive models by secretly abetting more extreme actions, such as antiministerial riots.

But the planter-elite burgesses could be outmaneuvered, and they were. Someone (probably *not* Henry) sent all the resolutions to the other colonies, where newspapers quickly published them. To readers beyond the Old Dominion's borders, the seven resolutions became known as Virginia's official position. Unsuspecting colonists presumed that even the cautious planters would countenance more than legal protest, that they were in fact calling for extreme defiance. And there were many popular leaders, especially in the North, who were willing to test the more explosive weapons of extralegal resistance.

Unlike many Virginians, citizens in Boston did not live in mortal fear of insurrections from chattel slaves. Moreover, the provincial political milieu there was more decidedly polarized between definable royalist "court" and popular "country" factions than in Virginia. Personal frustrations and petty hatreds gave politics in the Bay colony a cohesive, intensely personal confrontational character, denoted by the royalist Bernard-Hutchinson-Oliver coterie, on the one hand, and the James Otis, Jr.-Samuel Adams popular faction, on the other hand.

Two trivial but formative incidents, which occurred in earlier years, had helped to evoke the intense bitterness which fed the awesome appetite for political rancor in Massachusetts during the 1760s. By circumstance as much as anything else, that petty local political factionalism was as important as any other factor in breaking down relations between the parent state and all of the colonies. It should not be underrated, nor should the incidents in question. The first incident had affected the very course of Samuel Adams's life. Late in the 1730s, Adams's father, the Deacon, became heavily involved in a plan to provide abundant paper currency for local commerce. Setting up a "land bank," and lending out currency in return for mortgages on land, the Deacon and other directors, all of whom were men of respectable means, faced belligerent opposition from the most prominent imperial-oriented merchants in Boston, among them Thomas Hutchinson. Out of fiscal orthodoxy and fear that paper money not backed by specie would rapidly lose its market value, Hutchinson was prominent among the group which demanded that the royal governor wipe out the land bank plan—and concomitantly the personal fortunes of men like the Deacon.

Samuel Adams was finishing his days at Harvard College in the midst of the land bank crisis; he reached adulthood at the very time when his family's personal financial standing was being shaken to its foundations. Finding no occupation that interested him, Samuel increasingly turned his attention to local politics. By the early 1750s, he was dividing his time between fending off his late father's creditors and stirring up resentment against favored royal officials and their local followers—no doubt reflecting his own personal disgust with men who had undercut his father's reputation. Each time the defunct land bank's creditors tried to wring more out of the Deacon's estate, his son received another reminder of how men like Hutchinson had shattered his family's standing, and how imperial officials in general seemed bent upon serving only themselves at the expense of politically weak but honest provincials. The younger Adams clearly developed a grudge, with Hutchinson and his friends—those favored by imperial authority—the prime targets for the wrath of the popular faction. Grenville's broadscale plans, as epitomized in the Stamp Act, made the local targets stand out that much clearer.

The second incident involved Hutchinson and the locally prominent Otis family of Barnstable. Hutchinson, an intelligent man of multifold talents and capacity for endless work, reveled in his burgeoning collection of political offices. After an assembly career he became a councilor and the province's lieutenant governor, while he also held local judgeships. Then, in 1760, the post of chief justice of the Superior Court, the province's highest judicial office, became vacant. The elder James Otis hinted loudly that a previous governor had promised the next vacancy to him but had not delivered. The new governor, Francis Bernard, in a moment of poor political judgment, chose the multiple officeholding Hutchinson, who apparently was not directly soliciting the office but who nevertheless accepted it. The Otis family was furious. Temperamental James, Jr., apparently told others that he personally would "kindle such a fire in the province as shall singe the governor, though I myself perish in the flames." He quickly "joined himself to the party which was jealous that the views of administration were unfavorable to the rights of the colony . . . and soon became its chief leader."[7]

Family pride, finances, political ambitions, and community recognition—all had been thwarted because of the seeming thirst of Hutchinson for preferment. Otis, Jr., vigorously defended American rights after 1760, before suffering from debilitating mental disturbances and losing his way. By 1765 Samuel Adams had begun to take over from the younger Otis as the *de facto* head of the popular faction. As Boston's less than demanding collector of local taxes, Adams had been making friends in the poorer districts by not pressing the growing numbers of downtrodden inhabitants for payments. Although his tax accounts were in arrears in 1764 by as much as £8,000, local currency, and he was facing legal prosecution, Adams was winning a loyal following among those who later formed the essential core of the Boston Sons of Liberty.

The destruction of Hutchinson's property in August 1765 thus may have served more than one purpose. Intimidation and violence not only reduced the slim prospects for administering the Stamp Act; it also allowed old hatreds, based on bad family blood, to be vented. To attack the Stamp Act had the residual benefits of embarrassing, humiliating, and possibly even destroying the careers of old local political enemies who, as imperial administrators, faced the prospect of heavy fines and summary dismissal from office for not properly implementing imperial legislation.

The heated style of local political vilification in Massachusetts, exhibited fully in Boston's Stamp Act riots, gained coherency during the 1760s from the world view of a conspiracy to destroy liberties. There had to be something in the interpreted reality of local politics that fitted the world view of conspiracy, or it would have been useless as an explanatory form. From the Adams faction's point of view, Hutchinson and his friends were precisely the kinds of men who were bent upon destroying liberties in their greed for offices and power. They were the sycophantic puppets of higher authorities in England, so explanations went, who readily grabbed at all types of preferment in return for willfully undermining American rights. They had become ministerial dupes; as such they had to be stopped before they reaped a full harvest of perdition.

Ever anxious John Adams, Samuel's Braintree cousin, who often yearned for the glories of high offices himself, encapsulated these perceptions and resentments during the riots of August 1765, after dutifully condemning the violence: "Has not his Honor the Lieutenant Governor discovered to the People in innumerable Instances, a very ambitious and avaricious Disposition? Has he not grasped . . . the most important offices in the Province into his own Hands? . . . Is not this amazing ascendancy of one Family, Foundation on which to erect a Tyranny?"[8] The multifaceted favoritism enjoyed by Hutchinson, too often gained at the expense of others who likewise sought recognition but who did not possess the appropriate imperial connections, was proof in itself of an insidious plot, even without the Stamp Act. Adams was not rationalizing; he was rather trying to explain the reality of conditions that he and others felt were overwhelming them.

To Samuel Adams, to Cousin John, and to other popular leaders in Massachusetts, toppling Hutchinson and his fellow malefactors of imperial preferment became a *sine qua non* for the preservation of

American liberties. At the same time also it would settle old family scores—which only made those images of tyranny more vivid and real. In addition, the organized, controlled, and selective violence that shook Boston in August 1765 proved to be the ingredient that activated the spirit of Patrick Henry's resolutions. Intimidation had become a most important extralegal tactic of resistance, making implementation of Parliament's will in the provinces virtually impossible, unless home ministers chose to use some counterforce, such as redcoated troops, in supporting imperial authority. That decision too, in time, would come.

Vituperative words and intimidating deeds, suggesting near frenzy if not virtual paranoia, reflected the perceptions of local leaders who were on the lower rungs of the officeholding hierarchy. Hutchinson and the Olivers, lodged on the upper provincial rungs, perceived matters very differently, although they employed the same conceptual framework. From their favored level, as men who personally benefited from imperial connections and who expected deference, not defiance, from the "meaner sort," it appeared that the "licentious democracy" of common citizens had got completely out of control. The threat of total anarchy from below could, in theory, destroy the balanced constitutional order. These diverging perceptions, ultimately irreconcilable, abetted the breakdown in communications that eventually became so severe as to result in open rebellion.[9]

The ill will manifested in Boston during August 1765 quickly spilled over into attacks upon those unfortunates named as stamp distributors in other colonies. Citizens elsewhere did not debate the reasons why selective property damage had occurred in the Bay colony's metropolis. Rather, they saw that Bostonians had utilized a most effective weapon in challenging Parliament's actions. A riot in Newport, Rhode Island, just before the end of August, ended the stillborn distributor's career of Augustus Johnson. The mood of violent intimidation kept spreading. By early September, designated distributors in New York and New Jersey had resigned, the former specifically alluding to the destruction of Andrew Oliver's property in explaining his timidity to an English official. He hoped that his dissociation with the Stamp Act had come soon enough to save his property. Zachariah Hood, the Maryland distributor-designate, was more courageous. He resigned and fled the province only after a large crowd tore down his house in early September.

By late October, the spirit of overt resistance had reached South Carolina. In Charleston, artisans and mechanics, affiliated with the popular leader Christopher Gadsden, who was attending the Stamp Act Congress in New York at the time, drove the stamp officials out of town. The "contagion" of violence meant that imperial officials had lost their ability to enforce plans of direct taxation in America.[10]

If petitions to Parliament resulted in gentlemanly sneers from home government officials, reports of violence clearly angered them. Neither tactic—the one too gentle, the other too harsh for making friends in England—was enough to get Parliament to reconsider its stand. It would be two other tactics, economic boycott and outright defiance of the law, that worked most successfully. New York City merchants were the first among many to agree to a systematic boycott of English goods. On October 31, 1765, the day before the Stamp Act was to go into effect, they pledged not to order "goods or merchandise of any nature, kind, or quality whatsoever, usually imported from Great Britain . . . unless the Stamp Act be repealed."[11] Within a month, merchants in the other major urban trading centers, including Boston and Philadelphia, signed similar pacts. This time the New Yorkers had abetted the popular leaders of Boston by broadening the basis of resistance. With the postwar British economy sagging, a nonimportation plan represented a serious threat to British merchants and manufacturers heavily involved in American commerce. The very threat turned them into a lobbying force in England among M.P.s; and their pressure definitely buoyed the American cause, in spite of the fact that, on the whole, the potential boycott created much bitterness in Parliament.

Outright defiance of the Stamp Act began shortly after November 1. Even though there were no stamps available for sale or designated distributors foolish enough to sell them, the colonists still hesitated to proceed with their daily business, as if the act did not exist. Especially important in this moment of hesitancy were the attitudes of newspaper editors. After October 31 they were not to publish their papers without stamped paper. On that date the *Pennsylvania Journal*, its front page draped in black borders with a coffin woodcut, announced that it was "Expiring: In Hopes of Resurrection to Life Again." But the editor continued to publish, and thereby supported resistance sentiment. Some editors, more timid, ceased publication for a time but then resurrected themselves. They were led by a newspaper published on December 10, which claimed to be "An Apparition of the late Maryland Gazette, which is not Dead, but only Sleepeth." As one contemporary observer somewhat cynically noted: "Printers . . . have generally arranged themselves on the side of liberty, nor are they less remarkable for attention to the profits of their profession. A stamp duty, which openly invaded the first, and threatened a great diminution of the last, provoked their united zealous opposition."[12]

The channels of public communication through newspapers remained intact, even if with clever contrivances. As November gave way to December and the new year dawned, the same pattern of outright defiance affected other activities. Courts first closed, then reopened. Trading vessels without stamped clearance papers remained in ports, then made their way out to sea. Citizens spoke about homespun, personal sacrifice, and working for the higher goals of the community. Although reluctantly, merchants with British trading connections heeded nonimportation agreements, hoping that goods in hand would last. By the early part of 1766, *local* trading activity was returning to normal, except of course for the boycott.

However, popular leaders remained uneasy. They feared that defiant protest could give way to popular indifference, if not resentment, over the inconveniences caused by interruptions in normal services and activities. Once more the Boston Sons of Liberty came to the rescue. In mid December, the Adams group again demanded that Andrew Oliver resign, on the ground that his commission as stamp distributor had finally arrived from England. Oliver desperately wanted to avoid more public humiliation, but the Sons ordered him to "appear under Liberty Tree, at 12 o'Clock [December 17], to make a public Resignation." "Your Noncompliance, Sir," they added, "will incur the Displeasure of *the True-born Sons of Liberty.*" The feared morning arrived—cold, windy, and raining. Street leader Ebenezer Mackintosh went to Oliver's home and escorted the aging merchant arm in arm to Boston's favorite tree, where a crowd of two thousand persons had gathered. The juxtaposition of the roughhewn cobbler and the highborn, wealthy provincial leader must have been striking. Bostonians cheered and jeered as Oliver arrived and once again recanted, stating that he only meant to serve the people through public office.[13] Reminders were not needed in other provinces. Even the fainthearted remained silently attached to the course of open defiance.

Provincials waited nervously but expectantly in early 1766 as Parliament addressed itself to the question of continuing the Stamp Act. A combination of factors were now working in the Americans' favor. George Grenville's ministry had fallen in July 1765; and the youthful, pro-American Lord Rockingham became the new cabinet head. Looking for supporters to strengthen what turned out to be a very feeble ministry, the Rockinghamites instinctively grabbed on to the

British merchants, who feared the potential economic devastation of a drawn out American boycott. Pressure from these worried businessmen, along with the open, vociferous support of William Pitt, the Great Commoner, assured the Rockingham ministry of its needed margin of votes.

Pitt shone in debate in the House of Commons. In his most persuasive speech, he asserted that "this kingdom has no right to lay a tax upon the colonies," yet he acknowledged "the authority of this kingdom over the colonies, to be sovereign and supreme, in every circumstance of government and legislation whatsoever." He appealed to his fellow M.P.s not to think of Americans as ignorant, combative adolescents, but as full "subjects of this kingdom, equally entitled with yourselves to all the natural rights of mankind and peculiar privileges of Englishmen." "The Americans," the Great Commoner thundered, "are the sons, not the bastards, of England!"[14]

George III reluctantly signed legislation nullifying the Stamp Act in March 1766. But he simultaneously approved a face-saving resolution, known as the Declaratory Act, which most colonists ignored during their victory celebrations. Many M.P.s willing to approve repeal of the Stamp Act demanded as their price some firm and formal expression of Parliament's supreme authority. Hence the Declaratory Act asserted in bold words that the King in Parliament "had, has, and of right ought to have, full power and authority to make laws and statutes of sufficient force and validity to bind the colonies and people in America, subjects of the Crown of Great Britain, *in all cases whatsoever*."[15] If Parliament had retreated out of expediency, it still specifically claimed the full power of taxation—and in language that was irreconcilable with the American position. The hope among friends of America in the cabinet and Parliament was that no one would test the difference between the two positions.

By the summer of 1766, several points should have been clear to all concerned. Americans wanted nothing to do with streamlining the Empire; they preferred the days of salutary neglect. The provincial assemblies had defined a constitutional position: taxation was their exclusive privilege. Even if M.P.s shrugged them off, petitions sent to Parliament consistently underscored that claim. Far more important for future events, a number of provincials were becoming worried that a conspiracy by power hungry English ministers and their willing American agents was threatening them with total despotism. In voicing perceived threats, popular leaders were constructing broad-gauged local political alliances, involving large numbers of people who had little or no political standing in the movement to stop imperial aggressions. The very intensity of these feelings, reflecting notions of rapidly declining provincial influence in the Empire, coupled with assaults on personal opportunity, kept many colonists alert to possible further attacks from above. Popular leaders stood ready in 1766 to meet new challenges, to lead in mobilizing widespread opposition (even if it meant crowd violence), and to defy the imperial will, which had become such a disheveled joke during the Stamp Act crisis.

But not all provincials had feelings of alienation. Great numbers of citizens, preferring above all else not to become involved, stood by indifferently. But a small number of gentlemen, especially those caught up in the web of imperial connections, were becoming very concerned about the possible loss of their favored standing. A fundamental split was occurring within the provincial elite. Some firmly believed that the provinces had no future without a stabilizing of imperial ties, and that the colonies would be crushed into submission by Great Britain if defiance proved too bold. In their minds there was also the specter of mob harassment. If the agitation began again, accepted hierarchical relationships, assuring the "better sort" their rightful place, might fall prey to popular anarchy, described so often as "democratic licentiousness." That could mean collapse and ruin from within, instead of from without. Men like Hutchinson and the Olivers could only hope in 1766 that the changing British cabinets would refrain from further provocative acts.

The full implications of the recent turbulent events could not be seen by even the most perceptive observers in 1766. People were too close to the Stamp Act crisis to gain needed perspective. While a small number of English leaders understood that a "cooling-off period" was essential, so that mature and rational decisions about the role of Americans within the Empire might be worked out, a majority of home officials still wanted stronger policies.

Rationality did not long prevail, and the immediate source of its demise was the fall of Rockingham's cabinet. George III had been maneuvering for months to have William Pitt become the head of government. Personal feelings aside (the King believed Pitt to be intolerably independent-minded), George III finally persuaded him to help in the construction of yet another cabinet, this time with a stronger majority in Parliament. The aging Pitt, suffering from deteriorating health and extreme pain from the gout, finally accepted the King's solicitations during the summer of 1766 in return for ennoblement as the Earl of Chatham. With Pitt in the House of Lords, others in the new cabinet had to sustain majorities in the Commons.

As it turned out, Chancellor of the Exchequer Charles Townshend, known widely as "Champagne Charlie," emerged as one major cabinet leader in the House.[16] As much as anyone else, the narrow-minded Townshend reopened the Anglo-American controversy. Caught up in financial problems and their details, as Grenville had been, Townshend was about to put forth another plan for picking money from American pocketbooks. More adept at political chatter than at serious thinking about the consequences of legislation, his grand scheme soon earned deserved opprobrium as the Townshend duties.

Whatever his capabilities, the determined Chancellor of the Exchequer believed that Americans had to be taxed—and on their terms. Townshend employed the logic of the irascible Benjamin Franklin, who was in England during the debates over repeal of the Stamp Act. Franklin, out of touch with the American position, gave the impression among M.P.s that the colonists objected only to direct, or "internal" taxes, but not to indirect, or "external" taxes. The latter could be defined as duties on trade for imperial revenue, rather than for the regulation of commerce. Appearing before the bar of the House of Commons, Franklin sustained the invidious distinction between the two types of taxes, clearly misrepresenting what had been written in the vast bulk of formal American petitions. Instead, he insisted that Americans were defiant only about internal taxes. Once drawn, the distinction took on its own life. Charles Townshend accepted it literally, even though he thought that it was foolish, and used it as the basis for his scheme. His disingenuous actions were about to precipitate another significant wave of American protest and resistance.

In June 1767, Parliament sanctioned a revenue act authorizing trade duties as indirect taxes. Now there would be even more import duties collected in American ports, specifically on British-manufactured glass, red and white lead, certain paints and papers, and tea (three pence a pound). Townshend proudly proclaimed that his duties would yield £35 to £40,000 a year "for defraying the charges of the administration of justice, and the support of civil government within all or any of the said colonies or plantations." Since Parliament in 1766 had lowered the duty on foreign molasses from three to one pence a gallon and extended that duty to British West Indian molasses as well, the trade-duties-as-taxation-approach seemed viable. Americans had not protested against the broadened molasses duty, and Townshend suspected that his new scheme would be too subtle in intent to engender much opposition. He was wrong.

The Townshend duties were not much different from the Stamp Act tax, except that provincial consumers would pay indirectly. Presumably, the duties would be less offensive because they would not be visible. In seeking sustained revenue, and in following Grenville's ill-fated path, Townshend forgot the many ways in which American commercial ties supported and stimulated the British economy. Concern and pressure on Parliament from English and Scottish businessmen at the time of the Stamp Act crisis should have proved that point. But Townshend was looking at the small picture; for a paltry sum he was begging provincial leaders to resharpen their tools of resistance. If anyone was shuddering in America after learning about the Townshend duties, it was the provincial officeholding group in the imperial orbit.

To make matters worse, Parliament in June 1767 also approved a plan to create an American Board of Customs Commissioners, to be located in the provinces and with all the powers enjoyed by home-based customs officials. The new American Board was designed to assure more efficient collection of all trade duties, including Townshend's. For some reason, the decision was made to locate the five-man American Board in Boston. The year of uneasy accommodation was about to come to a close.[17]

American popular leaders had learned that defiant, extralegal protest could make Parliament back down. The Stamp Act's repeal set an obvious precedent designed to encourage further resistance. But popular leaders were also discovering in the fall of 1767 that now it was much more difficult to muster concerted colonial opposition. Not only were the royalist targets charged with implementation less noticeable (except for the Customs Board Commissioners in Boston) but also, unlike the Stamp tax, the Townshend duties affected only small numbers of people. Except for tea, the duties were on luxury items rarely used by most colonists. Moreover, it did not take long for industrious provincial merchants to circumvent the tea duty by expanding smuggling operations with Dutch merchants. Tea consumption did not lessen, but the source of its supply changed dramatically. Getting Americans to defend themselves against this new parliamentary assault on their liberties, then, was a difficult task.

The provincial legal and constitutional arguments surfaced almost immediately. John Dickinson, a wealthy Philadelphia lawyer, who also had extensive landholdings in Delaware, restated the basic provincial position in his *Letters from a Farmer in Pennsylvania*. First published as newspaper essays during late 1767 and early 1768, then collected and circulated widely in pamphlet form, Dickinson's skillful arguments attacked Townshend's basic assumption. The "Farmer" pointed out that the distinction between internal and external taxes was spurious. Both were taxes—just that. American representatives had to make it clear that there was a difference between duties "for the regulation of trade"—facilitating the proper flow of imperial commerce—and duties *"for the single purpose of levying money upon us."* Even though Parliament had the unquestioned power to establish duties to promote the "mutually beneficial intercourse between constituent parts of the empire," taxes disguised as trade duties represented "an innovation; and a most dangerous innovation." They signaled the end of liberty and the beginning of political slavery.

Legislation which turned the colonists' "boasted liberty" into "a sound and nothing else" had to be challenged. However, Dickinson did not advocate violent resistance. Careful in his logic, the cautious "Farmer" feared the repercussions that might follow if the democracy of citizens acted too often out of doors. Thus Dickinson urged his fellow provincial leaders to avoid the path of internal social convulsions, which portended the end of stable governments, of deferential politics, and of hierarchical relationships. Instead, he advocated a concerted petitioning campaign and argued that reasonable leaders in England would respond to American grievances. If given time, they would cease to attempt to tax the colonists. The "Farmer" did not, however, mention that an earlier petition campaign against the Stamp Act had got the colonists nowhere.[18]

The widespread publication of Dickinson's *Letters* prompted the Massachusetts General Court in February 1768 to send a circular letter to the other assemblies. For Samuel Adams, now ensconced in the General Court, the Circular Letter seemed a relatively mild form of protest. But it was protest, and attempts to utilize more extreme forms of resistance were lagging. The Circular Letter, in Adams's own words, not only denounced Townshend's scheme as a violation of constitutional rights; it also lashed out at Parliament for seeking to use the tax revenue to pay the salaries of royal officials in America. (The Stamp tax had been earmarked for regular army soldiers.) Assemblies traditionally had employed their right to appropriate annual salaries as a means of exacting full gubernatorial cooperation in legislative decisions, especially when those decisions favored local over imperial interests. Controlling gubernatorial salaries had aided the assemblies over the years in building up their strength vis-à-vis the prerogatives of the governors. The Circular Letter stressed that salaries paid "independent of the people . . . subvert the principles of equity, and endanger the happiness and security of the subject." Obviously,

American assemblies were already taxing citizens to pay those salaries. Now Parliament would assume that right and, in the process, make royal governors more independent in the administration of imperial authority. The Circular Letter concluded by urging other assemblies to join formal protest efforts.[19]

The most important reaction came from England—from Lord Hillsborough, another gentleman-politician who possessed limited knowledge about the provinces, and who had recently accepted the new cabinet post of Secretary for American Affairs. Infuriated over what he interpreted as the General Court's impudence, Hillsborough overreacted by insisting that Governor Bernard make the General Court rescind its Letter. If it refused (and it did), Bernard was to dissolve that body and call for new elections. At the same time, Hillsborough sent out instructions to the other provincial governors ordering them not to permit their assemblies "to receive or give any countenance to this seditious paper." Else they, too, would be dissolved, and the governors would be forced to inconvenience incumbent representatives by calling for new elections.[20] If Hillsborough sought submission, his actions were inept at best. The new assembly elections only swelled the ranks of those who were willing to stand firm against imperial policies and manipulative crown officials.

By now—the spring of 1768—Hillsborough was seething over more than the Circular Letter. He was also disturbed by reports concerning the rough treatment of the five-man Board of Customs Commissioners and other customs collectors in Boston. The board members quickly had become targets of local abuse. When one of them landed in Boston on November 5, 1767, a large crowd carrying effigies of "devils, popes, and pretenders, through the streets, with labels on their breasts, Liberty, and property, and no commissioners" greeted him.[21] It was Guy Fawkes's day, and the parade was only an orderly warning from private citizens. The commissioners soon discovered, however, that it was virtually impossible to carry out their responsibilities without ongoing harassment. To ferret out smuggling and to condemn vessels in the vice admiralty court was to invite intimidation. Serious rioting finally broke out on June 10, 1768, when a mob beat up customs people who had seized John Hancock's sloop *Liberty* on charges of carrying smuggled goods. The commissioners expeditiously fled to Castle William, a fort in Boston harbor, and settled for writing more angry reports about the breakdown of law and order.

Governor Bernard joined in the fretting over democratic licentiousness. His perceptions of events reveal key thought patterns, especially of those officials in the imperial orbit. After the *Liberty* riots, he wrote that redcoats might be necessary "to rescue the government out of the hands of a trained mob." It was not the first time that the Governor had hinted about the necessity for military intervention. Boston, according to Bernard, had been "under the uninterrupted dominion of a faction supported by a trained mob from August 14, 1765." He had written to his superiors as early as 1764 that he had proof of a concerted plan "to lay a foundation for connecting the demagogues of the several governments in America to join together in opposition to all orders from Great Britain."[22] By 1768, Bernard believed that the crisis of relationships was at hand. The anarchy of the masses, if not contained, would destroy the vital constitutional balance among the traditional orders in society. The threat had become that of a popularly based tyranny of the majority. The only answer seemed to be redcoats, but Bernard could not bring himself to ask for their presence in Boston.

Bernard was not alone in conjuring up images of popular convulsions from below. Thomas Hutchinson expressed similar fears on numerous occasions. In early 1769 that beleaguered man wrote: "There must be an abridgement of what are called English liberties. . . . I doubt whether it is possible to project a system of government in which a colony 3,000 miles distant from the parent state shall enjoy all the liberty of the parent state." Hutchinson concluded that "some further restraint of liberty" was mandatory, "rather than the connection with the parent state should be broken." He was sure that a breach would prove "the ruin of the colony."[23] If events pointed toward a political Armageddon, then Hutchinson would have to fight with all his might against those fomenting the disaster. To him, the stabilizing imperial connection was all that remained to save the people from chaos.

Hutchinson's words have particular meaning because they were written shortly after hundreds of regular troops had debarked in Boston. Lord Hillsborough, gnashing his teeth about the Circular Letter and the rough treatment meted out to customs officials in Boston, took the initiative himself and ordered General Thomas Gage, commander in chief of royal forces in America, to move redcoats to the Bay colony metropolis. Hillsborough's decision came in early June 1768, just before the *Liberty* riots. As Bostonians mourned the passing of the unconstrained days of yore, the troops began arriving during the fall of 1768. No one missed the implications. Hutchinson was referring to the soldiers' presence when he spoke of "an abridgement of . . . liberties." Popular leaders fulminated over tyranny; a standing, professional army, even if subject to civilian officials, was all the proof that Samuel Adams and his supporters needed to give legitimacy to their harangues about despotism. Adams went so far as to call for armed resistance to prevent the troops from landing, but calmer heads, realizing that a bloodbath might result, prevailed.

The presence of regular army soldiers in Boston as a stabilizing police force did help somewhat in galvanizing unfocused American opposition to the Townshend duties. The duties had been law for over a year, but resistance, beyond petitions and the turmoil caused by Hillsborough's reaction to the Massachusetts Circular Letter, remained negligible. Human targets for intimidation were not that easy to identify outside of Boston, since collection of the duties did not depend upon individual administrators like the stamp distributors.

One threatening tactic remained—that of a direct economic boycott through nonimportation pacts. Popular leaders had tried to promote the idea of another nonimportation movement during the summer of 1767, but the most powerful merchants in the major ports resisted the call. Many of them did not want to endanger the prosperity that was finally returning after the postwar economic downturn. Also, mercantile magnates in one port feared that merchants elsewhere would not cooperate, thereby making huge profits at the expense of those who were foolish enough to become committed to protest. Many wealthy merchants, moreover, were still recoiling from earlier mob activities, which could be directed against them if resistance efforts got out of hand. Like Bernard and Hutchinson (and even John Dickinson), they feared the specter of democratic despotism, especially if the "common herd" became too presumptuous in its out-of-doors political role.

The breakthrough in assuring at least some tactical resistance came during a well-managed meeting on August 1, 1768, at Faneuil Hall in Boston—in the aftermath of the decision to place regular troops there. Subscribers to this nonimportation pact agreed to cut off British imports, except for a few vital goods, for at least the year 1769, or until Parliament gave in. New York City merchants soon followed suit, partially out of pique over a local order that customs duties in that port were to be collected in hard money rather than in heretofore acceptable promissory notes. Popular pressure also helped to persuade the merchants to make their decision. Philadelphia business leaders had to be accused in print of favoring personal monetary gain over liberty before they signed articles of nonimportation. They inaugurated economic boycott in that port on February 1, 1769. It took many more months and sustained pressure from local artisans and mechanics before Charleston merchants comprehended the significance of the constitutional crisis and joined the cause, but they, too, finally came around during the summer of 1769. With the major provincial cities closing off trade, many lesser coastal communities followed suit.

Nonimportation, though leaky, clearly hurt British merchants and manufacturers (including the Scots). In 1768, New Englanders imported £430,807 worth of goods from Britain; in 1769 the figure dropped to £223,694. New Yorkers were even more rigorous. In 1768, they imported £490,673 in goods from Britain, but only £75,931 the next year. Pennsylvanians followed suit, though less dramatically, dropping from £441,829 in 1768 to £204,979 in 1769. Carolinians, given Charleston's late entry, bought as much in 1769 as they had in 1768. The 1769 import figure was £327,084; but in 1770 the figure dipped to £168,500. Only in the tobacco-planting colonies of Maryland and Virginia did the value of British imports increase, rising from £669,523 in 1768 to £714,943 in 1769. Over-all, though, the quantity and value of British imports declined significantly as the economic boycott took effect.[24]

There was an added dimension to the nonimportation movement which should have improved the position of the poor, especially in the cities. The boycott, had it been sustained, was a potential long-term stimulant for American manufacturing, especially the production of woolens. Repeated pleas went out to prosperous provincials to join the poor in wearing homespun clothing, even if that meant foregoing the latest cuts in fashionable cloth from London. Patriot leaders called upon "genteel ladies" to learn the arts of spinning and weaving. All "Daughters of Liberty," urged the *Boston Gazette*, must

> *First then throw aside your high top knots of pride*
> *Wear none but your own country linen*
> *Of Economy boast. Let your pride be the most*
> *To show clothes of your make and spinning.*[25]

Generally, upper-class women, while complaining to each other about the itchiness of homespun, disdained working at spinning and weaving. But for poorer women, especially in the cities, the boycott meant piecemeal employment, sometimes at home and sometimes in local shops. Yet the opportunity for extra family income did little to improve their economic circumstances. The prices paid for homespun goods remained quite low, since an abundance of cloth quickly appeared in the marketplace. Poorer women virtually gave their labor to the cause. The boycott built itself upon a general attitude of sacrifice, and, for poorer women, whose labor could be so easily exploited, the calls for sacrifice took on vivid meaning.

Those English businessmen engaged in American commerce reacted quickly, as they had done in early 1766. The provincial nonimportation movement threatened short-term profit losses and long-term economic disaster. American manufacturing, if given a sufficient start, would not easily die out, especially if the boycott lasted for several years and nascent provincial industry grew deep roots. Nonimportation would also reduce the huge private trading debt that provincials had accumulated, since the annual value of their British imports far outweighed that of their exports. Provincial manufacturers might enter into direct competition with British firms; in fact, the colonies might even become economically independent.

Alarmed home merchants and businessmen thus appealed to the ministry for help. Their argument was simple. They could not imagine how £40,000 sterling a year in Townshend duties could be worth a several hundred thousand pound loss in the value of trade. Sympathetic Lord North, who had taken over from the hapless, confused remnants of the Pitt coalition in January 1770 (Townshend died shortly after his duties became law) tried to pave the path toward accommodation.

In temperament, North seemed to be the kind of person that George III had been searching for as cabinet head for several years. North, personally amiable and a skillful debater in Parliament, was willing to submit to the King's judgments regarding legislative decisions. North would be the King's agent and would permit George to play more fully the role that Lord Bute had outlined so clearly during the King's adolescent years. George, as a committed constitutional monarch working on behalf of all his subjects, had built up a sizable parliamentary following by scattering around quite a few titles and offices. Now North, somewhat indecisive and indolent, was to be George's champion on the floor of the Commons. From 1770 to 1782, North served as the King's loyal minister, unlike previous cabinet heads who had acted primarily as Whiggish adversaries standing on guard (for public purposes, at least) against new outbreaks of potential monarchical tyranny.

Nearly ten years had passed since George had acceded to the throne; now he was to have a stable cabinet, at least in terms of longevity. The stability of North's ministry, however, could not in the long run undo the damage already done to Anglo-American relations. The instability of the ministries of the 1760s had unleashed trends too powerful to be brought easily under control.

North, who, incidentally, bore a striking physical resemblance to George, wanted to put a stop to the adversarial relationship with America. He and the King had enough problems with confrontational politics at home, especially with the London radical John Wilkes, who enjoyed significant popular support in his vituperative attacks against the King and his supporters. One Wilkes assault, printed as *North Briton No. 45*, resulted in his removal from Parliament in 1763. But Londoners still adored their popular hero; in the late 1760s, after Wilkes returned from exile in France, they reelected him to Parliament. But the House of Commons, under direct pressure from the King, continued to bar Wilkes because of his reputedly libelous statements. Serious rioting resulted, while men like Lord North shuddered in the face of the democracy's turmoil at home.[26]

Yielding to English merchants, manufacturers, and American boycotters thus seemed an easy way to reduce some of the disorder in the larger realm. Accordingly, on March 5, 1770, North urged the House of Commons to rescind the Townshend duties. He argued that the duties were foolish at best and of no real value. Parliament heeded the ministerial leader's advice, declaring them null and void, except for the 3 pence a pound duty on tea. North and the King's Parliament thought that the tea duty should be maintained as a symbolic reminder to Americans that Parliament still maintained full powers of taxation, as well as the right of full legislation over all matters affecting the provinces.

Indeed, George and North were making a consciously conciliatory move, primarily for the promotion of political stability. But Americans thought that their economic boycott had been the key factor which forced Parliament to back down again. Even though a few radical diehards in the provinces insisted that the boycott should remain in full force until Parliament abolished the tea duty, resistance collapsed in the face of a rush of new orders for British goods. To knowledgeable observers, it appeared that Lord North had prevented a more intense confrontation, and that his conciliatory tactics had produced the cooling-off period which contentious ministers such as Townshend and Hillsborough had undermined through their narrowly gauged actions. In fact, it seemed that a new era of harmony in Anglo-American relations was dawning. But the ramifications of earlier decisions could not be stopped.

The King's troops, for example, were still in Boston, where the local populace had readily taken to troop baiting as their new sport. Yet it was more than sport. Agitating the redcoats also reflected the direct competition for unskilled jobs between off duty soldiers and struggling day laborers, whose economic plight was reaching another new low in terms of community property distribution. Tension mounted throughout 1769, erupting into occasional fist fights and beatings. Then a particularly vile incident occurred. On Friday, March 2, 1770, an off duty soldier looking for work visited John Gray's ropewalk establishment. Eyeing the soldier up and down, one employee sarcastically asked: "Do you want work?" The soldier meekly replied: "Yes, I do, faith." Apparently not one to pass up an opportunity to hurl an insult, the employee retorted: "Well, then go and clean my shit-house." The soldier snorted back: "Empty it yourself." Outnumbered, the soldier backed off as other workers surrounded him. He went for help and returned with friends from the 29th regiment. In what turned into a pitched battle, the soldiers pitted their clubs against the workers' rope-twisting sticks. The fight ended in a draw, even though the workers drove the soldiers from Gray's establishment. The incident, however, was only the beginning of a far more memorable confrontation.[27]

Over the weekend there were sporadic, isolated clashes between more soldiers and workers. Then came Monday, March 5, the very day that Lord North urged Parliament to repeal the Townshend duties. The daylight hours passed quietly, perhaps because it was bitterly cold with snow piled high everywhere. Early in the evening, however, small groups of apprentices, day laborers, and merchant seamen began to congregate in the streets. At first they milled about; then they moved, seemingly without any over-all direction, toward King Street. There a small detachment of the 29th regiment under Captain Thomas Preston, including the soldier who had asked for work at Gray's ropewalk, was on guard duty in front of the Customs House.

To this day no one knows exactly what happened. The growing crowd pressed in on the soldiers; musket shots rang out. According to the pro-American *Boston Gazette,* Preston's troops had overreacted when the howling throng pelted them with snowballs. "On this," the *Gazette* reported, "the Captain commanded them to fire; and more snowballs coming, he again said, damn you, fire, be the consequences what it will!"

Captain Preston, a forty-year-old Irishman, remembered the details of what became known in the colonies as the "Boston Massacre" somewhat differently: The crowd was shouting, "Come on you rascals, you bloody backs, you lobster scoundrels, fire if you dare, God damn you, fire and be damned, we know you dare not." One soldier "having received a severe blow with a stick, stepped a little to one side and instantly fired." It was a warning volley, commented Preston, but the mob, further enraged, began a "general attack . . . by a great number of heavy clubs and snowballs . . . by which all our lives were in imminent danger." Preston later explained that three or four soldiers fired into the crowd in total panic, but justifiably so, in order to protect their lives.[28] Before the shooting had stopped, civilians were dying, among them seventeen-year-old apprentice Samuel Maverick, black merchant seaman Crispus Attucks, and rope maker Samuel Gray. All told, five men lost their lives as a direct result of the shooting.

The names of some of those killed led some crown-supporting citizens to suspect that the Boston Massacre had been something more than a spontaneous, unorganized uprising. Samuel Gray, possibly a relative of John Gray, had participated in the ropewalk melee of March 2. Samuel Maverick was a half-brother of the wife of Boston's workingman street leader, Ebenezer Mackintosh. It is at least possible—extant records do not clarify the issue—that the Adams men encouraged the confrontation on March 5—a logical conclusion in light of their earlier failures to focus crowd opposition squarely against the Townshend duties. Turning the soldiers into bloodstained killers would force imperial officials to remove the troops from Boston. Their presence had reduced the ability of popular leaders and their followers to walk all over the Hutchinson-Oliver group. In any event, because of the Massacre, the troops soon would be withdrawn from Boston, some being confined to Castle William and others being sent to New Jersey.

Whether a confrontation planned by popular leaders, a spontaneous uprising, or an organized assault by the poor themselves in an effort to strike back at their economic competitors, the Massacre drew to a head tensions which had been building toward the boiling point for well over a year. More important for the course of events, blood had been spilled on Boston's streets; the imperial political crisis had claimed its first martyrs; and images of impending tyranny had become more compelling.

Thomas Hutchinson, serving as acting governor in 1770 (after Francis Bernard had resigned his office in disgust the previous summer and had sailed for England as a crowd literally cheered from the docks), acted quickly and wisely to avoid further violent repercussions. He succumbed to pressure from popular leaders and ordered the regiments removed. In turn, Captain Preston and his men eventually came to trial. The men had fired without an order from a local magistrate present at the scene, which was the mandatory procedure unless the populace had been declared to be in a state of open rebellion.[29] Ambitious John Adams "volunteered" to serve as one counsel for the defense. What appeared to be a magnanimous act for a man with political ambitions may also be interpreted as a maneuver on the popular party's part to have one of their own in a position to cover up embarrassing evidence about the Massacre's causes. No popular leader wanted to face a formal courtroom charge of inciting a riot that had resulted in bloodshed. Through two trials, one for Captain Preston and one for the soldiers, Adams worked to avoid comments from witnesses regarding possible organized activities in the streets before the actual confrontation had taken place. Captain Preston and all but two of his men were acquitted. The jury at the soldiers' trial found two of them guilty of manslaughter, and they paid the penalty of having their thumbs branded before being set free. With Samuel Adams's vital support, Cousin John shortly thereafter appeared for the first time in the General Court. Paradoxically, defending the troops had abetted the Braintree Adams's political career.

In the end, questions about the cause of the Massacre were not as important as its effects. March 5 became a local holiday, an annual time for remembering the first martyred victims of Britain's tyranny. Each year until the mid-1780s, when July 4 came into vogue as a commemorative holiday, Bostonians gathered to hear a Massacre oration in which the images of tyranny reached unparalleled dimensions. The actual incident lost all sense of proportion as local citizens bowed each year in memory of the slain. Most effective, because of its inflammatory language, was Dr. Joseph Warren's oration in 1772. Warren, Samuel Adams's lieutenant and a superb propagandist, implored the throng not to forget *"the fatal fifth of March, 1770."* "The horrors of *that dreadful night* are but too deeply impressed on our hearts. Language is too feeble to paint the emotions of our souls," recalled Warren, "when our streets were stained with the blood of our brethren; when our ears were wounded by the groans of the dying, and our eyes were tormented with the sight of the mangled bodies of the dead." So much for what had happened! For Warren there were other, far more serious dangers, and the good Doctor readily pointed them out in staccato fashion. Warren's "imagination presented" to the spectators "our houses wrapped in flames, our children subjected to the barbarous caprice of a raging soldiery; our beauteous virgins exposed to all the insolence of unbridled passion." Nor could Warren exclude from his apocalyptic vision "our virtuous wives, endeared to us by every tender tie, falling a sacrifice to worse than brutal violence, and perhaps, like the famed Lucretia, distracted with anguish and despair, ending their wretched lives by their own fair hands."[30] The cause of liberty obviously demanded ongoing vigilance.

This emotional language cannot be dismissed as heated rhetoric. Comparing Warren's choice of words with those of Patrick Henry in his formal resolutions or with those of John Dickinson in the *Farmer Letters*, an important pattern emerges. Petitioners and pamphleteers, using sophisticated, legalistic, and learned reasoning, sought to communicate primarily with leaders on their own socioeconomic and political level. Through elaborate and extended argumentation, they sought to persuade the well-educated and the powerful, depending upon the logic and the rectitude of their propositions. But Warren, in standing before the gathered throng, was using a vocabulary which the ordinary people could understand, one stripped of quotations from the classics and other formalities. His language contained striking images which all citizens, not just an educated elite, could appreciate. He wanted to communicate with and influence those who, under normal circumstances, were expected to defer to the better sort in political judgments. The Adams men depended upon popular participation in protest efforts; public rhetoric like Warren's, when compared to more learned documents, undergirded and gave even greater cohesion to the popular alliance against tyranny.[31]

Warren's phrases also conveyed a sense of burning passion, if not consuming frustration, coming at a time when there were no new major imperial issues to frighten New Englanders, only the shadowy remnants of old controversies. In 1772 George III and Lord North were holding firm to the course of conciliation. Popular leaders seemed to be drifting, struggling almost by inertia or out of personal vengeance against various royalist leaders to find targets of opposition in defending American rights. Incidents, when they did occur during the so-called "issueless years" of 1770–1773, often had a parochial cast, suggesting that some provincials were trying to keep the flames of protest burning on any pretext. Other incidents, largely local confrontations, such as the Wilkes Fund controversy in South Carolina and the *Gaspée* incident in Rhode Island, had a much broader impact.

In December 1769, the Commons house of the South Carolina assembly ordered the provincial treasurer to send £1,500 from the public treasury to the Society of the Gentlemen Supporters of the Bill of Rights in London. That *ad hoc* group had assumed responsibility for paying the debts of John Wilkes. South Carolina's royal governor and "placeman" councilors in the upper house balked at the assembly's action, arguing that the Commons house did not have the exclusive right to disperse public funds without approval by higher provincial authorities. Since the lower house had exercised this privilege before with no complaints, it was obvious that the issue really centered on Wilkes, the home government's most effective critic at that time. The royal governor appealed to the ministry and got back exactly the answer that he wanted. The angry ministers ruled that the assemblymen had exceeded their authority and violated gubernatorial prerogatives. The ministry ordered that any treasurer who acted only on assembly directions in the future would be removed from office and fined triple the amount initially issued. Commons house leaders were irate, and normal decision making virtually came to a standstill in South Carolina for the rest of the colonial period.

Many Commons house leaders, generally the wealthier planters and merchants, were also bitter about the ministerial practice of naming placeman outsiders rather than native elite leaders of local distinction to higher appointive royal offices in South Carolina. Like their counterparts in the other assemblies, they were seething with frustration over the comprehensiveness of recent imperial policies which appeared to circumscribe their personal opportunities, no matter in what direction they turned. And through popular leaders like Christopher Gadsden they had developed links with the artisans and mechanics of Charleston who would vigorously support them in throwing off constraining imperial ties during 1775 and 1776.[32]

Far to the north in Rhode Island, tensions mounted because of the burning of *Gaspée*, a royal naval vessel engaged in running down local smugglers. *Gaspée* had been patrolling in Rhode Island waters and had been successful in harassing local violators of the trade acts. The ship's crew and its haughty commander, Lieutenant William Dudingston, made themselves obnoxious, moreover, by their bullying tactics. By 1772, some Rhode Islanders had had enough of Dudingston and his aggressive crew. A smaller coasting vessel, giving the appearance of a smuggler, flaunted itself before *Gaspée*, a much larger vessel, on the afternoon of June 9. As the smaller sloop sailed closer to the shore, Dudingston gave chase and ran his own ship aground. That evening a mob disguised as Indians descended on *Gaspée*, further immobilized by an ebbing tide, and set it on fire. To make matters worse, one enthusiastic participant paid Dudingston the highest disrespect by firing a musket ball into his buttocks!

Rhode Islanders cheered the burning, but English officials, including Lord Hillsborough, demanded satisfaction for such blatant destruction of the King's property. Hillsborough appointed a special commission to look into the incident and threatened full legal prosecution of all offenders. The commission got nowhere in ferreting out the local "Indians." On the contrary, its investigation turned out to be counterproductive for the Crown, because three younger Virginia burgesses—Patrick Henry, Thomas Jefferson, and Richard Henry Lee—convinced their less truculent planter elite colleagues that the House of Burgesses should establish a standing committee of correspondence to communicate with the other assemblies when new possible threats to liberty occurred. The older, more cautious burgesses had long since become accustomed to Henry's rantings. They might have found him boisterous and distasteful, but they went along with the suggestion because they thought that they could control the committee's membership. By the spring of 1774, the only provincial assembly lacking a standing committee of correspondence was Pennsylvania's. A formal intercolonial communications network, ready to spread news of undesirable home government decisions, had grown out of the *Gaspée* incident. It proved to be a valuable network as events heated up in the months ahead.

Another communications network, closer to the grass-roots level, also began to take shape during 1773. It arose out of the ongoing, petty turmoil in Massachusetts politics. When Thomas Hutchinson and Andrew Oliver became governor and lieutenant governor respectively in 1771, word spread that their salaries were to be paid out of customs revenues, in the spirit of the Townshend duties program. In 1772, the ministry extended its salary coverage policy to the Superior Court, now headed by Peter Oliver. The Adams men kept exhorting the populace, warning everyone of doom, but with little response. Finally, in October 1772, they persuaded the Boston town meeting to set up its own standing committee of correspondence. That body's purpose would be to communicate regularly with the interior towns, warning them not "to doze, or sit supinely indifferent on the brink of destruction, while the Iron hand of oppression is daily tearing the choicest fruit from the fair Tree of Liberty."[33] Many interior communities, rather than investigating such charges impartially, responded by establishing their own committees. They were now poised and ready for news from Boston about further acts of tyranny.

Through all the particularist turmoil, Lord North held steady to his course of not tampering with the provinces. Yet old and festering sores continued to plague the colonies. One incident significantly heightened local tensions and produced confrontational feelings which would be played out in a broader context not many months ahead. In Massachusetts, the royalist-popular party feud took another provocative turn in 1773, when the Adams group published private letters which Thomas Hutchinson had earlier sent to well-placed English correspondents, letters which commented on the turbulence in the Bay colony. An enemy of Hutchinson in England passed them back to friends in Boston through the willing hands of Benjamin Franklin, who was close to the end of a long stay in London as a lobbying agent for several colonies and for his own interests, including western lands. It was in one of those sequestered letters that Hutchinson spoke out about "an abridgement of what are called English liberties." Hutchinson was mortified and Franklin thoroughly embarrassed. The Philadelphian even lost his lucrative position as deputy postmaster general for the colonies as a result of his part in the affair. What was more important was that the letters confirmed once more, for those who needed convincing, that there was still an active, dangerous plan of despotism afoot to destroy American liberties.[34]

Attitudes and perceptions on all sides clearly had hardened in the years of protest and tactical resistance. Local leaders with high personal aspirations and with grudges stood ready for further assaults from above. The corrupting hand of power seemed to guarantee that new attacks would come. Further attempts to shackle the popular leaders and their followers and to strike at them economically, socially, or politically would have far more serious repercussions; the sheer weight of events over the past decade had become too stifling and threatening. It is ironic that Lord North, the minister of general conciliation, misread the temper of the times so completely when he went before Parliament in May 1773 over a problem that only indirectly touched upon American interests.

Notes

1. "Journal of a French Traveller in the Colonies, 1765," *American Historical Review*, 26 (1920–1921), 745. For the most recent investigation of Henry's life, see Richard R. Beeman, *Patrick Henry: A Biography* (New York, 1974).

2. The resolutions are contained in *Prologue to Revolution: Sources and Documents on the Stamp Act Crisis, 1764–1766* (ed. E. S. Morgan, Chapel Hill, N.C., 1959), 47–50. See also Edmund S. and Helen M. Morgan, *The Stamp Act Crisis: Prologue to Revolution* (rev. ed., New York, 1962), 120–136.

3. *The Rights of Colonies Examined* (Providence, R.I., 1764), reprinted in *Tracts of the American Revolution* (ed. Merrill Jensen, Indianapolis, Ind., 1967), 43.

4. The Stamp Act Congress petitions may be found in Morgan, ed., *Prologue to Revolution*, 62–69. Savelle, *Seeds of Liberty*, 313–318, discusses embryonic notions about divisible sovereignty.

5. See the sources cited in note two. For the crisis from the British side, see

Ian R. Christie and Benjamin W. Labaree, *Empire or Independence, 1760–1776: A British-American Dialogue on the Coming of the American Revolution* (New York, 1976), 46–94.

6. For a discussion of Henry's revivalistic speaking manner, see Rhys Isaac, "Preachers and Patriots: Popular Culture and the Revolution in Virginia," Young, ed., *The American Revolution*, 127–156. See also Martin, *Men in Rebellion, passim.*

7. William Gordon, *The History of the Rise, Progress, and Establishment of the Independence of the United States of America* (4 vols., London, 1788), III, 140–141. See also John J. Waters, Jr., *The Otis Family in Provincial and Revolutionary Massachusetts* (Chapel Hill, N.C., 1968), 76–131.

8. Diary entry, August 15, 1765, *The Adams Papers: Diary and Autobiography of John Adams* (4 vols., ed. L. H. Butterfield *et al.*, Cambridge, Mass., 1961), I, 260. For a discussion of the emerging worldview of conspiracy, see Bailyn, *Ideological Origins*, 94–143.

9. James Kirby Martin, "The Rights of Man and the American Revolution: Samuel Adams, Thomas Hutchinson, and John Dickinson," *Men, Women, and Issues in American History* (ed. H. Quint and M. Cantor, Homewood, Ill., 1975), 63–83. An excellent example of perceptions that a conspiracy was developing to destroy the system from below may be found in Peter Oliver's *Origin & Progress of the American Rebellion: A Tory View* (ed. Douglass Adair and J. A. Schutz, San Marino, Cal., 1961), *passim.*

10. Morgan and Morgan, *Stamp Act Crisis*, 187–204.

11. Jensen, ed., *English Historical Documents*, IX, 671–672.

12. David Ramsay, *The History of the American Revolution* (2 vols., Philadelphia, 1789), I, 61–62. See also Arthur M. Schlesinger, Sr., *Prelude to Independence: The Newspaper War on Britain, 1764–1776* (New York, 1958), 67–84.

13. *Boston Gazette*, December 23, 1765. See also Henry Bass to Samuel P. Savage, Boston, December 19, 1765, Colonial Society of Massachusetts *Publications*, 26 (1927), 355–356.

14. The debates between Pitt and Grenville, occurring on January 17, 1766, may be found in William Cobbett and T. C. Hansard, *The Parliamentary History of England* (London, 1806–1820), XVI, 95–108.

15. Jensen, ed., *English Historical Documents*, IX, 695–696. (Italics mine).

16. Sir Lewis Namier and John Brooke, *Charles Townshend* (London, 1964), *passim.* See also Christie and Labaree, *Empire or Independence*, 95–118.

17. Jensen, ed., *English Historical Documents*, IX, 701–703, reprints the Revenue Act of 1767 (June 26) and the Act creating the American Board of Customs Commissioners (June 29).

18. The heart of Dickinson's constitutional argument is in Letter II, Jensen, ed., *Tracts of the American Revolution*, 133–139.

19. Jensen, ed., *English Historical Documents*, IX, 714–716.

20. *Ibid.*, 716–717. For more on Hillsborough, consult Christie and Labaree, *Empire or Independence*, 119–130.

21. Ann Hulton, *Letters of a Loyalist Lady* (Cambridge, Mass., 1927), 8.

22. Bernard to Lord Barrington, July 23, 1768, *The Barrington-Bernard Correspondence and Illustrative Matter, 1760–1770* (ed. Edward Channing and A. C. Coolidge, Cambridge, Mass., 1912), 167–168; Bernard to the Board of Trade, June 29, 1764, quoted in Merrill Jensen, *The Founding of a Nation, 1763–1776* (New York, 1968), 122–123.

23. Boston, January 20, 1769, quoted in Clifford K. Shipton, *Sibley's Harvard Graduates*, VIII (Boston, 1951), 179.

24. Price, "New Time Series for Scotland's and Britain's Trade," *William and Mary Quarterly* (1975), 324–325. Still an excellent summary of nonimportation is Arthur M. Schlesinger, *The Colonial Merchants and the American Revolution: 1763–1776* (New York, 1918), 77–239.

25. November 9, 1767, quoted in Joan Hoff Wilson, "The Illusion of Change: Women and the American Revolution," Young, ed., *The American Revolution*, 398.

26. For further information, consult George Rudé, *Wilkes and Liberty: A Social Study of 1763 to 1774* (Oxford, 1962), esp. 105–190.

27. Incident quoted in Hiller B. Zobel, *The Boston Massacre* (New York, 1970), 182–183.

28. *Boston Gazette*, March 12, 1770; Preston's account, dated March 13, 1770, is in Jensen, ed., *English Historical Documents*, IX, 750–753, which also contains the *Boston Gazette* analysis, 745–750.

29. John P. Reid, "In a Constitutional Void: The Enforcement of Imperial Law, the Role of the British Army, and the Coming of the American Revolution," *Wayne Law Review*, 22 (1975), 1–37.

30. Hezekiah Niles, *Principles and Acts of the Revolution in America* (2nd ed., New York, 1876), 20–24.

31. For a discussion of the emerging art of public rhetoric, see Gordon S. Wood, "The Democratization of Mind in the American Revolution," *Leadership in the American Revolution* (Washington, 1974), 63–88. See also Eric Foner, *Tom Paine and Revolutionary America* (New York, 1976), 71–106.

32. Jack P. Greene, *The Quest for Power: The Lower Houses of Assembly in the Southern Royal Colonies, 1689–1776* (Chapel Hill, N.C., 1963), 399–416.

33. *A State of the Rights of the Colonists* (Boston, 1772), Jensen, ed., *Tracts of the American Revolution*, 235–255, attributed to Samuel Adams, went to the interior towns; it contained the call for committees. A probing monograph by Richard D. Brown, *Revolutionary Politics in Massachusetts: The Boston Committee of Correspondence and the Towns, 1772–1774* (Cambridge, Mass., 1970), should also be consulted.

34. The most thorough account of the letter publishing incident may be found in Bernard Bailyn, *The Ordeal of Thomas Hutchinson* (Cambridge, Mass., 1974), 221–259.

IV

Rebellion and the Call to
Revolution, 1773–1776

Numerous violent incidents had occurred during the years of protest and resistance in the major port towns—Boston, New York, Philadelphia, and Charleston. In these urban areas popular leaders had been particularly effective in mobilizing everyday citizens, especially the propertyless poor, against imperial acts and officials. Those unfortunate individuals in the provinces charged with implementing parliamentary programs had been turned into "devils, popes, and pretenders" in the popular imagery of conspiratorial tyranny. In some cases, the patriot crowds had acted in close conjunction with popular leaders, as during the Stamp Act riots. Popular leaders, who almost never participated directly in selective acts of violence against property and personal intimidation, normally guided the thrust of incidents in general planning sessions before releasing their street leaders. In other situations, crowds had acted on their own, or privately, which may have been the case with the confrontation that led to the Boston Massacre because of direct economic competition between local citizens and off duty soldiers.[1]

Whether incidents of violent protest had a public or private character, the effect on high-placed observers, more important, was essentially the same. By 1774, British cabinet leaders had become convinced that anarchy was threatening to erupt everywhere in the colonies, but nowhere more menacingly than in Boston. Indeed, imperial officials in America had repeatedly emphasized the role of Boston—and New England more generally—as the center of provincial disaffection. The voluminous flow of complaints from Bernard, Hutchinson, and others in the Bay colony, besides the reports of many royal officials elsewhere, created the distinct impression in London that "democratical" leanings were a malignant disease among the "licentious" New Englanders. After the Stamp Act disturbances in Charleston of October 1765, for example, the royal governor there explained to his London superiors that, "by the artifices of some busy spirits," the thoughts of citizens there were "universally poisoned with the principles which were imbibed and propagated from Boston and Rhode Island (from which Towns at this time of the year, vessels very frequently arrived)."[2] The royal governor obviously wanted it understood that forces outside his community had duped the normally deferential Charleston workingmen.

Home ministers took these accusations with mounting seriousness. Lord Hillsborough's impolitic decision during 1768 to place troops in Boston was evidence of such thinking. The soldiers were to do more than prop up Bay colony royalists. They were also to make sure that rabidly democratical Bostonians no longer had the opportunity to set anarchical examples for unthinking provincials elsewhere.

Even though these perceptions simplified real conditions, they also had some validity. Nowhere in the provinces was local politics more intense than in the Bay colony. There all the bad family blood had spilled over with virulent force into the popular-royalist factional split. Of even greater significance, there was no major countervailing force to ease the intensely confrontational character of politics. In Charleston and the South more generally, the specter of slave revolts tended to assuage differences. The fear among white leaders that violent protest against British policies would serve as a model for angry black slaves restrained some popular leaders. Christopher Gadsden specifically worried about being trapped between two forms of slavery, the one political and the other economic and social—and being consumed by both.[3]

Although some violent incidents of protest did occur in New York City and Philadelphia between 1765 and 1773, they lacked the sustained intensity of Boston's belligerency. Again, countervailing forces were at work. New York during the 1760s had two competing Whiggish factions led by the Livingston and DeLancey family clans and their supporters, with each of the clans vying for control of the assembly. The Livingston-DeLancey divisiveness even carried into the streets, where the two elite groups competed for on-the-scene crowd leadership. Not until the early 1770s did a semblance of crowd fusion occur. At that time, Alexander McDougall, a privateer during the Seven Years' War who had become a petty New York merchant, began to unite all of the people in his role as a Livingston clan street leader. But by then Boston had been stereotyped as the leading den of democratical iniquity.

Philadelphians found themselves facing even more bewildering circumstances. It was unclear whether a truly popular faction really existed there, at least before the mid 1770s. The Quaker party, of which Benjamin Franklin was a leader during the 1760s, was basically more interested in challenging the Penn family-proprietary group and its title to Pennsylvania's rich land resources than in checking ministerial tyranny. The Quaker group had launched a campaign in England designed to undercut the Penns and to turn Pennsylvania into a royal province. Using the crowd in Philadelphia to resist home officials would not have helped that campaign. Consequently, violent incidents often had anti-Quaker as well as antiministerial characteristics. Only in 1776 did a popular grass-roots leadership group become strong enough to take charge and push Pennsylvania with a jolt into the intercolonial rebellion.[4]

The Adams men in Boston, not having to contend with these kinds of confusing crosscurrents, were able to focus exclusively on enemies to liberty in Massachusetts and England. Yet even in 1773 they were not thinking in terms of independence, despite charges from the opposition. Their goals were far more mundane—to thwart constraining imperial policies and to drive local enemies from royal offices. Persistent harassment had been their weapon, but the harassment was about to go too far in the minds of George III and his ministers. The crisis over tea as it embroiled the Bostonians was the opening round in a far more significant clash—pointing directly toward rebellion and the call to revolution.

At the beginning of 1773, the King and his cabinet leaders had no way to sense that an awesome crisis was nearing. In fact, they were optimistic because of the general trend toward greater imperial harmony. For example, commerce had long since passed its pre-nonimportation movement levels. Imports from Britain to the colonies for the period 1771–1774 were up by nearly 50 percent over the period 1765–1768. A pleased Lord North was not much concerned with American questions in early 1773. For him, a far more pressing problem was another troublesome agency of empire—the East India

Company, that infamous joint-stock concern whose officials had controlled British interests in India and the Far East for well over a century and a half.

The company, normally very profitable, had fallen upon hard times during the 1760s. Americans exacerbated the situation when they stopped buying company tea and turned to smuggled Dutch blends in reaction to the Townshend duties. In gross figures, English tea exports to the provinces dropped from a high point of 868,792 pounds in 1767 to a low point of 108,629 pounds in 1770. Despite the upward spiral in the value of British imports after 1770, tea sales did not approach pre-nonimportation levels, being only 359,153 pounds in 1771 and 263,140 pounds in 1772 for all the provinces combined.[5] Americans had not reduced their tea consumption; in some cases they processed their own bitter-tasting redroot bush blends; but for the most part they were purchasing Dutch tea from provincial smugglers.

Britons had also taken to drinking smuggled tea, which was much cheaper on the British market than the company's product. As a result, by the end of 1772 the East India Company had nearly 18,000,000 pounds of surplus tea in its warehouses. At the same time it owed the Bank of England and the government £1,300,000. Directors faced the prospect of bankruptcy. The primary question was whether or not the North ministry could find a solution to the company's fiscal crisis by mobilizing support in Parliament (which contained many stockholders). The East India directors, desperately needing financial assistance, forced the issue in March 1773 by asking for a £1,500,000 public loan.

As the company's request made its way through Parliament, the debate broadened and touched on related American problems. Inadvertently, it can be argued, Lord North reopened Pandora's box by supporting the company's request that tea be shipped directly to the provinces so that it would not have to pass through England, where costs of unloading, wharfage, storage, auctioning, and reloading added significantly to the final American price. Eliminating such costs would make the company price competitive with that of smuggled Dutch tea. Lord North calculated that company tea, even with the three-pence-a-pound Townshend duty, would now be as cheap, if not cheaper, on the American market. Americans, while paying no more for company tea than Dutch blends, would be acknowledging painlessly the Townshend duty and Parliament's right to tax, without being threatened or humiliated.

Lord North foresaw few problems. He pointed out that Americans seemed willing to pay the duty, if no one embarrassed them about it.

After all, they had purchased some 600,000 pounds of English tea in 1771 and 1772 with the Townshend tax. He thought that he was masterfully solving several imperial problems with one ingenious stroke. He should have heeded the M.P. who warned "the Noble Lord now if he don't take off the duty they won't take the tea."[6] But North, in changing his hands-off course, ignored all warnings.

Parliament approved the ministry's Tea Act in May 1773. The financially straitened company quickly prepared to get its tea into the American market. By July, the directors named special agents in Boston, New York, Philadelphia, and Charleston—local merchants of distinction who would accept shipments of company tea for regional distribution at a commission of 6 percent. Within another two months tea shipments totaling over 600,000 pounds (valued at £60,000 sterling) were ready for shipment. The directors, who had also received a large loan from Parliament, anticipated full economic recovery. Lord North foolishly dreamed of enhanced imperial revenues and looked forward to American recognition of parliamentary sovereignty.

What North and others did not understand was that the Tea Act of 1773 would become one more piece of evidence supporting a provincial worldview of insidious, never ending ministerial plotting. Popular leaders had been upset by the widespread purchase of du-tied company tea after the collapse of the economic boycott in 1770. Now the Tea Act highlighted their fears and grievances anew. Philadelphians, at a mass rally on October 16, 1773, summarized the essential arguments. Paying the tea tax had "a direct tendency to render assemblies useless and to introduce arbitrary government and slavery." All citizens were accordingly urged to demonstrate "a virtuous and steady opposition to this ministerial plan of governing America . . . [in order] to preserve even the shadow of liberty."[7] Elsewhere, colonial leaders clamored against the trading monopoly that was being created; they objected especially to the selection of a few favored provincial merchants as tea consignees.

In Boston, the Adams men were particularly angered by reports that Thomas and Elisha Hutchinson, the sons of their hated rival in the governorship, were to be among the Bay colony tea consignees. The presence of Hutchinson's sons in that group became quintessential proof that the plot was being broadened. When not politically gluttonous, it seemed that the Hutchinsons were economically avaricious. Either way, liberty appeared always to be hanging in the balance.

Popular leaders in all the major ports prepared for resistance, but they were the busiest in Boston. Since the conspirators against liberty were identifiable and known (as had been true in 1765), intimidation and the threat of mob violence was obviously the most available and tested form of response. Late in October, word started circulating through Boston's streets that no company tea was to be landed. Then handbills appeared demanding the tea consignees' presence at the Liberty Tree on November 3 for a commission-resigning ceremony. Memories of the riots in August 1765 gave these invitations a particularly ominous cast. The tea consignees refused public humiliation; they did not appear. They had nothing to resign because they had not yet received commissions. They had no intention of being held accountable for a problem of someone else's making. Some workingmen in the Liberty Tree crowd of November 3, not appreciating such distinctions, responded by going to Richard Clarke's warehouse, where the consignees had gathered to bolster each other. There was a slight outburst of violence when some crowd members rushed the main door and broke it down. The consignees quickly retreated, however, and no significant property damage occurred.

It was a pyrrhic victory at best for Boston's popular forces. The fact that direct intimidation had failed may have strengthened the royalist faction's determination to face down its opposition—before it was too late. A small crowd by earlier standards (only about five hundred) had gathered at the Liberty Tree, which may have been interpreted as a lack of widespread popular support. For whatever reasons, royalist supporters this time were not backing off in the face of pressure. If any group was fretting about what might happen next, it was the Adams men.

The catalyst which finally set off the local showdown occurred on November 28, the day the first tea ship, *Dartmouth*, docked in Boston's harbor. Harassed customs commissioners fled to Castle William, and the local committee of correspondence placed guards on *Dartmouth* and the other two tea ships when they cleared the harbor a few days later. The Adams faction fulminated about the tea ships and insisted that they return to England. They declared that they would not allow the Townshend duty to be collected, no matter how trivial an infringement upon American rights it might be. Moreover, Samuel Adams was not going to let his old adversary, Thomas Hutchinson, defeat him publicly.

By the end of November all eyes had turned toward Hutchinson. He had at least one alternative open, had he wanted to avoid another confrontation: he could issue papers permitting *Dartmouth* and the other vessels to leave port without unloading their tea. Hutchinson refused this alternative in the conviction that the popular faction not only could but also had to be beaten. He knew that the general rules of trade specified that unclaimed cargoes, once ships had docked, had to be seized by customs officers after twenty days if customs duties had not been paid. The goods then would be held in storage until claimed by their owners. If not claimed within a reasonable period, they would be sold at auction, with some of the revenue being used to pay their duties. Hutchinson also knew that the tea consignees would not be foolish enough to claim the waiting tea. Thus he presumed that customs officers would land the tea after twenty days and eventually sell it at auction. (*Dartmouth's* twenty-day waiting period would end on December 17.) In the process the Adams men would be defeated and, in time, Bostonians would adjust to the reality of reinvigorated royalist rule.

Hutchinson clearly underestimated the intensity of feeling among his opponents. He had desperately sought to preserve a modicum of imperial authority. His opponents had made a mockery of it far too often; they had also embarrassed, humiliated, and tormented him, members of his family, and several of his close friends. To Hutchinson, it was time to put a stop to what he perceived as the monstrous force of democratic licentiousness in the form of popular ill will. If the Empire and stable political relationships were to have any chance at all in the future, a line had to be drawn somewhere before the Adams men completely destroyed imperial ties. It appeared as though the popular faction's cause was languishing; so the timing seemed appropriate. Hutchinson chose to defend the imperial connection by not allowing the £10,000 worth of East India Company tea to leave the harbor. Confrontation thus became inevitable.[8]

The twenty-day waiting period was an anxious time for Bostonians. Again and again pleas went out to the governor urging the signing of clearance papers, but Hutchinson doggedly refused. On the morning of December 16, a reported five thousand people (some from outlying towns) attempted to crowd into Boston's Old South Church. The assemblage sent an emissary to Hutchinson at his country home in Milton, but the Governor did not waver. Late in the afternoon the emissary reported that Hutchinson still refused to approve the clearance papers. The crowd, pressing for a showdown, grew restive. Finally, Samuel Adams gained everyone's attention. "This meeting can do no more to save the country," he reportedly shouted.[9] Quickly the assemblage dispersed. Several dozen men followed a preplanned course and dressed up in Indian garb; then they rushed to the vessels and dumped 342 chests of tea into the harbor. It had taken them three hours to drown imperial harmony in the harbor along with the tea.

Similar incidents occurred in the other ports as the beginning of 1774 unfolded. Philadelphians used liberal threats of tar and feathers to convince any doubters that the first tea ships should be sent back to England. South Carolina's royal governor outmaneuvered the local Charleston populace and managed to get the tea consignments landed, but to little avail. The tea lay rotting in a warehouse and never reached the marketplace. Provincials in New York City geared themselves for similar action but had to wait until the spring of 1774 for a tea ship to attempt docking. Then they cheered heartily as the captain accepted threats at face value and fled for England.

The Bostonians thus had demonstrated once again their genius for baiting the English. But this time neither side in the local political war had bowed to pressures from the other, and both sides after all looked foolish. After it was all over, Governor Hutchinson, groping for explanations, concluded meekly: "It would have given me a much more painful reflection if I had saved it [the tea] by any concession to a lawless and highly criminal Assembly."[10] Blaming the Tea Party on Hutchinson's stubbornness, Samuel Adams wrote confidently: "I think we have put our Enemies in the wrong, and they must in the Judgment of rational Men be answerable for the Destruction of the Tea, which their own Obstinancy rendered necessary."[11] Cousin John perceived the implications more broadly when he apprehended "a Dignity, a Majesty, a Sublimity in this last Effort of the Patriots." "This Destruction of the Tea," he added, "is so bold, so daring, so firm, intrepid, and inflexible, and it must have so important Consequences, and so lasting . . . as an Epocha in History."[12]

John Adams was a good prophet. The Boston Tea Party was both an end and a beginning. It ended the heated personal factionalism between the Adams men and the Hutchinson forces, so often carried out within the setting of broader imperial issues affecting America and explained on both sides in terms of plots and conspiratorial ideas. Defeated for the last time, Hutchinson accepted a leave from the governorship and sailed for England in June 1774. Hutchinson was only seeking rest and solace after years of turmoil. As it turned out, he found himself residing permanently in England as a loyalist refugee, one of the first of the thousands who fled their homes out of allegiance to the Crown. Resistance was slowly becoming rebellion, and, as the crisis deepened, Hutchinson prayed that the redcoats would quickly reestablish the old imperial order that had been so good to him. He dreamed incessantly of returning to his beloved Massachusetts but died forlorn and forgotten in England, an outcast from his homeland, in 1780.

George III and Lord North seethed with anger when reports of the Tea Party reached them in late January 1774. Like John Adams, North thought that the Bostonians had been daring and intrepid; but, unlike Adams, he felt that they had been defiant once too often. Those deeply embedded perceptions of Bostonians as rabble-rousers were at work. The King and his ministers wanted the Bay colonists singled out and punished severely before their licentious example did irreparable damage to Anglo-American relations. Parliament would not be allowed to capitulate again. George III felt strongly that Parliament had erred seriously in backing down the first time during the Stamp Act crisis. Now it would have to establish its sovereignty once and for all, with the support of military force if necessary. As North explained to the House of Commons, when he introduced the first of the "Coercive Acts" in March 1774, "We are considered as two independent states" in Boston.[13] All the possible explanations gave way to that straightforward statement. It was time for Massachusetts to become an example, one that colonists elsewhere would not want to emulate.

A metaphorical expression of what was happening in the Empire may be found in the events surrounding the death of Andrew Oliver, Hutchinson's lieutenant governor, who passed away in March 1774. Oliver was given a state funeral in Boston, and a large crowd gathered to watch the interment. As his remains were lowered into the grave, the crowd erupted in cheers. Such barbarity shocked royalist family members, especially Andrew's brother, Peter, who wrote bitterly: "The Vengeance of the Faction was carried to, and beyond the Grave. . . . *Could Infernals do worse?*"[14] To John Adams, though, who did not mention graveside insults, Oliver's death was "but the second . . . which has happened among the Conspirators, the original Conspirators against the Public Liberty, since the Conspiracy was first regularly formed, and begun to be executed, in 1763 or 4."[15] The family-oriented factionalism in Massachusetts politics had culminated in a total breakdown of communications. It had produced an all-pervading atmosphere of hatred in which there was to be no room for reason or compromise. It was the old imperial connection that was buried symbolically with the remains of Oliver.

Lord North, ignoring warnings about striking back too hard out of pique over Boston, insisted upon several parliamentary acts of retribution. The first was the Boston Port Act, signed into law by a most willing George III at the end of March 1774. By this act, Boston would cease to exist as a commercial port on June 1, or until Bostonians paid for the destroyed tea. May brought the Massachusetts Government

Act and the Administration of Justice Act. The first altered the charter basis of the government of Massachusetts. It vastly increased gubernatorial powers and abolished the old elective council (upper house), replacing it with a royally appointed council to be handpicked by the King's officials. The governor would now have the exclusive right to make all-important local political appointments without having to heed the council's advice. Town meetings, moreover, were not to be held without the governor's permission, except for the annual spring election meetings. The Justice Act gave imperial officials in Massachusetts, especially customs officers, greater legal protection. For example, should they maim or kill anyone while carrying out their duties or while putting down riots, this legislation guaranteed them a fair trial in another colony or in England, if the Massachusetts governor did not feel that impartial local juries could be assembled.

Even before these two acts became law, the cabinet called on General Thomas Gage, the soft-spoken, tolerant, and cautious commander in chief of British military forces in North America, to assume the Massachusetts governorship. In personal instructions to Gage, who arrived in Boston just before Hutchinson's departure, Lord Dartmouth, the new American Secretary, warned the commander about "the present state of disorder and commotion within that province," and told him to use his troops, if necessary, to support "your authority as the first magistrate" and "fully to preserve the public peace."[16] The Crown wanted political stability, and it was virtually creating a military dictatorship to achieve it. Nor was it offering any guarantees that normal civil relations would return, even should the Bostonians pay for the tea.

One other widely misunderstood act was part of Lord North's coercive package. It was a bill, approved early in June 1774, which amended the Quartering Act of 1765. The law of 1765 had outlined procedures to be followed in locating housing for regular troops. It specifically exempted occupied private homes. The amendment of 1774 gave military commanders more authority in bargaining for soldiers' quarters. In effect, soldiers could now be located anywhere, despite the obstructionist tactics which local civil officials might employ, and at fair rental rates. But even the amendment did not permit the forcible quartering of troops in occupied private residences. That occurred only after full-scale military operations were under way.[17]

Often included with the Coercive Acts, although not so intended, was the Quebec Act, which Parliament also adopted in June 1774. This legislation had been in the making for several years; the goal was the rational administration of conquered Canada. The new law specified that the government of Quebec would consist of a royal governor and a large appointive advisory council, but no popularly elected assembly. Roman Catholicism was to remain the established form of religion for French speaking inhabitants; and Parliament designated the Ohio River as Quebec's southwestern boundary.

The Quebec Act had no connection with the disciplining of Massachusetts, but it nevertheless confirmed for thousands of Americans up and down the whole eastern seaboard their worst fears about the "intolerable" spate of legislation. The Crown was seemingly denying the right of local representative government, thereby taking the next logical step beyond the militarily oriented revision of the government of Massachusetts. Political liberties and the rule of law simply could not exist or have any meaning without popularly based institutions. The Quebec Act thus suggested that there might be an even broader imperial attack in the making on all American assemblies. Likewise, it sanctioned a religious faith that provincial Protestant dissenters equated with an oppressive state church. The strong fear of Catholicism, epitomized in the effigies often carried by prerevolutionary crowds, took on new meaning. And the act cut into western lands which provincial speculators viewed as an important future area of expansion and personal profits. The Quebec Act, perceived as one more piece of denigrating and constraining legislation, caused thousands of persons beyond Massachusetts to accept Parliament's coercive challenge.

With or without the Quebec Act, the North ministry badly miscalculated when it proceeded beyond the Boston Port Act. Punishing recalcitrant Bostonians was one thing. Many Americans thought that their Bay colony brethren were too aggressive and too democratical—that they deserved to be chastised. Other provincials might have been willing to let the Bostonians stand alone in their clash with King and Parliament. Lord Dartmouth, a cabinet level friend of America, argued vigorously against legislation beyond the Port Act. But undiscriminating anti-New England feeling had peaked among home government leaders in the wake of the Boston Tea Party.

Those few English voices which suggested that Parliament was goading the provinces into broader forms of resistance were correct. There was something in the coercive package to offend almost every provincial. The laws seemed to violate the sanctity of colonial institutions, to distort the normal administration of justice, to raise military government out of the funeral pyre of civil authority, to condone "Popery" and state religion, and to put another barrier in the way of the fertile western lands which were deemed so essential to future economic opportunity. The total effect of the Coercive Acts was to unite, more than ever before, the conspiracy-minded colonists. Popular leaders felt a new rush of support during the summer of 1774. North's abandonment of conciliation for retaliation had reduced the range of possible responses to only one—resistance verging on open rebellion.

However, during the late spring of 1774, responses in the provinces were at first very disjointed. When word of the Port Act reached Boston in mid May, the more staid, imperial-oriented merchants urged quick payment for the lost tea. Samuel Adams, gloating over his victory over the Hutchinson forces, insisted upon total economic boycott as the appropriate response. He was not thinking in terms of independence; he also disdained sentiment favoring an intercolonial congress because it could delay, or even completely stifle, united nonimportation efforts. In fact, the Adams men sent Paul Revere riding off to Hartford, New York City, and Philadelphia with this advice. Revere was received cordially and gained some pledges to support Boston with basic supplies after the port was closed on June 1, but he was not overwhelmed with sympathy for his city's plight. Wealthy merchants in particular did not relish the prospect of further losses should nonimportation be invoked for the third time since 1765. Thus it was only during the summer months, as provincials learned of the full extent of Parliament's actions, that Boston's cause metamorphosed more fully into the American cause.

The Virginia House of Burgesses was in session when news of the Boston Port Act reached Williamsburg. The more militant assembly-men urged the burgesses, at the very least, to adopt a mild resolution calling for a day of fasting and prayer in sympathy for their northern brethren. The governor, John Murray, who as a member of the Scottish peerage held the title of Lord Dunmore, overreacted by dissolving the burgesses for what he interpreted as a flagrant slap at King and Parliament. Infuriated by Dunmore's audaciousness, many burgesses remained in Williamsburg. They met extralegally, and at one session in the Raleigh Tavern, the former burgesses produced a series of significant resolves. Condemning the home government for its taxation policies, they recommended some form of comprehensive intercolonial nonimportation effort and instructed their standing committee of correspondence to write to other assemblies and urge the calling of a continental congress. As the summer temperatures rose, other provinces responded by electing delegates who were to meet at Philadelphia in early September. Only Georgia failed to heed the call.[18]

Even if many Americans at all levels of society were pulling together during the summer of 1774 in not letting Massachusetts stand alone, they still lacked central direction in shaping an effective response. The main problem facing the delegates to the first Continental Congress was just that—coordinated direction in protest. The men who traveled to Philadelphia held a variety of opinions about the most appropriate form of resistance. Among the more radical members of the Congress were Samuel and John Adams, Patrick Henry, and Richard Henry Lee. They were ready to take an uncompromising stand against perceived imperial tyranny. Then there were individuals like George Washington, a substantial Virginia tobacco planter, who waited to be persuaded. Diametrically opposed to the radicals were the more cautious gentlemen, such as Pennsylvania's royalist-oriented speaker of the house, Joseph Galloway, or the wealthy, brilliantly logical New Yorkers, James Duane and John Jay. They were looking for a way to accommodate differences and restore Anglo-American political equilibrium. They believed that a clear definition of constitutional relationships between the parent state and the American provinces was fundamental to the renewal of imperial stability and harmony. As men of exceptional socioeconomic standing, too, they believed that the imperial connection was essential for continued internal political stability. They feared that the masses would become too involved in local decision making if the course of events continued. In that sense, their concerns were similar to those of Hutchinson and other denigrated royalist supporters. While the radicals wanted to force Parliament to back down and to return to the days of salutary neglect, the accommodationists sought harmony with the home government before all was lost to the masses.

Given the delegates' varied persuasions, it is not surprising that political maneuvering began even before the Congress officially opened its sessions. As the delegates convened in early September, the accommodationists favored holding meetings in the Pennsylvania State House, but the radicals insisted upon Carpenter's Hall, a gathering place for Philadelphia's workingmen. The delegates voted for Carpenter's Hall. Congress would identify symbolically with the people rather than with British authority, since the government of Pennsylvania functioned in the State House. Next, the radicals urged that Charles Thomson, a Philadelphia merchant of moderate means who had been active in organizing resistance, be named the recording secretary. Thomson was elected. The accommodationists were thus on the defensive and losing ground even before the delegates turned to the issues. A rout of the more conservative delegates followed in the next month and a half.[19]

All the representatives, lacking a clear sense of direction, floundered for a few days over what should be the focus of their concerns. Finally, they established a committee to draft a statement of American "rights, grievances, and means of redress." The radicals, aware that petitions had not resulted in any parliamentary concessions during the previous decade, wanted something more. If they were going to get only a petition out of Congress, however, they wanted it to be as strongly worded as possible, rather than just another obsequious rationale of the American position. Thus, while the accommodationists preferred to base provincial complaints on two grounds—the British constitution and the colonial charters—the radicals demanded that Americans also justify themselves on a third basis, that of the "immutable laws of nature."

The radicals, drawing upon the writings of the seventeenth-century English political theorist, John Locke, knew that references to the laws of nature implied that citizens had come together at some earlier, mythical time to form civil society and governmental institutions by compact for the protection of each individual's life, liberty, and property. In a state of nature, there could be nothing but anarchy, with no protection for life and property. The transition from a state of nature to civil society, therefore, was the means by which threatened people found protection against untamed despoilers of liberty, even if it also meant giving up the right to do exclusively as one pleased. When individuals had entered into a compact for civil society, they also had formed governments and had elected magistrates to represent them in order to guarantee political stability and to protect personal safety, essential liberties, and basic property rights. But when governments and magistrates abused their trust, citizens, after exploring all other means of legal and extralegal protest—from petitioning over grievances to out-and-out intimidation and violence—also possessed the *right of revolution* in order to insure governments consonant with compacted purposes.

In attempting to tax Americans without granting them direct representation in Parliament, English leaders had been guilty of violating the compact maxim that only duly elected representatives could attach portions of individuals' estates for the greater good of the whole. By not recognizing American assemblies as appropriate agencies for taxation, English ministers in theory were violating the compact which was the foundation of the provincial rationale for those governments. The radicals, by insisting that American grievances be based upon the laws of nature, wanted to make it clear, even if indirectly, that revolution was a legitimate, albeit extralegal, means of ending tyrannical decision making by willful magistrates.

Accommodationists on the "rights and grievances" committee thought that they had a solution to the dilemma. They argued that Parliament's sovereignty should extend over all legislative matters affecting America, except taxation. Yet there was nothing new in that position. The radicals countered by declaring that Parliament had no right to legislate at all upon internal provincial matters. Parliament's only function, they argued, was to maintain and support whatever general rules were necessary for imperial harmony.

In the end, Congress in full session sided with the radicals by approving "The Declaration of Colonial Rights and Grievances." In its final form, it proclaimed that provincial assemblies had jurisdiction over "all cases of taxation and *internal polity*, subject only to the negative of their sovereign." Parliament seemingly had lost its right to legislate for the colonies in any direct capacity. As the Declaration summarized it: "We cheerfully consent to the operation of such Acts of the British Parliament, as are *bona fide*, restrained to the regulation of our external commerce." And Congress based its position concerning Parliament's abuse of authority and American grievances on "the *immutable laws of nature*, the principles of the English constitution, and the several charters or compacts."[20] The provincial radicals had been triumphant. That should have been taken as a serious warning in England.

The victory of the radicals did not, however, occur without heated verbal battles and well-organized political chicanery. In the Boston area, a mass gathering of Suffolk County residents, still angered over the Coercive Acts, adopted on September 9, 1774, resolutions written by Dr. Joseph Warren. The resolutions encouraged the Massachusetts citizenry to pay no taxes to governments under royal authority. They called for new vigor in local militia organization, although only for defensive purposes. They also insisted upon a plan of total economic boycott. It was a preplanned coincidence that the citizens of Suffolk County chose to base their grievances on the immutable laws of nature, as well as on other arguments. Equally uncoincidental was the long, hard ride that the insurgent silversmith, Paul Revere, made in carrying the Suffolk Resolves from Boston to Philadelphia. Once that expression of popular sentiment was placed before Congress by mid September, the accommodationists were put on the spot. To reject the Resolves was to flout what appeared to be a united popular feeling. Congress approved them. Saddled with this endorsement several days before the "Declaration" took final form, the accommodationists had no alternative but to go along with a petition appealing to the laws of nature. Otherwise, the delegates would have appeared to have been hopelessly divided and confused, destroying the facade of unity which everyone wanted to convey to the British ministry. Manipulation and careful timing had assured success to the radicals.

In endorsing the Resolves, Congress moved rapidly toward approving what was soon called the Continental Association. It specified that nonimportation of British goods would begin on December 1, 1774; nonconsumption of British trade goods on March 1, 1775; and nonexportation of American products, if necessary, on September 10, 1775. Every provincial community was to establish its own committee of observation and inspection to monitor local citizens. Association violators would face social ostracism, since the committees were directed to "cause the truth of the case to be published in the gazette; to the end, that all such foes to the rights of British America may be publicly known, and universally condemned as the enemies of American liberty; and thenceforth we respectively will break off all dealing with him or her."[21] In reality, the Association became the radicals' test of loyalty to the cause. Citizens throughout the provinces soon were facing crises of personal allegiance, as events kept pushing toward rebellion. Many citizens who had the courage to stand up to the Association's methods of forcing community consensus would pay dearly for their loyalty to England—with their lives in some cases, as well as with their fortunes.

The only major accommodationist countercharge during the first Continental Congress was Joseph Galloway's Plan of Union, which was debated at the end of September. Galloway, who joined the most militant loyalists within months, was searching for some means of settling Anglo-American constitutional differences once and for all. Thus he proposed a structural reformation in the imperial government. Each colony was to have its own assembly; but a central coordinating body in America, consisting of a "grand council" headed by a "president general," would be placed over all of the assemblies. The president general was to be a Crown appointee who would serve "during pleasure," while the grand council was to be elected every three years by provincial assemblymen. Although the grand council was to be "an inferior and distinct branch of the British legislature," all parliamentary programs affecting America had to be approved by the grand council and the president general—the converse was the case for grand council legislation—before becoming law.

Galloway's plan, which offered a positive alternative to the confusion over the distribution of imperial power, foreshadowed the commonwealth organization of the future British Empire. But in 1774 provincial insurgents were seeking submission from Parliament, not structural reform. In a close vote, Galloway's Plan of Union went down to defeat. Later Charles Thomson had all references to the plan deleted from the official congressional record, ostensibly to give the appearance of American unity in the face of British tyranny.[22]

When the first Continental Congress dissolved itself at the end of October 1774, it had nothing more substantive to show for its efforts than the defiant phrases of the "Declaration" and the intimidation inherent in the Continental Association. The radicals had not offered a positive program to facilitate reconciliation with the parent state. Rather, they had clearly established that the issues behind the problems faced by Massachusetts were everyone's problems. The delegates had not called for political independence. That would have been much too extreme. But they had notified British leaders that the bulk of Americans would no longer accept imperial restrictions on their socioeconomic and political freedoms. If the King and Parliament refused to take Americans seriously and to capitulate again, then radical provincial leaders were getting ready to mobilize citizens for a far more serious challenge to imperial authority than had ever been mounted before. The delegates seemed to sense their belligerent course as they adjourned. One of their last resolutions was to call for a second Congress to meet on May 10, 1775, "unless the redress of grievances which we have desired, be obtained before that time."[23]

Conditions deteriorated rapidly between the end of October 1774 and early May 1775. Although a sprinkling of American friends still could be found in Parliament, King George, North, and the vast majority of M.P.s scoffed at the work of the first Continental Congress. Parliament reacted by appropriating yet more funds for troops. Three new commanders—Generals William Howe, John Burgoyne, and Henry Clinton—were named to join General Gage and his expanding regiments in Massachusetts. Then came a parliamentary act restraining New England's trade by limiting it to Britain, Ireland, and the British West Indies. This was in direct reaction to the Continental Association. Since American trade routes often stretched beyond the Empire into the Mediterranean, Africa, and the French West Indies, the M.P.s intended to disrupt the American export economy. The restraining legislation also made it clear that the British mercantile community would not come to the Americans' rescue this time. Later, in April 1775, Parliament extended the restraining act to include all the provinces except New York, Delaware, North Carolina, and Georgia, where the North ministry believed loyalist sentiment to be still quite strong, if not dominant. Thus Parliament reacted to American defiance with yet more confrontational legislation.

Lord North also made sure that conciliatory plans developed by pro-American leaders in England were not adopted. He even co-opted one idea and rather insincerely turned it into his own "conciliatory proposition." North proposed that colonial assemblies which taxed provincial citizens for the support of redcoats as well as for royal civil officers in provincial government, and which turned those taxes over to Parliament for regular disbursement, should not be subject to direct or indirect parliamentary taxes. No one on either side of the Atlantic gave this scheme serious consideration.

Indeed, North had long since passed out of his conciliatory mood. He was loyal to his king, who wanted complete submission and believed that no one, especially rude Americans, could stand up to well-trained British soldiers. George believed that earlier compromises had only encouraged the provincials to bolder acts of defiance. He wrote privately: "Had the Americans in prosecuting their ill grounded claims put on an appearance of mildness it might have been very difficult to chalk out the right path to be pursued; but they have boldly thrown off the mask and avowed that nothing less than a total independence of the British Legislature will satisfy them."[24] The King saw only one alternative—the use of military force. His curt words to Lord North of September 1774 had an ominous ring: "The die is now cast, the colonies must either submit or triumph."[25] And it was this polarized reasoning that resulted in the parliamentary statement of February 1775 declaring Massachusetts in an open state of rebellion. If the troops now shot down civilians without civilian magistrates first reading the riot act, they would be acting well within the law. The troops were now treating the civilians as rebels, men and women beyond the protection of due process.

The North ministry, by demanding complete submission, was pursuing an openly belligerent course with the Bay colony, which it perceived as the source of American turmoil. Cautious General Gage, by comparison, was advocating that the Coercive Acts be suspended until British arms were powerful enough in their concentrated presence for rigorous enforcement. More militant cabinet members mocked Gage's timidity and his suggestion that "inferior" provincial citizens could withstand the might of armed British soldiers.

Indeed, as Parliament paved the way financially for the military buildup in America, the North cabinet in late January 1775 prepared secret orders for Gage. He was not to tolerate continued "violences committed by those who have taken up Arms in Massachusetts Bay, . . . a rude *Rabble* without plan, without concert, and without conduct." The cabinet insisted that he use his army "to arrest and imprison the principal actors and abettors" of rebellion, if possible without bloodshed. But if that proved to be impossible, Gage was to put his redcoats into the field to demonstrate once and for all the futility of continued American resistance. Cabinet members confidently assumed that Bay colony residents would be "unprepared to encounter with a regular force" and would quickly submit, at last, to imperial sovereignty.[26]

General Gage received the cabinet's secret orders on April 14. He had already made general plans for sending a regiment into the countryside and had only been waiting for the ministry's backing. Gage, realizing that it would be next to impossible to run down popular leaders, gave his subordinates a specific target: the town of Concord, located several miles northwest of Boston, where local citizens had been collecting and storing gunpowder and other military supplies. Late in the evening of April 18, seven hundred British regulars under Lieutenant Colonel Francis Smith and Major John Pitcairn moved out across the back bay of Boston under cover of darkness. But the provincials knew of the troops' whereabouts; the plan and the target at Concord were no secret. Paul Revere and William Dawes went hurrying into the countryside, warning citizens of the military incursion. By the time the troops debarked across the bay in Cambridge and began their march toward Concord, local farmers were hoisting arms and making last minute preparations for whatever might come.

It was at Lexington, five miles east of Concord, that excited words over how to confront the British had their greatest significance. In the midst of the Lexington tavern crowd were Samuel Adams and John Hancock, fresh from meetings of the provincial congress, the colony's extralegal governing body which was operating in open defiance of the languishing imperial authority. The lack of enthusiasm in recent sessions was discouraging to both men. They feared that indifference over defending liberties was setting in and would undermine resistance efforts. But events during the next few hours changed those feelings dramatically. British columns had taken to the field, and they were bearing down on Lexington.

The local militia commander, Captain John Parker, had seventy men. Just before dawn on April 19 they lined up across the village green, having determined to act as an army of observation. They would be there to tell the British commanders that they were trespassing on free soil. Once they had made their point, they would leave the field, hoping somehow that the redcoats would return to Boston rather than pursue a collision course. The Lexington militia moved into a tightly drawn line formation just before the British advance column under Pitcairn bore down on the village green in the hazy early morning light. Perhaps Pitcairn and Parker exchanged words. Then a mysterious shot rang out, very likely as Parker's men turned to leave the green. Pitcairn's soldiers reacted with a volley of indiscriminate fire, and eight "embattled farmers" lay bleeding and dead, a number of them shot in their backs. Several other farmers had been wounded. Almost mechanically, the British columns regrouped and surged forward down the road toward Concord, hardly aware of the clash that had just occurred or its real meaning.[27]

The rest of the day was a disaster for the British. Colonel Smith's men, reaching Concord, searched for arms and gunpowder. A contingent moved toward North Bridge; again there was gunfire, but this time the British soldiers fell back with some of their comrades slain. Smith finally ordered a general retreat, but only the appearance of a one-thousand man relief column from Boston saved the redcoats from hundreds of Massachusetts farmers who, hiding behind trees and fences, ripped Smith's units to shreds. Final casualty figures showed an estimated 273 British regulars dead or wounded, compared to only 95 Americans. All the home government's assumptions about the superiority of British arms meant nothing in light of this day's grim body count. Well-trained militiamen had taken advantage of British military arrogance and made a mockery of it.

The significance of the battles of Lexington and Concord ran much deeper. The skirmishing instantaneously clarified the American position. Britain had attempted to use the ultimate tool of tyranny, a standing army in the field and against the people, the popular leaders argued, and had been beaten by determined defenders of liberty. The loss of American lives could not go unanswered. The response must be clear and determined. The alternatives some provincials saw were now the same as those suggested earlier by George III: total submission or total triumph.

The cause, at least in New England, surged with new vigor after April 19. Dr. Warren hurriedly prepared an "unbiased" account of the tragedy in the form of a circular letter. He reiterated that "the barbarous murders committed on our innocent brethren . . . have made it absolutely necessary that we immediately raise an army to defend our wives and our children from the butchering hands of an inhuman soldiery." "An hour lost," warned Warren in terms paralleling those of his Boston Massacre oration of 1772, "may deluge your country in blood and entail perpetual slavery upon the few of your posterity who may survive the carnage."[28] Hard upon Warren's circular report, the Massachusetts provincial congress sent out a call for eight thousand citizen-soldiers. In response, men and women from all over the countryside moved into hastily organized military camps surrounding Boston. Even with reinforcements on their way from England, Gage and his redcoats found themselves trapped. In reality, they were cowering on the peninsula of Boston, not stealthily planning a second foray, as Warren had predicted.

The Massachusetts provincial congress convened with awakened vigor. It tried to make sense out of the military situation. But the gentlemen who gathered in Philadelphia from all the colonies in early May 1775 for the second Continental Congress, although shocked by Lexington and Concord, still were not prepared as a group to declare independence. The New England men, especially Samuel and John Adams, were finally readying themselves for that decision, given the latest extreme in belligerence, yet the large majority of delegates still hoped for an accommodation of differences. They were not going to let their fiery New England associates force a declaration of rebellion without having first explored all possible channels of reconciliation. Indeed, the second Congress found itself locked between a numerically superior reconciliationist faction, headed informally by John Dickinson, with overwhelming support from middle colony delegates, and a smaller number of emerging advocates of independence. Both factions fought over each specific issue as if it would determine the broader question. Above all else, the reconciliationists did not want to offend British officials to the point of destroying all possibilities of renewed Anglo-American harmony. The congressional reconciliationists, far more coherent a group than the accommodationists of the first Continental Congress (the prevention of independence gave them a common goal), maintained their control of the second Congress well into the spring of 1776. Then the weight of events occurring outside Philadelphia completely overwhelmed them.

A major congressional controversy developed in June 1775 over the matter of providing central military planning and coordination by the creation of an intercolonial army. Most delegates agreed that some military direction was necessary. The New England contingent viewed central-army organization as one effective means of involving the rest of the colonies in what was still a localized war. Physically imposing George Washington had his own way of letting other delegates know that some Virginians, at least, were ready to commit themselves. As John Adams noted to his wife Abigail, "Colonel Washington appears at Congress in his Uniform."[29] Washington's less than subtle sartorial statement paid off. He was a Southerner, unlike John Hancock, who desperately wanted the post of commander in chief. Moreover, Washington had had military experience, even if it was of a mixed quality, in the French and Indian War. With Washington's appointment to head the Continental army, the South (or at least Virginia) symbolically became involved in the war.

The reconciliationists clearly perceived the implications of central military organization. Forming a continental military establishment and naming a full complement of high-level officers seemed an obvious first step toward offensive warfare without the word "independence" attached. Although the reconciliationists, led by Dickinson, accepted the buildup as a necessity, they demanded that Congress adopt a statement explaining why it had occurred. The delegates in early July 1775 thus adopted the "Declaration of the Causes and Necessity for Taking up Arms," to be forwarded to England. The reason for the Continental establishment was not "to dissolve that union which has so long and so happily subsisted between us." Rather the Continental army would function solely to *defend* American liberties, lives, and property until "hostilities shall cease on the part of the aggressors, and all danger of their being renewed shall be removed, and not before."[30]

And so the debate would go on during the next several months. The reconciliationists wrote petitions, explained, cajoled, and begged; but they did not allow undeclared insurgency to become declared rebellion. Typical of their efforts was John Dickinson's "Olive Branch" petition, endorsed a few days after the "Declaration of the Causes." In almost saccharine tone, this petition begged George III to intervene with Parliament to preserve English liberties in America. Dickinson wrote that "our breasts retain too tender a regard for the kingdom from which we derive our origin" to desire independence.[31] The Olive Branch served mainly to infuriate the radical faction; George and his ministers ignored it. They seemed to want only statements of complete penance and submission, not self-effacing petitions. In fact, the King called for an even greater military buildup during the fall of 1775 for the massive campaign effort of 1776. George's agents started hiring Hessian mercenaries for the American theater, and Parliament declared all the colonies to be in a state of rebellion.

The radical faction, despite lack of numbers, never stopped maneuvering. The provision for effective forms of governments in the provinces became a pressing concern, since royal authority was collapsing in many locales. One by one the colonies elected men to provincial congresses that substituted for regular assemblies. More and more citizens became involved directly in daily defiance. During the summer of 1775, Massachusetts asked the Continental Congress for advice about creating a more enduring government beyond the *ad hoc* provincial congress. The delegates in Philadelphia demurred, knowing that a new government, especially one based on a written constitution, would be interpreted in England as another sign of *de facto* independence. After New Hampshire insurgents ousted their royal governor during the same summer, the local activists, like those in Massachusetts, sought Congress's advice. Finally, a report came out of committee in early November in response to New Hampshire's plea. The Continental delegates cautiously advised that New Hampshire should set up "such a form of government, as . . . will best produce the happiness of the people," but only in conjunction with a written constitutional provision that such a government would exist until "the present dispute between Great Britain and the colonies" ended.[32] To the reconciliationists, new governments could be erected, but for the main purpose of guarding against democratic anarchy in the face of an armed parent state. No one in England, however, should assume that these governments were to be permanent.

Just in case anyone became confused, the reconciliationists managed to get a statement from the assembly in Pennsylvania that instructed that colony's congressional delegates to "dissent from, and utterly reject, any propositions . . . that may cause or lead to a separation from our Mother Country."[33] Within weeks New York, Delaware, Maryland, and South Carolina sent similar instructions to their representatives. If the reconciliationists had their way, maneuvering delegates were not going to be permitted to force a vote on the question of independence.

For once, the more radical popular leaders were not in control, even if their mounting desire for formal independence made the most strategic sense for a cause needing comprehensive goals. The tenor of the times demanded cohesive leadership, not division and bickering at the core. It needed coordinated direction that went beyond perfunctory references to defending liberties. John Adams specifically blamed John Dickinson for congressional faintheartedness in the face of an enraged parent state. In unguarded language, Adams wrote that "a certain great Fortune and piddling Genius [Dickinson], whose Fame has been trumpeted so loudly, has given a silly Cast to our whole Doings. We are between Hawk and Buzzard."[34] It did not improve relations among congressional factions when the British captured Adams's letter and gleefully published it.

With Congress virtually at a stalemate, it turned out to be the weight of events outside Philadelphia that finally forced a resolution of the question of independence. Since the late fall of 1774, communities in all the colonies had been forming local committees of observation and inspection, involving people by the thousands in the task of sorting out neighbors who were defending liberties through the trade boycott from those who refused to support the Association. The committees were not kind to residents who wavered in the cause. The Wilmington, North Carolina, committee, for instance, went "in a body" to "wait on all Householders in Town." People who refused to sign the Association were declared "Enemies to their Country . . . and treated with the contempt they merit." Eleven citizens defied the committee; in retaliation, the committee circulated their names throughout the area; and at a minimum these nonconformist souls experienced social ostracism. The Caroline County, Virginia, committee concentrated on local merchants who were not only selling English goods but also raising their prices in the midst of scarcities. Six merchants faced charges of price gouging. Sensing their fate, they quickly submitted. In New Cambridge, Connecticut, committeemen singled out people "unsound in their political sentiments," interviewed them, and warned them that ostracism would follow for nonconformity.

By "purifying" the landscape, the local committees were instructing citizens in the need to conform for the greater good of the cause. The local committees also prepared residents for actual material sacrifices which would of necessity come should united resistance lead to a formal state of rebellion. In keeping with the spirit of the Association, most inhabitants accepted spartan restrictions on their personal behavior. Many committees went so far as to halt social frivolities, such as concerts, plays, dances, horse races, cock fights, county fairs, and anything else that was superfluous to the cause. Lavish clothing began to be interpreted as a badge of disloyalty; homespun again came into vogue, at least for the lesser sort. Committees banned ostentatious funerals and the wearing of mourning clothes. In turn, they instructed citizens how to save and stretch basic commodities. In some locales no one was to slaughter sheep; every last pound of wool would be needed for clothing. Gentlemen shared knowledge about processing a molasseslike substance from pumpkins so that hard liquor would still be available in spite of nonimportation. One distinguished Virginia planter claimed that he knew a formula for making beer from cornstalks. Tea drinkers again turned from mild bohea to bitter redroot bush blends; at least one committee let it be known that varieties of imported teas were routinely used in other countries for embalming fluids. Invariably, committees called for more home manufactures, and in some areas societies sprang up to offer encouragement to nascent American manufacturing efforts, especially the production of crude woolen clothing products.[35]

Generally, poorer citizens paid most heavily for such efforts by giving their labor for next to nothing in wages. Everyone was to sacrifice, but some sacrificed more than others. In the end, determining who was displaying spartan virtue (and humiliating those who were not) helped to build a wall of sentiment at the grass-roots level for united defiance, at least until the stubborn parent state decided to redress American grievances.

Actions by royal officials also abetted widespread popular feeling that independence might be the necessary long-run choice. No royal official in the provinces was more precipitate than the determined Lord Dunmore of Virginia. After his hasty decision in May 1774 to dissolve the House of Burgesses, Dunmore rapidly lost control of government in the Old Dominion. In early June 1775, he left Williamsburg for the last time and raised the royal standard aboard a naval vessel in Chesapeake Bay. The issue, as Dunmore saw it, was simple. He had to reassert royal authority over defiant Virginians, especially those planter elite leaders who had seized the reins of government and who were meeting in extralegal sessions of the provincial congress. Specifically, Dunmore knew that he had to humble the often arrogant planter elite. Pondering many alternatives, he finally concluded that turning Virginia's slaves against their masters was the only way to break the back of the resistance movement.

Lord Dunmore took this final step on November 7, 1775, by issuing a modified emancipation proclamation: "And I do hereby further declare all indent[ur]ed servants, Negroes, or others . . . free, that are able and willing to bear arms." The desperate Governor urged slaves to join "His Majesty's Troops, as soon as may be, for the more speedily reducing the Colony to a proper sense of their duty, to his Majesty's crown and dignity."[36] Needing soldiers, Dunmore speculated that Virginia's slaves would rise up in mass, throw off their chains, embrace the royal standard, and teach their former masters that cries about liberty had a hollow ring when so many human beings remained locked in chattel slavery.

Dunmore's Proclamation frightened the tobacco-planting gentry as no other action could have done. Possible slave insurrections, at the heart of southern fears about civil anarchy, conjured up images of blacks brutalizing, maiming, and killing whites. The legal structure had been designed to make insurrections virtually impossible. It inhibited the movement as well as the formal education of slaves in the hope that ignorance would keep potentially rebellious Afro-Americans in chains. In one bold stroke, Dunmore was thrusting at the heart of the plantation system, at the planters' leisured life-style, and at the economic basis of their gentlemanly existence. If some Virginians dreaded open rebellion against England because it might set a bad example for militant slaves, they feared even more royal officials who would foment a race war to keep the tobacco-producing elite in its proper subordinate place within the Empire. More and more distinguished Virginians gave serious contemplation to formal independence after Dunmore's Proclamation.

In the meantime, the planters used several tactics to suppress the Proclamation and keep their slaves under control. They systematically destroyed as many copies as they could find. They denied rumors of its existence. They voiced it about that Dunmore really intended to send blacks to the West Indies, which had a reputation for extremely brutal working conditions and unusually high mortality rates. The Virginia provincial convention quickly resolved to pardon all runaways who returned within ten days, but erstwhile slaves taken in arms were to be sold to the West Indies, if planters did not choose to flog them into submission and humiliation as examples to others.

Despite overwhelming odds, which were intensified by the heavy geographic concentration of slaves on large plantations where they could more easily be watched by a frightened white populace, an estimated one to two thousand Afro-Americans had joined Dunmore by the summer of 1776. Probably the Governor's inability to reestablish himself on land was as important as any other factor in holding down the numbers who fled from their masters. In early December 1775, Dunmore's hastily assembled "Ethiopian" regiment challenged the Virginia militia at Great Bridge and took a severe beating. Retreating again to vessels in Chesapeake Bay, Dunmore watched over a growing flotilla of boats, numbering over one hundred at its peak. The Governor, white loyalists, and black freedmen kept looking for the right moment for another strike; but smallpox swept through the flotilla, causing hundreds of deaths. Dunmore finally put out to sea in the summer of 1776, leaving behind a united planter class guarding its slave population more closely than ever before while girding itself for the war in the name of liberty against imperial tyranny. The irony of it all could not have been more striking.

The reality was the same everywhere that one looked, as winter turned into spring in 1776. Spreading rebellion was undermining the congressional reconciliationists. New England was an armed camp. Virginia potentially faced a race war. Local committees were suppressing loyalists, hounding them out with the epithet of "tory." Royal authority was a mockery across the landscape. George III, Lord North, and Parliament were making vague hints about sending commissioners to the provinces to discuss grievances in full, but their actions suggested far different purposes. They continued to order up vast numbers of new troops. In late December 1775, they approved the American Prohibitory Act, closing all American ports until provincials laid down their arms. This measure also mentioned the peace commission, but the commissioners in the end were the Howe brothers, William and Lord Richard. The former had replaced Gage as head of His Majesty's forces in America. The latter had assumed command of the British fleet in American waters. William Howe would be offering loyalty oaths to citizens as he and his redcoats moved through the countryside later in 1776, but he lacked effective instructions to deal with specific or general grievances.

As bright springtime colors broke out along the American seaboard, provincial resistance still lacked a unifying focus, and the reconciliationists still dominated the Congress. They found themselves caught between what they considered two equally undesirable alternatives—tyrannical rule from above or the threat of anarchical, popular rule from below. From their perspective (by and large that of wealthy, propertied citizens who were still trying to be good Englishmen) an independent republic, free of stabilizing imperial ties, would succumb to internal chaos as soon as the democracy of citizens fully realized their newfound decision-making authority and challenged the deferential norm.

Both inside and outside of Congress, reconciliationists believed that the violence of the masses would not stop with rebellion but would inevitably consume the cause from within, if Great Britain were not standing by to help suppress violence. Thus John Dickinson insisted in his last arguments against independence: "First we ought to establish our governments and take the regular form of a state. These preventive measures will show deliberation, wisdom, caution, and unanimity."[37] The creation of strong internal governments, fully capable of controlling the people and keeping them in their places, had become the primary reconciliationist goal if independence could not be stopped. Propertied gentlemen specifically wanted to prevent a social revolution from developing out of the movement for independence.

The words contained in Thomas Paine's *Common Sense,* while striking the imagination of so many thousands in the general population, had only increased the determination of the reconciliationists to stand pat. *Common Sense,* published in January 1776, assaulted monarchism in England ("the folly of hereditary right in Kings, is that nature disapproves it . . . by giving mankind *an Ass for a Lion*"); denounced the reconciliationists ("I have heard some men say, many of whom I believe spoke without thinking, that they dreaded an independence, fearing that it would produce civil wars"), and preached fervently for independence and revolutionary commitment ("O! ye that love mankind! . . . Every spot of the old world is overrun with oppression. . . . O! receive the fugitive, and prepare in time an asylum for mankind.")[38]

Paine, who was in his late thirties, had been in the provinces for slightly over a year when his electrifying pamphlet appeared. Since his childhood in England, he had struggled against poverty, a fight he seemed to be losing when he embarked for America in 1774. All of a sudden, the former staymaker's apprentice had become famous. By the standards of the day, *Common Sense* was an explosive bestseller. It went through twenty-five editions before the year was out. The people who had not read portions or had portions read to them undoubtedly were exceptions to the rule.

No set of reasons will ever fully account for the pamphlet's success. Of especial importance, however, was Paine's forceful, biting language, crafted as it was in the popular rather than in the more learned phrases of the day. With its strident, cutting logic, it touched human hearts in exhorting people to renounce the reconciliationists and to strike out toward a bold new future through independence.[39]

Common Sense had a significant impact in breaking the British hold on North America. But the deepening military crisis, more than anything else, was overwhelming the reconciliationists. No matter what some said, the war, once unleashed at Lexington and Concord, kept expanding. Typical was the ill-fated provincial military invasion of Canada. The motives for such a venture varied with the individual telling. Some in Congress, despite their assurances about waging war only for defensive purposes, clearly were expansionists. Others simply wanted to have more allies. Then there were those who believed that taking Montreal and Quebec would effectively block the path of a large invading British force bent upon severing the rambunctious New Englanders from the rest of the provinces.

Whatever the reasons, Congress launched a two-pronged invasion during the fall of 1775, which eventually resulted in the deployment of some one thousand men under Richard Montgomery and Benedict Arnold before the town of Quebec. An all-out assault under cover of a driving snowstorm—just a few hours before the New Year—resulted in a rout. Montgomery was killed; Arnold was seriously wounded; and the dream of drawing Canada into the fray had failed, at least for the moment.

The provocative incidents kept piling up, and they finally took their toll. A short bloody battle between loyalists and insurgents at Moore's Creek Bridge in North Carolina (February 27, 1776) not only led to a mauling of the local tories; it also persuaded frightened members of the provincial congress to reverse its earlier order prohibiting its delegates in Philadelphia from voting for a plan of national government (and by implication, independence). Unanimously, the convention in mid April instructed its congressional delegation to agree to a resolution for independence, should the question be presented and debated. Next, the Virginians, still reeling from the effects of Dunmore's actions, voted the same. Then the scrappy Rhode Islanders became impatient with all of their colonial brethren and declared independence for themselves. In completing the cycle, the reconciliationists in the Continental Congress suffered their most serious setback to date on May 10. John Adams had proposed a resolution recommending that "where no government sufficient to the exigencies of their [the united colonies'] affairs have been hitherto established, to adopt such government as shall, in the opinion of the representatives of the people, best conduce to the happiness and safety of their constituents in particular, and America in general."[40] Over rapidly declining reconciliationist opposition, the Congress was urging that separate, *independent* American state governments be established.

On June 7, 1776, Richard Henry Lee presented the resolutions from the Virginia provincial convention and forced the issue of independence on the floor of Congress. The Virginia resolutions read as follows:

> That these United Colonies are, and of right ought to be, free and inde-
> pendent States, that they are absolved from all allegiance to the British
> Crown, and that all political connection between them and the State of
> Great Britain is, and ought to be, totally dissolved.
>
> That it is expedient forthwith to take the most effectual measures for
> forming foreign Alliances.
>
> That a plan of confederation be prepared and transmitted to the respec-
> tive Colonies for their consideration and approbation. [41]

During the next few days independence advocates in Congress
quickly moved ahead, establishing committees on independence and
on the organization of a national government. Attempting to pacify
Dickinson, the delegates named him head of the latter committee.
John Adams, Benjamin Franklin, Robert R. Livingston, and Roger
Sherman joined Thomas Jefferson on the independence committee.
Reluctantly, the shy, redheaded Virginian took primary responsibility
for writing the text that the Congress formally and unanimously
adopted on July 4, 1776. The only major objection to Jefferson's draft
came because he blamed the continuing slave trade on the King. Such
a clause stretched reality too far; the delegates voted to drop it as a
superfluity. Jefferson also wanted to repudiate friendship with the
British people; Congress struck out this paragraph.

The Declaration of Independence, in attacking George III rather
than Parliament as the perpetrator of tyrannical rule, may be interpreted in various ways. When the Declaration spoke of all men being
created equal, it meant all human beings. Generally, Jefferson was
working within a Lockean framework; and he was saying specifically
that royal monarchs were not set above other people by some special
birthright, which gave them the power to enslave citizens and destroy
their liberties. Monarchs were nothing more than high level magistrates, who came into the world like everyone else, and who had an
obligation to serve their people according to the compacted rules of
government. No person, however exalted, could disobey the compact
without causing the citizenry to rise up justifiably in protest, even to
the extent of rebellion and the formation of new governmental institutions when less extreme forms of protest failed. Since George III,
according to the Declaration, was now a tyrant, Americans were jus-
tified, even obliged, to declare their independence and create a new
nation in which liberty would henceforth prevail.

Exclusive focus on the King, instead of on power hungry, corrupted ministers and members of Parliament, was an important de-
viation from the earlier presentations of England's country Whigs. To
the world beyond, however, the pure Whig argument had a far more

familiar, less paranoid sound. Thus George III, cast as the tyrannical magistrate rather than the people's servant, had to accept the blame in the Declaration's summary list of grievances. He had, among other heinous crimes, denied provincials their right to westward expansion; obstructed and distorted justice; tampered with the right to trial by jury; placed standing armies of hired professionals among peaceful subjects; and waged war without adequate provocation. In his thirst for power, the King had provoked the rebellion. Only independence and the formation of a separate nation could end such lustful tyranny in America.

Yet Jefferson wanted the Declaration to be much more than an attack upon a willful king. As a result, he also went beyond standard theoretical bounds. He wrote of "certain unalienable rights" that could not be compromised short of political slavery, among them being "life, liberty, and the pursuit of happiness." In modifying the Lockean trilogy, Jefferson substituted "happiness" for "property." The Virginian, in urging his peers to set their sights upon something higher than a mere transfer of power and authority from Britons to Americans, was calling his fellow citizens to revolutionary goals. He envisioned a wholly new system of relations among peoples, based on "a new Government, laying its foundations on such principles and organizing its powers in such form, as to them shall seem most likely to effect their safety and happiness." Jefferson was urging that a purer political state, what could be called a republican order in which all citizens devoted themselves to the greater good of the whole, should emerge out of the corruption of the old imperial system. It would be a new system in which all citizens would commit themselves to achieving more perfect human relationships and the rule of law and human decency would replace the corrupting hand of abusive power and tyranny. Jefferson was asserting that Americans should dedicate themselves to much more than a movement for independence. It should be a revolution in the very character of political society as well.

In asking for so much, in imbuing the rebellion against imperial authority with revolutionary ideals, the Virginian had acknowledged that the rebellion, if it was to have lasting meaning, had to reach beyond the petty, factional feuding and self-interested behavior that had played such a crucial part in the slow ebbing of imperial relations. So much of the pace-setting furor had centered in Boston, where the Adams men, supported by the city's poorer citizens, had sought to destroy their perceived political enemies, or at least to drive them from their favored offices by casting them as fomenters of tyranny.

All of the rancor had come to a head with the Boston Tea Party, after which more profound issues became far more preeminent. Jefferson wanted something significant and of lasting value to come out of all of the bickering and turmoil.

Thus the Declaration of Independence was both a highly interpretive summary of recent events within the British Empire and an eloquent plea for improving the human condition through revolution. Perceptions of stifling human greed, ambition, and conspiratorial tyranny from above had helped to produce the Declaration of Independence. But the critical question lingered: Could Americans achieve in deeds what Jefferson now envisioned in words?

Notes

1. Dirk Hoerder, "Boston Leaders and Boston Crowds, 1765–1776," Young, ed., *The American Revolution*, 235–271, makes the valuable distinction between types of crowds.

2. Governor William Bull, quoted in Richard Walsh, *Charleston's Sons of Liberty: A Study of the Artisans, 1763–1789* (Columbia, S.C., 1959), 36–37.

3. Christopher Gadsden to William Samuel Johnson, Charleston, April 16, 1766, *The Writings of Christopher Gadsden, 1746–1805* (ed. Richard Walsh, Columbia, S.C., 1966), 69–74. See also Pauline Maier, "The Charleston Mob and the Evolution of Popular Politics in Revolutionary South Carolina, 1765–1784," *Perspectives in American History*, 4 (1970), 172–196.

4. On Whiggish divisions in New York, see Patricia U. Bonomi, *A Factious People: Politics and Society in Colonial New York* (New York, 1971), 229–286, and Roger J. Champagne, *Alexander McDougall and the American Revolution in New York* (Schenectady, N.Y., 1975), 11–66. For Pennsylvania, see James H. Hutson, *Pennsylvania Politics, 1746–1770: The Movement for Royal Government and its Consequences* (Princeton, N.J., 1972), *passim*, and R. A. Ryerson, "Political Mobilization and the American Revolution: The Resistance Movement in Philadelphia, 1765 to 1776," *William and Mary Quarterly*, 3rd Ser., 31 (1974), 565–588.

5. Benjamin Woods Labaree, *The Boston Tea Party* (New York, 1964), 331. For a general discussion, see Lucy S. Sutherland, *The East India Company in Eighteenth-Century Politics* (Oxford, 1952), *passim*. For the whole incident in succinct form, see Christie and Labaree, *Empire or Independence*, 163–182.

6. William Dowdeswell, on the floor of the House of Commons, quoted in Labaree, *Boston Tea Party*, 71.

7. Jensen, ed., *English Historical Documents*, IX, 773–774.

8. Bailyn, *Ordeal of Thomas Hutchinson*, 259–263, points out that Hutchinson hoped to make some personal profit on the tea consignments through his trading company, managed by the Governor's sons. But the possibility of personal monetary gain, even though undoubtedly a factor, does not fully explain Hutchinson's desire to confront his adversaries over tea.

9. These words may be apocryphal, but Adams did demand action during the meeting.

10. To Francis Bernard, January 1, 1774, quoted in Labaree, *Boston Tea Party*, 147.

11. To James Warren, December 28, 1773, *The Warren-Adams Letters* (2 vols., ed. W. C. Ford, Boston, 1917–1925), I, 19–20.

12. Diary entry, December 17, 1773, Butterfield, ed., *Diary and Autobiography of John Adams*, II, 85–86.

13. For North's full comments, made on March 7, 1774, see Cobbett and Hansard, *Parliamentary History*, XVII, 1159–1167.

14. Adair and Schutz, eds., *Peter Oliver's Origin & Progress*, 112.

15. Diary entry, March 6, 1774, Butterfield, ed., *Diary and Autobiography of John Adams*, II, 90.

16. Instructions, dated April 9, 1774, Jensen, ed., *English Historical Documents*, IX, 785–789.

17. The Coercive Acts have been reprinted in *ibid.*, IX, 779–785. See also Jack M. Sosin, "The Massachusetts Acts of 1774: Coercive or Preventive?", *Huntington Library Quarterly*, 26 (1963), 235–252, and Christie and Labaree, *Empire or Independence*, 183–196. For a valuable look at Virginia politics, see George M. Curtis, III, "The Role of the Courts in the Making of the Revolution in Virginia," *The Human Dimensions of Nation Making: Essays on Colonial and Revolutionary America* (ed. J. K. Martin, Madison, Wisc., 1976), 121–146.

18. For events during the summer, see David Ammerman, *In the Common Cause: American Response to the Coercive Acts of 1774* (Charlottesville, Va., 1974), esp. 19–51.

19. A standard analysis of the first Continental Congress and its factions is Merrill Jensen, *The Articles of Confederation: An Interpretation of the Social-Constitutional History of the American Revolution, 1774–1781* (Madison, Wisc., 1940), 54–73. Jensen uses different descriptive labels in sorting out the factions.

20. "Declaration," dated October 1, 1774, *Journals of the Continental Congress, 1774–1789* (34 vols., ed. W. C. Ford *et al.*, Washington, 1904–1937), I, 63–73. (Some italics mine)

21. Association, dated October 20, 1774, *ibid.*, I, 75–80.

22. Plan of Union, dated September 28, 1774, *ibid.*, I, 49–51.

23. Resolution, dated October 22, 1774, *ibid.*, I, 102.

24. Personal memorandum, December 1774 or January 1775, *The Correspondence of King George the Third* (6 vols., ed. Sir John Fortescue, London, 1927–1928), III, 47–48.

25. To Lord North, September 11, 1774, *ibid.*, III, 131. See also Bernard Donoughue, *British Politics and the American Revolution: The Path to War, 1773–1775* (New York, 1964), *passim.*

26. Lord Dartmouth to General Gage, January 27, 1775, *The Correspondence of General Thomas Gage*, II (ed. C. E. Carter, New Haven, Conn., 1933), 179–183. (Italics mine)

27. See in particular Robert A. Gross, *The Minutemen and Their World* (New York, 1976), 109–132. For a more "conspiratorial" explanation, see Arthur B. Tourtellot, *William Diamond's Drum: The Beginning of the War of the American Revolution* (Garden City, N.Y., 1959), 57–143.

28. Circular letter, dated April 20, 1775, quoted in *ibid.*, 215–216.

29. May 29, 1775, *The Adams Papers: Adams Family Correspondence* (2 vols., ed. L. H. Butterfield *et al.*, Cambridge, Mass., 1965), I, 207.

30. "Declaration," dated July 6, 1775, Ford, ed., *Journals of the Continental Congress*, II, 140–157.

31. July 8, 1775, *ibid.*, II, 158–162.

32. November 3, 1775, *ibid.*, III, 319.

33. Instructions, dated November 9, 1775, *American Archives*, 4th Ser., III (ed. Peter Force, Washington, 1840), 1407.

34. To James Warren, July 24, 1775, Ford, ed., *Warren-Adams Letters*, I, 88–89.

35. Incidents described and quoted in these two paragraphs are from Ammerman, *In the Common Cause*, 103–124.

36. Quoted in Benjamin Quarles, "Lord Dunmore as Liberator," *William and Mary Quarterly*, 3rd Ser., 15 (1958), 494–507. See also Quarles, *The Negro in the American Revolution* (Chapel Hill, N.C., 1961), 19–32.

37. July 1, 1776, Jensen, ed., *English Historical Documents*, IX, 873–877. See also Christie and Labaree, *Empire or Independence*, 257–281.

38. *The Writings of Thomas Paine*, I (ed. M. D. Conway, New York, 1894), 81, 96, 100–101.

39. Foner, *Tom Paine and Revolutionary America*, 71–87. See also David Freeman Hawke, *Paine* (New York, 1974), 1–5.

40. Ford, ed., *Journals of the Continental Congress*, IV, 342.

41. *Ibid.*, V, 425.

2

Convulsions from Below

The evils we experience flow from the excess of democracy. The people do not want virtue; but are the dupes of pretended patriots.
　　　　　　　—Elbridge Gerry of Massachusetts, speaking before the Constitutional Convention, May 31, 1787

THE WAR FOR AMERICAN INDEPENDENCE

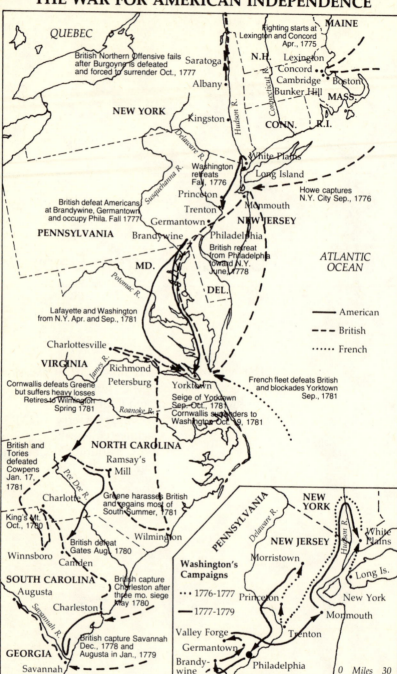

QUEBEC

Fighting starts at Lexington and Concord Apr., 1775

MAINE

British Northern Offensive fails after Burgoyne is defeated and forced to surrender Oct., 1777

Saratoga

N.H.

Lexington
Concord
Cambridge · Boston
Bunker Hill

MASS.

Albany

NEW YORK

Kingston

Hudson R.

Connecticut R.

CONN.

R.I.

Delaware R.

White Plains

Washington retreats Fall, 1776

Long Island

Howe captures N.Y. City Sep., 1776

Princeton

Susquehanna R.

Trenton

Monmouth

British defeat Americans at Brandywine, Germantown and occupy Phila. Fall 1777

Germantown

NEW JERSEY

PENNSYLVANIA

Brandywine

Philadelphia

British retreat from Philadelphia toward N.Y. June, 1778

ATLANTIC OCEAN

MD.

Potomac R.

DEL.

Lafayette and Washington from N.Y. Apr. and Sep., 1781

——— American
– – – British
······· French

Charlottesville

VIRGINIA

James R.

Richmond

Cornwallis defeats Greene but suffers heavy losses Retires to Wilmington Spring 1781

Petersburg

Yorktown

French fleet defeats British and blockades Yorktown Sep., 1781

Roanoke R.

Siege of Yorktown Sep.-Oct., 1781 Cornwallis surrenders to Washington Oct. 19, 1781

British and Tories defeated Cowpens Jan. 17, 1781

NORTH CAROLINA

Ramsay's Mill

Pee Dee R.

Charlotte

Greene harasses British and regains most of South Summer, 1781

King's Mt. Oct., 1780

Wilmington

British defeat Gates Aug. 1780

Winnsboro

Camden

SOUTH CAROLINA

British capture Charleston after three mo. siege May 1780

Augusta

Savannah R.

Charleston

GEORGIA

British capture Savannah Dec., 1778 and Augusta in Jan., 1779

Savannah

PENNSYLVANIA

NEW YORK

Delaware R.

NEW JERSEY

Hudson R.

White Plains

Morristown

Washington's Campaigns

····· 1776-1777
——— 1777-1779

Princeton

New York

Monmouth

Long Is.

Valley Forge

Trenton

Germantown

Brandywine

Philadelphia

Wilmington

0   Miles   30

V

At the Precipice:
March 15, 1783

George Washington stood in front of his rebellious officers as a man looking down the barrel of a loaded musket. They confronted each other on March 15, 1783, in Newburgh, New York, the last cantonment of the Continentals before the army disbanded later that year. The officers, provoked by unredressed grievances, had assembled to decide upon a course of action against civilian leaders and citizens of the new republic, which the army had originally been organized to help create. Talk of mutiny had been running high. There was even the chance of a military *coup d'état*—a march to Philadelphia, seizure of power from the Continental Congress, and establishment of a dictatorship.[1]

In March 1783, the war was at a standstill. Since October 1781, when a British army of 8,000 under Charles, Lord Cornwallis, had surrendered at Yorktown, the conflict in the North American theater had been winding down. After Yorktown, Commander in Chief Washington moved the main body of Continental forces northward from Virginia to Newburgh, New York, a few miles above West Point, on the Hudson River's west bank. There the Continental troops, some 10,000 war-wearied veterans and their officers, along with nearly 1,000 women camp followers, settled in and waited for news of a peace settlement that would lead to final evacuations of British troops, particularly from their main base in New York City. The

107

American army remained intact and alert through the long months of 1782 and early 1783, in order to guard against possible incursions while peace commissioners in Europe labored for official recognition of American independence.

As 1782 wore on, Washington's officers and common soldiers kept themselves ready for action, but rarely did they have enough activity to occupy themselves. One project that the soldiers had been ordered to carry out in late 1782 was that of building a meeting house for officers, later called the "Temple of Virtue." Since men from every state line had a hand in the construction, the temple was supposed to symbolize unity among the creators of the new nation. Virtue referred to the restraint and glory which the Continental army had exhibited, even when poorly supported by its civilian masters. The principle was that a republican order could not withstand the test of time unless all citizens, including military personnel, subordinated their personal interests to the higher good of the whole community. Ironically, Washington was confronting his disgruntled officers in the Temple of Virtue.

The officers, like the rank and file, were restive over the issue of pay, or lack of it. In 1780, the Continental Congress, reacting to threats from the officers about resigning *en masse*, promised them half-pay pensions for life at the war's end. But the officers knew that the national government lacked the permanent tax revenues necessary for paying those pensions. Congress could only ask the states for funds, and the states, struggling to control their own war debts, were generally unresponsive to pleas from the weak central government. Congress did not have the money to fulfill its promises. The common soldiers were being paid irregularly. In addition, the officers' recent demand that their promised pensions be commuted into five years of full pay as severance allowances had not been heeded by Congress. Officers and men during March 1783 thus had something in common: Both feared that, when final peace terms were ratified, the army would be discharged and a forgetful citizenry would neglect its financial obligations to those devoted veterans who had contributed so much to winning the war and to making the experiment in republicanism possible.

Over the years of military conflict, Continental officers and common soldiers alike had grown increasingly perturbed over the indifference of civilians and the lack of governmental support. In 1780 one angry officer wrote indignantly: "It really gives me pain to think of our public affairs; where is the public spirit of the year 1775? Where are those flaming *patriots* who were ready to sacrifice their lives, their fortunes, their all, for the public?"[2] Citizen virtue seemed to be wanting. High ranking Continental officers spoke harshly of self-serving civilians who grew wealthy from war profiteering while the army suffered and starved for lack of bare necessities. As the angered General Alexander McDougall summed up his disillusionment in 1779, when commenting on Philadelphians, "I am sorry to hear of the dissipated Manners of that Capital. It 'augurs' ill to America. Can the Country expect Spartan Virtue in her army, while the people are wallowing in all the luxury of Rome in her declining State. . . . The Consequence is obvious."[3]

Bad feelings within the Continental ranks kept simmering after 1779. In January 1781, soldiers in the Pennsylvania line rebelled. They began an overland march to Philadelphia from the army's winter encampment site near Morristown, in northcentral New Jersey. The Pennsylvanians wanted out, among other reasons because their pay, when they received it at all, was in rapidly depreciating paper money. They contended that their terms of service were over, even though civilian authorities claimed that they had signed on for the duration. But the Pennsylvanians were insisting that they would reenlist only if they received hard money bonuses comparable to those being meted out to lure new recruits. Scurrying civilian officials met the Pennsylvania soldiers' demands, but many of the men were so disgusted by continuing civilian indifference to the army's plight that they still refused to reenlist. They went home.

Close on the heels of the Pennsylvanians, the New Jersey line revolted. Washington, fearing that his army was about to disintegrate around him over such basic matters as adequate food, clothing, and supplies, issued harsh orders insisting upon forceful subjugation of the Jersey malcontents. A party of loyal soldiers caught the Jerseymen by surprise and quickly ordered that three ringleaders should be arbitrarily singled out for court martial. Death by firing squad was the penalty; twelve other mutinous leaders were ordered to administer the execution. Washington, considering the bitterness of his soldiers, found in January 1781 that this was the only way to keep his rank and file under some semblance of control.

After Yorktown, with peace at last a possibility, the officers at Newburgh wanted guarantees that they would be rewarded for their sacrifices. Many had suffered personal financial losses in order to remain in the field during the war. In a strongly worded petition to the Congress in December 1782, the officers pleaded: "We have borne all that men can bear—our property is expended—our private resources are at an end." Then they explained that their friends were "wearied out and disgusted" with their endless applications for credit. They demanded five years of full pay; else, they ominously warned Congress, "any further experiments on their patience may have fatal effects."[4]

The officers obviously were hinting that they would resort to military force, if necessary, to exact at least a minimum of personal financial justice from civilian authorities, even if that meant destroying the cause of republicanism. Increasingly, officers and soldiers perceived republicanism as a sham, anyway. It permitted private citizens to reap handsome war profits while others sacrificed and suffered. Even before March 1783, some officers and civilian officials had talked openly of making General Washington a virtual dictator, so as to bring some order out of the chaos of American affairs. The Commander in Chief rebuffed the idea. He concluded that it was too dangerous to supplant civilian with military authority, even for a short time, and still hope for the flowering of institutions dedicated to popular as opposed to despotic sovereignty.

In this milieu of massive disillusionment, Washington stood before his officers on, of all dates, the Ides of March 1783. The Commander, groping for the right words, urged patience and assured his officers that in time they would receive justice, recognition, honor, and financial recompense. He promised to do everything possible to see that each Continental veteran gained his due. Yet the officers did not seem convinced; their anger did not abate. Washington knew that he was not touching the hearts of his men. But he kept trying. Out of desperation, the Commander mentioned that he wanted to read a letter. He reached in his pocket and pulled out a pair of eyeglasses. The men were startled; none of them had ever seen Washington wearing glasses before. Sensing their surprise, he calmly explained: "Gentlemen, you must pardon me. I have grown gray in your service and now find myself growing blind."[5]

His words and their larger meaning caught the officers off guard. He verbalized for all of them their sense of personal sacrifice. Something far greater than repairing the shattered finances of any single individual was at stake. The soldiers, Washington was suggesting, had already established the fact that the concept of virtue, upon which the republican order must rest, already existed among certain citizens. It was the soldiers' example that mattered above all else now, even though many civilians had abused their obligations. The assembled officers understood; many began to weep openly.

The peak of the crisis was over. By calming his men and reminding them of their unshakable dedication, Washington had averted possible disaster at the precipice. The army could restrain its bitterness and wait for justice. It would not pursue the dangerous course of military intervention in civilian decision making, whether or not Congress satisfied its grievances.

Even though the Continental army disbanded peacefully later in 1783, the frustrations, temporarily abated at Newburgh, lingered on. The war had been won, and satisfactory preliminary peace terms had been achieved. But something still seemed amiss, especially to men like Washington and his highest ranking officers. They continued to suspect that a less than virtuous citizenry was undercutting, if not actually destroying, the possibility of creating an independent republican nation worthy of respect among other nations. Action had to be taken before it was too late—before some vicious act of self-interest propelled America into the bottomless pit of anarchy and chaos.

Notes

1. Recent investigations of the Newburgh crisis include sections in Merrill Jensen, *The New Nation: A History of the United States during the Confederation, 1781–1789* (New York, 1950), 67–84; E. James Ferguson, *The Power of the Purse: A History of American Public Finance, 1776–1790* (Chapel Hill, N.C., 1961), 155–168; and Forrest McDonald, *E Pluribus Unum: The Formation of the American Republic, 1776–1790* (Boston, 1965), 22–32. The most effective and thorough over-all analysis is that of Richard H. Kohn, "The Inside History of the Newburgh Conspiracy: America and the Coup d'Etat," *William and Mary Quarterly*, 3rd Ser., 27 (1970), 187–220. Criticisms along with replies by Kohn include Paul David Nelson, "Horatio Gates at Newburgh, 1783: A Misunderstood Role," *ibid.*, 29 (1972), 143–158, and C. Edward Skeen, "The Newburgh Conspiracy Reconsidered," *ibid.*, 31 (1974), 273–298.

2. John Paterson to William Heath, West Point, March 31, 1780, *The Heath Papers*, Massachusetts Historical Society *Collections*, 7th Ser., V (Boston, 1907), 44–45.

3. To Nathanael Greene, Peekskill, March 24, 1779, Nathanael Greene Papers, American Philosophical Society Library, Philadelphia.

4. "Address and Petition of the Officers," dated December 1782, Ford, ed., *Journals of the Continental Congress*, XXIV, 291–293.

5. Quoted in Douglas Southall Freeman, *George Washington: A Biography* V (New York, 1952), 435.

VI

The War for American Independence, 1775–1783

Between 1763 and 1776, a deep-rooted consensus among provincial Americans on the value of citizenship in the British Empire had been shattered. By July 1776, the protest movement had fully metamorphosed into an avowed rebellion and the proclamation of a new nation. Many Americans, however reluctantly, seemed willing by the summer of 1776 to strike out upon an independent course. Yet a numerically significant minority, perhaps as much as one third of the population drawn from all classes and groups, was either latently or explicitly loyal to Great Britain. In addition to these loyalists (or "tories," as the insurgents sneeringly referred to them), there were incalculable numbers who were ready to follow wherever others might lead, so long as that did not involve personal pain or sacrifice. These individuals, best described as neutrals or the uncommitted, no longer revered British citizenship as they once had but were not ready to immerse themselves fully in the cause of independence. As a matter of fact, neutrals may have been far more numerous than loyalists. Such a diverse group had no official spokesman, but one Philadelphian gave voice to their feelings when he stated: "Let who would be king, he well knew that he should be a subject."[1] Involving these neutrals, or at least controlling them, was essential if the War for American Independence was to be won.

In addition to fear, apathy, or lost enthusiasm, one reason why so many Americans chose neutrality was that they could not imagine that anyone, especially provincials from thirteen disparate colonies, could stand up for long against British men in arms. Waging full-scale war against well-trained, well-armed redcoats appeared to be a hopeless task. In many ways it was. Great Britain had demonstrated in earlier eighteenth-century wars that its combined land and naval forces were capable of defeating such major powers as France and Spain and exacting significant territorial concessions as the price of peace settlements. Subduing the rebellious provinces should have taken no time at all.

But the neutrals were not considering the full range of vital factors. Most important, they underrated the characteristic separateness, diffuseness, and sheer geographical size of the rebellious colonies. For British military leaders, the essential problem was that of reestablishing Parliament's sovereignty by force over a huge area of North America. The burden of proof in 1776 was on Great Britain. His Majesty's military units had to demonstrate the ability to regain citizen allegiance through the full application of military power, for Parliament's sovereignty had not been sustained through accepted forms of political accommodation.

Indeed, it may be argued that Britain from the outset had little chance of winning the war, unless there were too many Americans who refused to become involved. Despite condescending overconfidence, British men in arms faced towering obstacles. An attempt to conquer much of the eastern edge of a continent stretching some 1,500 miles from Maine to Georgia was beyond ordinary eighteenth-century military capabilities. More important, the provinces lacked a strategic vital center which, if captured, would end the rebellion. Conquering one city, such as the nominal capital, Philadelphia, or even one region, such as New England, would not guarantee total American submission. Like an ever changing amoeba, there was no real way to render the Americans completely helpless through one decisive military stroke, so long as there were enough rebels in other areas who would continue to fight. Only a general collapse of the will to resist would make British victory possible. As it turned out, maintaining that will was no small task.

Indeed, the assignment from the British side could have been viewed as lying beyond the accepted military means of the times. Yet British ministers in 1775 were not thinking in such realistic terms. Despite the embarrassment of Lexington and Concord, they believed that American citizen-soldiers would scatter in mortal fear whenever the vaunted regulars entered the field. As a result, British officials did not perceive the implications of the situation facing them. They worked away instead on such mundane matters as naming field generals, planning the details of their massive campaign effort of 1776, and collecting sufficient manpower and supplies to make that campaign a success. Also, they were preparing the navy to blockade the American coast. Through it all, the ministers presumed that, with one well-executed show of force, they would reestablish Parliament's sovereignty over the provinces. They were miscalculating by a wide margin.

In fact, it is possible that their last real military chance ended with the campaign fiasco of 1777, which resulted in the capture of "Gentleman" Johnny Burgoyne's army at the Battle of Saratoga in upstate New York. With that humiliating defeat, Britain found itself involved in a world war, ultimately having to fight France, Spain, and the Netherlands as American allies. Because of America's distinct advantages, it is astonishing that Great Britain came so close to subduing the American rebels before the serious setback of 1777. What is equally astonishing is how close Americans came to losing the war after 1777, when massive international support buoyed a cause suffering seriously from less than enthusiastic popular support. It was an unsettling paradox for all involved.

Why the British lost and why the rebels won the war cannot be explained by concentrating exclusively on specific battles. The major battles on the American continent, adding up to about thirty days of uninterrupted fighting over a seven-year period, obviously were important. However, they must be treated as the most vivid symbols of more subtle factors which, over time, tipped the scales in favor of the Americans. Those factors included a mixture of psychological, sociological, and strategic elements which sorted themselves out in a war that may be divided roughly into two geographic components: the northern phase of 1775–1778, and the southern phase of 1778–1781. In the North, the scale of disadvantages worked against British men in arms; in the South, Americans (in cooperation with the French) finally proved that they were unconquerable.[2]

The northern phase started with the battles of Lexington and Concord, an ignoble beginning for the British when compounded with the carnage of Bunker Hill. Disorganized but enthusiastic New England militia, besieging British-held Boston after April 19, put steady pressure on General Gage and his 5,000 redcoats. In time, the Americans moved out on to the Charlestown peninsula, across the back bay and north of Boston. Gage, "reinforced" by three high ranking field generals, John Burgoyne, Henry Clinton, and William Howe (who unlike Gage had virtually no respect for American fighting prowess), found himself having to face the New Englanders in battle once more—or lose all credibility. His decision was to demonstrate Britain's military superiority through a massive open-field frontal assault. The assumption was that Americans would wither once they confronted standard European military formations and battlefield maneuvers. Three times in close-order formation on June 17, the British ranks, directly under Howe's command, charged the advanced American position ahead of Bunker Hill on Breed's Hill. The third charge, bayonets glittering, finally dislodged the well-entrenched Americans, who suffered at this point from exhaustion and a shortage of ammunition.

The British, having driven the rebel forces off Charlestown peninsula, claimed total victory in what was the war's bloodiest battle. The King's casualties amounted to 1,054 wounded or killed, slightly over 40 percent of the troops committed to battle. American casualties (including Dr. Joseph Warren) totaled 400 (30 percent of the rebels engaged). The British casualty rate had been far too high for an army that could replace its fallen manpower only with difficulty. Even if the rebels conceded the peninsula by abandoning Bunker Hill, British field tactics had resulted in unusual carnage. Men of raw courage had faced soldiers with superior military training and had not gone down to easy defeat. It was a lesson that the British command should have taken more seriously.

Howe later confessed that he went through *"a moment that I have never felt before"* as he faced the possibility of battlefield extermination.[3] A cautious person, Howe seemed to be even more dilatory and less willing to run risks after Bunker Hill. Howe's heightened timidity became a subtle but important factor favoring the inexperienced Americans because he soon replaced General Gage as commander in chief of British forces in North America. (Gage had made himself expendable; among other reasons, he respected American fighting prowess, even if it had unconventional qualities and was inconsistent with the most up-to-date procedures in training manuals.) Perhaps Howe avoided major, extended frontal assaults during the critical campaign season of 1776 because of the personal trauma that he had experienced at Bunker Hill. If it was grudging respect, it grew out of the fear that standard close-order volleys followed by bayonet charges against well-entrenched rebel soldiers would cost the British too many men and so drain available manpower reserves in the field that it would be impossible to continue the war effort effectively.

While American manpower reserves were theoretically unbounded, Great Britain's were not, as was evidenced by the presence of so many Hessians in the British ranks. Thus Howe chose the option of deploying his soldiers cautiously in the months ahead. He did not permit his troops to be needlessly slaughtered in a showdown battle; and he maintained his numerical superiority in rank and file manpower in making sure that Americans did not enjoy their self-proclaimed independence too soon.[4] Howe's decision to save his army rather than to use it at critical moments helped to spare Washington's army from annihilation in 1776. It also may have saved the American cause.

As a rule, British field commanders mixed undue caution with attitudes of disdain toward everyone else's military capabilities. That unnatural combination produced mixed results from the campaign seasons; it injured as much as it helped the goal of restoring parliamentary sovereignty. "The native American is an effeminate thing, very unfit for and very impatient of war," wrote one high ranking British veteran of the Seven Years' War. To another, the rebels were "a set of upstart vagabonds, the dregs and scorn of the human species."[5] As General Burgoyne remarked when landing in besieged Boston, "Well, let *us* get in, and we'll soon find elbow room."[6] Several months later he did find his "elbow room." In March 1776, Howe abandoned Boston as indefensible, retreated by sea to Halifax, Nova Scotia, and prepared to assume leadership of the massive land campaign of 1776.

But even retreating by sea did not alter attitudes. "The contempt every Soldier has for an American," noted one English officer in 1779, "is not the smallest. They cannot possibly believe that any good Quality can exist among them."[7] British generals basked in their sense of military superiority, regardless of their initial setbacks. They too often failed to follow up on obvious battlefield advantages during the months ahead. After that it was too late.

In many ways it was too late after 1776, the year in which Britain put forth an awesome military effort by the standards of the time. The initial planning was sound. The strategy was that of concentration of forces. The target was New York City, an excellent base port for maintaining supply lines with England. New York would then become the base from which the surrounding countryside could be reconquered. In time, the King's forces could move northward and take the Hudson Highlands region, severing New England from the other states—thus isolating for conquest the area which had been the initial hotbed of defiance. British forces could also move with ease southward and westward across New Jersey, providing a regional land base, not only for food supplies, but also for loyalists who could come forward and help to reinstitute civilian authority under the Crown.

By the spring of 1776, the ministry was moving well along in its preparations for sending some 27,000 troops (over half of them Germans) to New York, where they would join William Howe's soldiers. The goal was to end the war with one massive show of force, optimistically within one campaign season. Looking back at the failures of 1775, the North ministry understood that it was vital to bring Americans to their senses before the rebels gained the support of France and Spain. Thus it was with a sense of urgency that the home government planned such a major military effort.

But the operation, once in motion, did not go smoothly. Assembling a fleet of over 400 vessels with naval escorts, providing for supplies, and outfitting the soldiers stretched the bureaucratic capabilities of the English government. Then there were interruptions. Because of the concerted insurgent attempt to seize Canada late in 1775, the ministry had to divert several thousand troops originally destined for New York City to Quebec. Thus the notion of concentrating manpower resources was compromised even before the main expedition was ready for service. Then the ministry sent out another force, this time against the southern colonies to link up with loyalists in order to subdue that region. That expedition turned out to be a failure, eventually suffering embarrassment and defeat at Charleston in the late spring of 1776 before sailing for New York to join Howe. Howe's forces from Nova Scotia had been gathering on Staten Island since late June. Yet the combined land-naval fleet coming from England was not in position to take the offensive against New York City until August, with more than half of the campaign season already gone.

Despite these delays and interruptions, the combined land-naval forces under William Howe and his brother, Admiral Lord Richard (in charge of naval operations), amounted to over 30,000 soldiers and sailors, including the troops which came with William from Boston via Halifax. American Continental and militia units in the New York vicinity, by comparison, totaled 28,000, but with only 19,000 troops ready for battle. More important, the Howes had Washington virtually trapped. Unwisely, the American commander, while awaiting the British attack, had split his forces—half on the island of Manhattan and half in Brooklyn. The royal navy landed British units at Gravesend, Long Island, on August 22. Naval maneuvering could have cut off Washington and half of his army simply by sailing Lord Richard's flotilla through New York harbor into the East River, thereby severing the rebels from their only possible escape route. However, undue caution and unfavorable winds held the British naval commander back. Even though the Americans took a drubbing, they escaped across the East River under cover of a foggy night. The plodding Howes, consistently failing to follow through, had just let pass one of the best chances that British commanders enjoyed during the war to capture or annihilate Washington's forces. Washington learned from his tactical blunder; once he had extricated his army from Manhattan, he never put his soldiers in such a dangerous position again.

The Howes missed other opportunities in other battles around New York during the remaining months of 1776. The conquest of the former provinces by the end of the campaign season may have depended upon destroying the Continental Army and ravaging the countryside around New York, that is, following a policy of annihilation with no quarter to shatter American confidence and will to continue. But William Howe acted like a man of conciliation, not like one who understood the necessity for a military reign of terror. It was not only his Bunker Hill experience that made him less than audacious. It was also his desire, as a person aligned with Whig leaders in England who had some sympathy for American grievances, to reconcile differences through military gentility rather than by tearing Washington's forces to shreds. The Howes carried instructions with them as Crown-appointed peace commissioners. Although they could not offer much in return for American submission, they wanted to restore harmony in the Empire with as little embittering bloodshed as possible. They no doubt held back from a course of calculated brutality in the hope that Americans would soon acknowledge British military superiority. To pursue peace and war at the same time was inevitably clumsy. It allowed Washington to divide his bruised and battered forces, to slip away, and to retreat in disorderly fashion southwestward through New Jersey and across the Delaware River into Pennsylvania.[8]

Howe had failed to bag his prey, a factor of enormous consequences in the light of coming events. While about one half of Washington's divided Continental army maneuvered for safety north of New York and then in northwestern New Jersey, Washington planned a desperate counterthrust. He decided to utilize his tattered, depleted forces—at most 6,000 troops, including militia—in a surprise foray against advanced British outposts on the Jersey side of the Delaware. On the icy Christmas evening of 1776, Washington led his men back across the Delaware, and overwhelmed a startled contingent of 1,500 Hessians at Trenton. During the next few days, the freezing Continentals outclassed British units a second time at Princeton. Howe responded by pulling his outposts into a narrower ring around the main British base of New York City. At the moment of ultimate despair, Washington had triumphantly regained much of New Jersey. Having kept a semblance of an army alive that was still capable of inflicting painful offensive thrusts, the satisfied American commander moved his forces northward to join the army's other wing and settle into winter quarters in New Jersey's Watchung Mountains, several miles west of New York City.

For the American cause, the Continentals' startling victories at Trenton and Princeton after four months of sustained humiliation clearly proved one point: an effective rebel army, however short of manpower, was still in the field with the ability to continue warfare in the future. In that sense, Britain's massive military effort of 1776 had failed, and for one basic reason: the unwillingness of British field generals to follow through to total victory when annihilation was feasible. Of equal significance was William Howe's abandonment of his distant Jersey outposts. He effectively undercut American loyalists, many of whom had risen up and taken loyalty oaths on the assumption that the British would maintain their control of New Jersey. Now the military protection was gone. These loyalists, having identified themselves, would be subjected to the retributive justice of local rebels. Time and again as the war progressed, British field generals undermined or used loyalists ineffectively by not holding the ground that they had taken. Britain, with so many potential supporters in the American population, failed to employ this vast reservoir of manpower effectively. By not capitalizing on people who could bear arms, reinstitute civilian government under the Crown, or grow foodstuffs necessary for supporting the main army, the British command increased redcoat dependency on supply lines stretching back to England, a dubious distinction at best.

As usual, rather than accepting failures and learning from mistakes, there were excuses. "Now as to the Hessians, they are the worst troops I ever saw," complained a British officer in excusing the Trenton setback.[9] The officer had missed the key point. Bringing Americans back into the Empire rested upon more than winning occasional battles. It depended upon making effective use of battlefield triumphs; and the British high command was not doing that. As a result, Britain had little to show for its massive campaign effort of 1776, except for control of New York and its environs.

Perfunctory generalship was one cause of the continuing British failure. An unswerving devotion to the standard military habits of the day, in terms of an army's nature and functions, also weakened the British military effort. The problem may be stated in sociological terms. Britain's was a "standing army," in which officers and soldiers served primarily for pay and individual glory in quasi-mercenary fashion. Life for the rank and file, though inherently brutal, was an alternative to filching in the streets, rotting in prison, or starving to death in some isolated hamlet. Ne'er-do-wells, the luckless, and the "poorer sort" in general filled the ranks. Rigorous discipline and training taught the men loyalty, even blind obedience, to their officers. For those who lacked economic opportunity elsewhere, the regular army provided food, clothing, and a modest income. Fighting the American rebels was merely one means of making a subsistence living. Common soldiers provided brute force, while gentlemanly commanders worried about holding the Empire together and keeping morale high among a rank and file that lacked much emotional commitment to fighting for intangible political goals.

While His Majesty's soldiers came largely from unprivileged classes, officers normally gained their commissions through family bloodline and personal connections. All high level British officers were drawn from the gentry and nobility, which had the financial means to buy commissions for large sums. Thus there was no relationship between rank and proved battlefield skill, tactical ability, or strategic know-how. Individuals progressed up the officer grades only as far as connections, personal influence, powerful patrons, corruption, and money took them. For instance, the Howe brothers, although competent commanders by the standards of their day, were related to George III through bastard family line connections; carefree Johnny Burgoyne was a wealthy cavorting dandy, a gentleman playwright, and member of Parliament. Since these men had access to the highest officials in the British government, they were the most visible products of an entrenched system of influence, favoritism, and nepotism—the very system which many provincial Americans had found so repulsive and destructive of liberty prior to 1776. If a truly gifted officer emerged in the top ranks, it was as much a matter of chance as anything else; it was rarely a matter of demonstrated ability.

Typical of the English patronage system was the elevation in 1775 of Lord George Germain to the post of Secretary of State for American Affairs, replacing Lord Dartmouth. Germain, a member of the powerful Sackville family, was single-mindedly unsympathetic toward Americans, whom he considered rude bumpkins. He was also a man with a sullied military past. In what may have been a frame-up, Germain had been courtmartialed and convicted of disobedience in carrying out battlefield orders during the Seven Years' War. Yet his personal political connections were powerful enough to secure the cabinet post charged with guiding the over-all military effort against America. Germain's efforts did little to help the Empire, especially when he issued vague, seemingly contradictory instructions, and when he encouraged his field generals to report in detail on each other's activities. Even though Germain was quite good at orchestrating broad-scale campaign planning (such as that of 1776), he did as much as anyone else to add confusion to the general war effort, largely because he insisted upon having his way at the wrong time.[10]

The upper-class generals, when not seeking personal advantages over one another or with cabinet-level officials like Germain, and when not leading their hired, lower-class troops in battle, saw to it that they lived as graciously as possible while in the field. Wherever they went, they insisted that their standing as gentlemen not be compromised. When General Burgoyne, for example, moved south from Canada in 1777 with an army of 9,500, he personally made sure that, among other "necessary" items, he had his silver-plated dining service, several cases of his favorite champagne, enough personal uniforms for looking splendid in the woods at all times, and other forms of private baggage which filled thirty slow-moving supply wagons. Just lugging the "necessities" of Burgoyne and his ranking officers through thick woods and along narrow trails made virtually impassable by resisting American militia helped slow Burgoyne's southward march to a crawl. Such dilatory movements eventually brought both defeat and disaster. Burgoyne, with his sumptuous life-style, paid a heavy price at Saratoga in October 1777.

If the British generals and their civilian superiors had worried as much about the art of conducting successful warfare and accomplishing strategic goals against the American rebels as they worried about rank, dress, and personal style, the outcome of the campaigns of 1776 and 1777 might have been different, perhaps less disastrous in the long run. There was enormous confusion, for instance, about how brutal Howe's virtually unstoppable forces should be. Germain wanted the army to act with vengeance in order to break American morale and provoke a quick cessation of hostilities on British terms. Yet others in the North ministry, and the Howes themselves, preferred milder intimidation simply through the army's concentrated and controlled presence in and around New York. No one could agree. Howe thus remained the gentleman in the field; he pursued his mistress, Mrs. Joshua Loring, with fervor, but he showed no interest in gaining a reputation as one of the horsemen of the apocalypse. Ministerial leaders seemed to be satisfied with Howe's initial string of victories, so much that the King awarded him knighthood status. There were some, however, who were sorry that the honor could not be revoked after learning about Trenton and Princeton—real signs that Howe had gained much less from so much effort than initially presumed.

All of the gentlemanly confusion over strategy and goals came to a head in 1777. Hoping to engage Washington's Continental forces in a major battle, Sir William tried to draw them out of their entrenched position in the Watchung Mountains. Fearing a repetition of Bunker Hill and debilitating manpower losses, Howe already had become obsessed with the idea of taking Philadelphia as one means of luring Washington into battle on more favorable terrain. Moreover, the British commander in chief thought that conquering the enemy's capital would seriously reduce the rebel will to resist. He treated Philadelphia as though it was a strategic vital center. He did not seem to know that the Continental Congress could move with ease to another site and continue to function. Rather than concentrating on a policy of cooperation with Burgoyne's forces and implementing the Hudson Highlands strategy of cutting off New England, Howe gave that logical choice second place in his campaign efforts of 1777. Germain only compounded the confusion by issuing vague general instructions. Inexplicably, Howe prepared to move on the enemy's capital. It may be that he did not want to support Burgoyne's troops unduly for fear that "Gentleman Johnny" would gain too much glory at home—at Howe's expense. As a result, the small contingent of British troops which eventually moved northward from New York City was too few and too late to save Burgoyne's entrapped army.

In focusing exclusively on Philadelphia and forsaking Burgoyne, Howe all but ended British chances of winning the war. Just to make sure, the myopic British commander, fearing that Washington would hound his flanks and supply lines if his troops traveled by land, moved some 15,000 redcoats by sea through Chesapeake Bay. In doing so, Sir William tied up large portions of the British navy assigned to the American theater, opening large holes in the attempted naval blockade of the coastline. Moreover, he had a large army at sea for nearly two months in the middle of a campaign season where it could not possibly be of any value. Only the weakness of the American forces permitted Howe to get away with such mistakes. Indeed, squandered time with an army at sea gave Washington an opportunity to release some men for duty against the beleaguered Burgoyne while moving the rest into position southwest of Philadelphia. Ostensibly, Howe appeared to have vindicated himself when he beat the Continental forces badly at Brandywine Creek (September 11, 1777), southwest of Philadelphia, and then marched unopposed into the city. But the British commander had captured an empty shell. Congress had already fled to York in the Pennsylvania interior. Even though Philadelphia loyalists cheered his presence, Howe began to realize that, while he had beaten Washington again and captured a pleasant spot for winter quarters, he had done so at the cost of Burgoyne's army.

Far to the north, Burgoyne's struggling units faced unremitting harassment from growing hordes of New England militia operating under the Continental army's Northern Department. Yet the British army desperately clung to the hope that a relief expedition from the South would fight its way to Albany. A small force from New York under Sir Henry Clinton did move up the Hudson corridor, but too lackadaisically and too late. Burgoyne's soldiers, hammered and exhausted in taxing engagements from mid September on, had to capitulate or face extermination. Burgoyne formally surrendered on October 17, 1777, to General Horatio Gates, the Northern Department commander. A British junior officer noted sadly in describing the scene that "we marched out, according to treaty, with drums beating and the honors of war, but the drums seemed to have lost their former inspiring sounds, . . . then it seemed by its last feeble effort, as if almost ashamed to be heard on such an occasion."[11] Unknown to this officer, Saratoga was the last drum sounding for Great Britain in its attempt to reconquer the erstwhile provinces. The capitulation of Burgoyne's army set the stage for France's formal entry into the war. The lack of coordinated planning and field action by Germain, Howe, Burgoyne, and Clinton, among others, had turned the campaign of 1777 into a shambles.

Since 1763, a handful of influential French citizens had relished the growing feud between England and her American provinces. The Treaty of Paris had swung the European balance of power heavily in Great Britain's favor, and there were many persons in France who saw in the Anglo-American rift an opportunity to strike back at their ancient foe. Some French leaders, especially the head of foreign affairs, the Duke de Choiseul, covertly encouraged the Anglo-American split. Breaking England's grip on its American provinces, Choiseul perceived, could restore the balance of power in Europe and once again elevate France to England's high stature. With that goal in mind, Choiseul sent spies to America who stirred the Anglo-American caldron and reported in detail on events. Choiseul was simultaneously encouraging his king, the debauched Louis XV, to spend massive sums to create a refurbished and powerful French army and navy. The new military buildup only further burdened a country suffering from unbearable tax levies on the poor; the nobility, exempt from taxation, did not seem to care as they cavorted stylishly at the King's court.

Louis XV died in 1774 with but little national mourning. His heir, Louis XVI, deferred in most policy matters to his queen, Marie Antoinette, who stoutly resisted those trying to bring the Crown's profligacy under control. He also gave a free hand to his foreign minister, the Count de Vergennes, who continued Choiseul's vengeance-oriented policy toward Great Britain. But while surreptitiously encouraging the split, the wily Vergennes kept his guard up against an Anglo-American trap. Until the Americans had proved themselves capable of sustaining warfare and of standing up militarily to Great Britain, he would keep France out of the conflict—at least formally. Most of all, Vergennes feared a quick reconciliation between Britain and America, with both warring parties suddenly turning on France. He did not want his country trapped in an overextended posture; yet he did want the Americans to succeed. Thus Vergennes's strategy after 1775 was to aid the American military effort informally and massively with war materiel, in turn helping to widen the breach between mother country and colonies beyond reconciliation. At that time formal intervention, if the Americans persevered, would set the stage for breaking Britain's international supremacy. Saratoga met all of Vergennes's tests for direct French intervention in the war.

Except for a few intellectuals (the *philosophes*) and hardheaded realists like Vergennes, the typical French citizen knew very little about the British provinces in North America, at least before the deepening crisis of 1775. Even the intellectuals were a bit fuzzy on the details. One popular theory held that Anglo-Americans were an emasculated people, a condition resulting from debilitating New World climatic and weather patterns. As late as 1771 the Abbé Raynal wrote stereotypically of "visibly degenerated" Englishmen in America. Raynal explained: "Their minds have been enervated like their bodies. Quick and penetrating at first, they grasp ideas easily; but they cannot concentrate nor accustom themselves to prolonged reflection. . . . Almost all of them have some facility in everything." Then he noted cautiously: "But none has a marked talent for anything. Precocious and mature before us, they are far behind when we have reached our full mental development."[12] The French environmentalists believed that degeneration rather than regeneration had occurred in colonial America. It was an image that had to be overcome in constructing a successful Franco-American alliance.

Unfavorable perceptions reached a fashionable peak between 1750 and 1770, but they quickly gave way in the mid 1770s to a far more positive image—that of aspiring republicans defending their liberties against arbitrary monarchical power. With vivid language, the excited *philosophes* turned the American provinces into a laboratory for testing Enlightenment principles, one of which was that vicious, self-serving monarchs stood in the way of human progress and happiness. French men and women of the Age of Reason were among those western peoples who were searching for universal laws and ideals which would improve the quality of human existence. In their quest, they often turned against traditional religious forms and faith in an all-powerful diety. They also made a new religion out of the capacity of human beings to solve their own problems through reason. As rationalists, they believed that serving the common good was an achievable goal, and they saw the institutionalization of republican government in America as an important step forward in the progress of mankind away from tyranny.

For the *philosophes*, provincial Americans suddenly turned into individuals who lived in harmony with nature. In the refurbished image of the 1770s, the Americans were people who felt deeply for the rights of man and who needed support in their bold attempt to preserve fundamental human liberties. If they succeeded, and republicanism triumphed over tyranny, Americans would demonstrate beyond reasonable doubt that a superior basis for human relationships could exist. They would also help to inspire others to bring willful monarchs, like those of France, more directly under popular control. The *philosophes* thus cheered as Americans moved toward a state of avowed independence. Enlightenment political ideals were now at last to have the chance to prove their efficacy somewhere, since the likelihood of overturning the *ancien régime* of France seemed remote in 1776.[13]

Unwittingly, the *philosophes* were lending numerical support at court to Vergennes, who, for far more mundane reasons, was encouraging American defiance. His agents kept sending him enthusiastic reports. As one spy overstated conditions near Boston late in 1775: "Everybody here is a soldier; the troops are well dressed, well paid, and well commanded. They have 50,000 men under pay and a large number of volunteers who desire none. . . . They are stronger than others thought. It surpasses one's imagination. . . . Nothing frightens them. Take your measures accordingly."[14]

With apocryphal reports from America and with growing support at home, Vergennes easily moved forward with his plans. His last major obstacle at court was Louis XVI's finance minister, Turgot. The latter argued vehemently that heavy fiscal involvement in the American cause would only speed the coming bankruptcy of the French government. It might also cause overburdened and overtaxed subjects at home to rise in protest or, worse yet, rebellion against the King himself. Turgot perceived the future accurately, but the wily Vergennes appealed to the strong current of anti-English sentiment and carried the day. Turgot's tight-fisted financial policies cost him his office in 1776, largely because Marie Antoinette disapproved of the crimp being placed on court expenditures. By that time, Vergennes was already preparing the way for massive French aid to the American cause.

From 1775 through 1777, the French Foreign Minister pursued a policy of covert assistance, knowing that if financial support helped to widen the Anglo-American breach beyond repair, France would be in a position to enter the war and crush the hated English. One of Vergennes's many agents, the dapper courtier Beaumarchais—he was better known as the author of the *Marriage of Figaro* and the *Barber of Seville*—went to London in May 1775 primarily in search of a wayward Frenchman who was reputedly selling state secrets to the North ministry. Beaumarchais also operated under orders to make contact with prominent Americans conducting business in England. He began meeting with acid Arthur Lee, Richard Henry's younger brother, and the two of them struck upon a plan for facilitating under-the-table French aid. Vergennes liked the idea. In the spring of 1776, a private mercantile firm, Roderigue Hortalez & Cie.—it was a front for Beaumarchais—began operations. With loans and financial grants from the French government, Hortalez & Cie. purchased materiel destined for American soldiers. In something over a year, for example, it collected an estimated 300,000 barrels of powder for cannons, 30,000 muskets, 3,000 tents, 200 cannons with full train, 27 mortars, 100,000 musket balls, 13,000 hand bombs, and clothing for 30,000 men. Admittedly, much of the merchandise was old and shoddy, but such bulk goods were better than nothing. These particular items passed through New England to upstate New York, where the Continental army's Northern Department distributed them to troops involved in defeating Burgoyne.[15] French loans, cash grants, and materiel thus were critical in creating those circumstances forcing Vergennes out into the open by early 1778.

While manipulating behind the scenes, Vergennes toyed in public with the American commissioners sent to France after the Declaration of Independence. Late in 1775, the Continental Congress had established a secret committee of correspondence to deal with matters relating to potential foreign support in the event that reconciliation did not occur. One of the members was Benjamin Franklin. Very much a man of the world with his international connections, he was a natural choice for service as a commissioner. Arthur Lee and the unscrupulous Connecticut merchant, Silas Deane, were the other two ministers plenipotentiary named as the original delegation to France.

Before sending Franklin overseas, Congress drew up model plans for foreign treaties and alliances. Basically, the articles demanded full recognition of American independence in return for the right to trade with Americans on a most-favored-nation basis. Any country acknowledging American independence would not be discriminated against with respect to port entry fees and duties on foreign commerce. In essence, Congress asked for everything in return for the prospect of uninhibited trading rights (presuming the Americans won the war). Publicly, it was the commissioners' task to sell France the future in exchange for the present. In reality, a willing Vergennes had been waiting all along in Versailles, looking for the proper moment to consummate the formal relationship.

No better person than Benjamin Franklin could have represented American interests. The aging Philadelphian was well-known to the *philosophes*, who considered him America's premier creative genius. In 1772 he had been elected to the French Academy of Sciences, primarily in recognition of his work on electricity. Far more important, Franklin seemed to prove through the power of his scientific experiments, practical inventions, and economic and political writings that republican-minded rustics did not necessarily degenerate mentally under American climatic conditions, but in fact could contribute valuable knowledge to mankind. With his simple clothes, fur hat, unkempt hair, and spectacles, Franklin came to embody the enlightened republican—the type of person who above all else was so free of Old World corruption that he could dedicate himself fully to improving the human condition through the defense of liberty. And Franklin reveled in his role. Witty and urbane as a diplomat, he enjoyed his celebrity status in France and gloated over the reproduction of his republican-looking countenance on such unlikely objects as

snuffboxes, handkerchiefs, rings, and watches. If the fawning attention he received flattered his ego, it also helped to cement Franco-
American relations in the months before the formal alliance.[16]
Franklin's rustic facade worked well with Vergennes's elaborate diplomatic machinations.

Personal public images aside, everything was not always harmonious or pleasant among the American commissioners, who seemed to
spend as much time fighting among themselves as pursuing a formal
alliance. Deane and Lee developed a loathing for one another that
centered on the latter's contempt for Deane's private business deals.
Lee also kept chiding Franklin about sloppy record keeping with respect to the delegation's finances; worse still, Lee complained that
secret documents were left about in Franklin's quarters as though the
elder American wanted every British spy in the vicinity to copy them.

And spies there were. Edward Bancroft, Franklin's personal secretary, and perhaps even Silas Deane himself, worked for the British
secret service. But rather than cooperate with Lee, Franklin took
Deane's side far too often in these petty disputes, raising charges that
Franklin was Deane's cohort in some rather dubious business dealings. Franklin considered Arthur Lee both haughty and arrogant. At
one point he told the Virginian that he had a "Sick Mind, which is
forever tormenting itself, with its Jealousies, Suspicions and Fancies
that others mean you ill, wrong you, or fail in Respect of you." Then
Franklin harshly warned Lee: "If you do not cure yourself of this
Temper it will end in Insanity, of which it is the Symptomatic Fore-
runner, as I have seen in several Instances."[17]

Petty quarreling among the American commissioners subsided
somewhat in 1778, after John Adams replaced the controversial
Deane. By that time, however, France and the United States had
worked out a full-blown alliance. On February 6, 1778, the parties
signed two treaties. The first, the Treaty of Amity and Commerce,
dealt with neutral rights in international commerce and put trade on
the most-favored-nation basis. In the second, the Treaty of Conditional and Defensive Alliance, France recognized American independence. Vergennes also agreed to renounce all French territorial aspirations in North America, including Canada, in return for unfettered
opportunity to conquer British islands in the West Indies. Each party
stipulated that no formal peace terms could be made with the British
enemy without the consent of the other. This clause guaranteed
France that it would have some voice in the matter, should serious
reconciliation attempts suddenly develop between America and England. The mutual consent clause eventually caused considerable

embarrassment for the American peace commissioners when negotiations began in 1782; but in 1778 no American minister could have avoided such a clause and got an alliance. It was Vergennes's protection against an Anglo-American trap.

The formal alliance, an essential factor in America's winning the war, gained final technical sanction when, on March 20, Louis XVI received the American ministers at court and ceremonially accorded the new nation diplomatic recognition. Many people realized that the alliance had unnatural qualities. New Englander Elbridge Gerry caught the contradictions vividly when he penned the following:

> What a miraculous change in the political world! The ministry of England advocates for despotism, and endeavoring to enslave those who might have remained loyal subjects of the king. The government of France an advocate of liberty, espousing the cause of protestants and risking a war to secure their independence. The king of England considered by every whig in the nation as a tyrant, and the king of France applauded by every whig in America as the protector of the rights of man! The king of Great Britain aiding the advancement of popery, and the king of France endeavoring to free his people from ecclesiastical power! Britain at war with America, France in alliance with her! These, my friend, are astonishing changes. [18]

Gerry may have been astute in his comments, yet the alliance was very real. The diplomatic turn completed its cycle in June 1778 when a French and British naval battle occurred in the English Channel. Declarations of war followed quickly. A rebellion had turned into a world war which would stretch British military resources and the will to regain the colonies beyond the breaking point.

Lord North's ministry had known from the outset that formal French intervention could mean the end of British hopes for reconquering the rebels by force. One indication that the stakes had suddenly changed was the hasty creation of the Carlisle Commission during the spring of 1778, with instructions to go to America and to promise everything short of independence. However, the Continental Congress ignored the commissioners. A second sign was an order from Lord Germain to Sir Henry Clinton, Howe's successor. Germain ordered Clinton to evacuate Philadelphia, to retreat with all British forces to New York City and, if necessary, to evacuate New York in the event that military pressures from allied troops became too great. By the fall of 1778, the home government was siphoning off manpower from Clinton for campaigning against the French in the West Indies and other vital points within the Empire.

Massive, direct French involvement now forced Great Britain to disperse its military resources throughout the world and to relocate many units closer home. No longer would it be possible to concentrate manpower and repeat the grand strategic objectives of 1776. Britain could no longer be sure when or where allied attacks might come. Indeed, strategy was no longer a matter of keeping American troops bottled up and on the defensive. Henceforth, the allies would be able to go on the offensive at almost any point. England itself was no longer invulnerable. The French even attempted to organize an invasion against the island kingdom, but confused field planning and turbulent weather thwarted that scheme.

If the formal French alliance did nothing else, it specifically helped to neutralize the powerful British navy, which had grown rusty in the decade following the Seven Years' War, but which was reaching a peak efficiency once again by 1778. Yet even before formal French intervention, the Royal Navy had been contending with ravaging American privateers in English coastal waters. Over persistent diplomatic protests, France gave the privateering adventurers outfitting and re-outfitting privileges in French ports. Once Louis XVI joined the war, England no longer could lodge complaints. Rather, its problems were far more serious, as was evidenced by the decision to draw the imperial fleet closer home. This left many extremities of the Empire unprotected.

Such actions seemed fundamental to survival, in light of events such as the raids of the daring John Paul Jones on ports in Scotland and Ireland during 1778. These forays unnerved a people heretofore isolated from the war. In addition, the great naval battle between Jones's weathered and aging *Bonhomme Richard* and the Royal Navy's well armed frigate *Serapis* off the English coast in September 1779 led many to question the capacity of British forces to provide protection of any kind in the European theater. It was the most memorable naval engagement of the war. Jones's outmanned and outgunned vessel eventually went down, but not before Jones had taken *Serapis* as a prize. Such incidents made it clear how difficult it would be for Britain to extricate itself from the war with any grace, especially when the ministers were no longer positive that the British Isles could be successfully defended, let alone valued holdings in the Caribbean or India.

The global dilemma that became the new reality for the North ministry was just becoming clear when Sir Henry Clinton evacuated Philadelphia and retreated across New Jersey in June 1778. Only confusion in the Continental army's command saved Clinton's forces from disaster when Washington attacked at Monmouth Court House

(June 28, 1778). With Clinton back in New York and Washington hovering nearby, the northern phase of the war had come to a virtual standstill. In the months ahead Clinton clung to his coastal base, and Washington hoped to recapture New York. However, the prime locus of the war in America was shifting to the South.

Washington's army, once again moving into New Jersey, had just barely survived the cruel winter at Valley Forge (1777–1778). After Clinton's retreat, Washington formulated his new goal—finding some means of striking a fatal military blow against his adversary— perhaps against New York City. Having survived on the defensive for so long, the crucial question was whether American men in arms, even with massive support from the French army and navy, could muster enough offensive punch to inflict a mortal wound and force the proud parent state to sue for peace.

Changing conditions eased Washington's burden, but still he faced a difficult assignment. Above all else, the Commander in Chief had serious manpower problems, and his army suffered from lack of popular support. No one seemed to want to feed and clothe or, worse yet, serve in the Continental ranks. There was a difference between keeping an army in the field to prove that the rebellion was still alive and building that army into a fighting machine capable of winning a major victory. There was a vast difference between following defensive-minded Fabian tactics and preparing for an offensive campaign to drive the British from New York into the sea.[19] As Washington gazed upon his bedraggled Continental soldiers before leaving Valley Forge, he felt enormous personal tension. His army simply did not have the numbers to take full advantage of opportunities when they arose.

Manpower had been a nightmarish problem for Washington since the late summer of 1776, when his forces took their first horrible beatings. As the desperate American units fled for the Delaware, soldiers by the hundreds deserted or refused to extend their enlistments. The army began to go hungry because the British paid specie to farmers for their produce while the Continental soldiers offered only paper dollars. New clothing seemed to be nonexistent. Why share goods with Washington's forces, the attitude seemed to be, when the British appeared destined to win anyway?

When Thomas Paine denounced "the summer soldier and the sunshine patriot" in his first *Crisis* paper, written late in 1776, he was exhorting the fainthearted to remain committed to the cause. "These are the times that try men's souls," Paine wrote urgently: "Tyranny, like hell, is not easily conquered; yet we have the consolation with us, that the harder the conflict, the more glorious the triumph."[20] Paine employed biting language in begging rebellious Americans not to abandon their military obligations at a grave hour. He was reminding them that a successful republican experiment depended upon a virtuous citizenry, willing to make any and all sacrifices. As it turned out, Paine's words stirred few Americans to action; after 1776, Washington's primary administrative task was that of finding enough persons willing to serve in Continental ranks, so that Congress could still honestly claim that an actual state of rebellion existed.

Contrary to popular myth, the hardy, independent yeoman farmer rushed home from the war rather than to the front lines in 1776. Many rejoined their local militia units and continued to give invaluable backup support to depleted Continental forces. They would turn out for harassment and the kill, as the militiamen did at Saratoga. But when the glory days turned to gore, Washington had to face some hard facts. To defeat the British, he would have to entice men into the Continental army with good pay and other incentives. He would have to build on the British model, creating, in other words, an American "standing army." Washington understood that a successful rebellion depended upon central military planning and direction. Scattered militia units, independently commanded, could not provide over-all guidance. Middle-class freehold farmers quickly retreated into these units, if indeed they had come out for Continental service at all. Washington also knew that there were a great number of poor and downtrodden people in America. They could help to solve his manpower problem. With backing from the Continental Congress, he promised them cash bonuses now and better lives at the end of the war, if only they would endure the brutality and rigorous discipline of military service. It was thus the lower orders, not the independent yeomen of mythology, who sustained the war effort in the Continental ranks. But no one seemed to remember that when the gory days turned back to glory.

The very term "standing army" had long conjured up the specter of tyranny to Americans. Ever since 1763, they had complained about the presence of British regiments during peacetime. Bostonians had interpreted the redcoats in their midst as a sign of absolute tyranny—the subversion of civilian authority by military autocracy. Samuel Adams summarized such feelings in 1776: "A standing army, however necessary it may be at some times, is always dangerous to the Liberties of the People. Soldiers are apt to consider themselves as a Body distinct from the rest of the Citizens." As Adams warned: "They have their Arms always in their hands. Their Rules and their

Discipline is severe. They soon become attached to their officers and disposed to yield implicit obedience to their Commands. Such a Power should be watched with a jealous Eye."[21]

Although common in Europe, standing armies were considered alien to the provincial military tradition. In the colonies, all white males between the ages of sixteen and sixty were expected to perform militia service, attend periodic muster meetings, and turn out to fight when enemies threatened hearth and home. The militia represented the ideal of a citizens' army. It rested upon the universal obligation of service, with each militiaman performing virtuous duty through short enlistments for the community. It insured that military power would be subordinate to civilian authority. Indeed, it was a reinvigorated militia system with citizen-soldiers at its core that had sent the red-coats retreating in disarray from Concord back to Boston. But it was not the kind of war machine that could defeat the British over the long haul, especially since it lacked an overarching command structure to plan fully orchestrated and coordinated offensive warfare. The Continental army was meant to be that centralizing mechanism.

To Washington, attempting to cope with the well-trained British professional force, a quasi-standing American army, paid to stay in the field for the war's duration, became the most viable option, especially after the severe manpower depletions of 1776. The Continental Congress would have to Europeanize its ideas about a central army, or the rebellion might collapse. Until his army was strong enough to win in battle and had broader popular support (the French would be critical on both counts), Washington knew that he would have to utilize Fabian tactics, in the hope of exhausting the British and breaking their morale while avoiding all-out confrontations. He would also have to pray that a well-trained standing American army would not explode in anger at a penurious civilian population, turning against that population and attempting to supplant civilian with military authority—thus destroying the goal of a free republican state in the process.[22]

Washington and the Continental Congress searched everywhere for long-term manpower. Congress reluctantly turned to hard sell recruiting, giving each state a quota to fill at the beginning of successive campaign seasons. In time, a conscription program was also instituted, but it contained a loophole for those who did not want to be forced into regular units. They could pay fines or find substitutes. As freemen bought their way out of service, black slaves, indentured servants, and propertyless day laborers normally took their places and soon formed a significant proportion of Continentals in northern regiments. Southerners were more reluctant to send slaves forward as substitutes, but they were not hesitant about felons and criminals. In time, even slaves appeared as southern substitutes, causing one gentleman to query why so many "Sons of Freedom" were willing "to trust their all to be defended by slaves."[23] The reality was that sacrifice seemed to be the burden only of those lacking property and wealth.

The draft system never worked efficiently or provided many regular soldiers. Hard sell recruiting remained the primary source of new manpower throughout the war. In January 1777, Congress for the first time offered each new recruit a cash bounty of twenty dollars, new clothing, and a hundred acres of free land in return for a commitment to serve for the duration. Each year after that, the bounties, often supplemented by state grants, went up, both to compensate for rapid inflation and to attract yet more manpower. Despite all these devices, most citizens preferred to fulfill their obligations through militia duty, entering Continental service only if they were unfortunate enough to draw the wrong number by lot when militia units became obligated temporarily to assist in filling draft quotas.

Despite all inducements, there was never any great rush into the Continental ranks. Those who came forward, voluntarily or otherwise, were overwhelmingly from the poor and unprotected groups in American society. After 1776 most Continentals were either persons who were in some sense trapped (slaves, servants, runaway apprentices, convicted criminals, and English/Hessian deserters and prisoners) or untrapped but poor (unemployed day laborers, uprooted tenant farmers, and the propertyless in general). Bounties, promises of decent clothing and regular pay, and free land at the war's end (plus personal freedom in many cases) were inducements with real meaning for those with little or nothing in life.[24]

In these people, Washington and the Congress found individuals who were willing to serve long enlistments and who could stand the brutal rigors of life in the field. They found individuals who could be deferentially obedient, counting on promises of a better lot in life after the war. It was as though the post-1776 Continentals had activated the American dream, with the army serving as the vehicle of upward mobility. As in the years before 1776, real deprivation had motivated many suffering people to become heavily involved in resistance efforts. Now the danger was that Washington's standing army, well-trained and fairly well-armed after 1778, might turn and attack the republican edifice it was helping to create, should an ungrateful citizenry not pay the men for services rendered to the new nation.

It is not surprising to find, then, that the goals of immediate survival and postwar prosperity, more than the defense of liberty, were the primary motivating thoughts among the Continentals. Some of the men joining the rank and file were like John Saunders, who in 1777 received the sentence of two public floggings for stealing horses. After the first beating, the dazed Saunders agreed to enlist in the Continental army; the judge generously remanded the second flogging. Then there was M'Donald Campbell, who "had formed an acquaintance with a young woman in Somerset County [New Jersey], of a very credible family, with whom I had been too intimate." Her father ordered Campbell to marry his daughter, which he did. Campbell, soon having second thoughts, fled to the Continental ranks.[25] While the details of such personal stories may be unique, the John Saunders and M'Donald Campbells had something to gain, both in the short and the long run, and little to lose by accepting the status of common soldier.

In contrast, Washington's field officers generally had been men of high community socioeconomic status before the war, with a clear stake in hierarchical relationships. So long as they kept the cause of independence and republicanism before them, and so long as they acknowledged civilian authority as the highest power in governmental decision making, they could act as a check upon soldiers trained to accept their every command in the face of the threat of severe punishment. (At one point the penalty for striking a Continental officer was five hundred lashes. No human being could survive such a beating.) But the peril was that the officers, too, might become so bitter that they would turn their soldiers against an indifferent population. However remotely, that danger was beginning to surface after the terrible winter at Valley Forge.

Washington had chosen Valley Forge as a campsite in the late fall of 1777 because it represented a hilly, defensible position only twenty-five miles from Howe's army in Philadelphia. That winter the American people seemed to forget that Washington's troops needed food, clothing, medical supplies, and decent shelter. As a result, many Continentals starved and froze in the midst of civilian prosperity. An average of four hundred soldiers died each month. Meat, however rotten, was rarely available; and three times, for short periods, food supplies simply did not exist. New clothing and shoes could not be found; old clothing disintegrated into worthless rags. In February 1778, Washington reported that at least 4,000 men were unfit for any kind of duty. Understandably, the desertion rate kept climbing. The army had every reason to be angry with civilians who not only let others do their fighting, but also did not support those who did fight. It was not the raw weather at Valley Forge that hurt so much. The Continentals faced harsher winters in New Jersey cantonments before the war was over. It was the popular indifference about the army's plight, which might not have been so great had the poor and indigent been less heavily represented in the ranks at Valley Forge.

Two unrelated but equally critical factors were vital in keeping Washington's forces together through that harrowing winter. First were the women, or "camp followers," who were an accepted element in any eighteenth-century army. Indeed, women as well as men were "on the ration"; that is, they were assigned duties in return for food and pay. In British armies during the War for Independence, there was approximately one woman for every ten men in the ranks. Most often from the lowest orders in society, they were sometimes married to common soldiers. But just as often they were in camp to carry out their assigned tasks of cooking, caring for the sick and wounded, washing and mending clothes, and burying the dead. Only rarely did they fight in battles. Some, most often prostitutes, were not on the payroll but followed along anyway.

What evidence there is suggests that Washington's army had proportionately fewer females on ration than did the British army. At Valley Forge, however, women were essential in keeping some semblance of order in the starving camp and in preventing starvation by scavenging for food. Their efforts kept large numbers of Valley Forge veterans alive. Washington was concerned primarily about outside females. Women in British pay kept appearing from Philadelphia to lure Continentals into desertion. Others, working for neither side, sneaked into camp and spread syphilis. Finally, the Commander ordered all possible routes from Philadelphia sealed off. But the problem never was fully solved. [26]

The second critical factor keeping Washington's forces together was improved training, thanks largely to the efforts of Friedrich von Steuben, who had held the rank of captain in the Prussian army. Unlike many European adventurers seeking high commands in the Continental service, Steuben, a pretended baron, proved to be invaluable. Thoroughly familiar with Prussian drill tactics and training practices that were capable of building discipline while welding soldiers into effective fighting units, Steuben pushed the men hard in training maneuvers. Speaking almost no English and barely recognizable French, he communicated through grunts and universally recognizable swear words. The soldiers quickly accepted Steuben's prodding. Focusing their attention on improved training convinced

great numbers that survival, winning, and postwar prosperity remained attainable goals. Steuben's drill tactics deflected the bitterness
and despair felt by everyone in camp, and a hardier, more resolute
army emerged in the late spring of 1778 from a terrible experience—
and with renewed determination to stand up and fight.

With hardened, trained veterans, with the French alliance and the
prospect of a French army to support his slim numbers, and with
militiamen willing to provide sporadic support, Washington could
actually begin to dream about winning the war. The Commander
could sense and feel victory, and he talked enthusiastically about
retaking New York. But it was better to hold defensible terrain near
Clinton's forces, which still far outnumbered Washington's. A precipitate battle might end in disaster. Manpower shortages, likewise,
still dictated that the Continentals practice more patience than many
of them would have liked, but prudence was necessary until conditions were right for a fatal blow.

While Washington maintained his cautious posture and looked
forward for French reinforcements, the British high command shifted
the focus of warfare to the South. French intervention, requiring that
British forces spread themselves more thinly across the globe, rekin-
dled interest in the use of American loyalists. The impression still
lingered that there were more loyalists in the South than in the North.
Whether accurate or not, British strategists made their plans on that
assumption. Redcoats once again would attempt to work with civilian
loyalists in subduing the rebels. The high command selected Charleston as the main base for southern operations. It could also serve as a
shipping point for war goods and manpower needed in contending
with French naval forces in the West Indies. The plan was to reconquer the whole South, using it thereafter as a staging area for retaking
the middle and northern regions. It was as though the campaign
strategy of 1776 had been redrawn for the South, but with the fundamental difference that more responsibility was to be placed upon
loyalists, both as soldiers and civilians.

The southern phase began successfully for the British in December
1778. Thirty-five hundred British, Hessian, and loyalist troops had
sailed from New York the previous month. Their target was Savannah. Joined by loyalists from the Floridas, they quickly subdued
Georgia. During 1779 British leaders went about the business of reestablishing royal government, depending upon deposed officials and
other local loyalists to provide leadership. In its first major assault,
the southern strategy worked perfectly.

Sir Henry Clinton, fearing a combined Franco-American movement against New York, was slow in following up on the Georgia campaign. Finally, he sailed from New York for Charleston with 8,000 troops in December 1779. Violent weather blew his fleet in all directions, but it reassembled and prepared for a long siege. Meanwhile, Charlestonians had been girding themselves for the assault. General Benjamin Lincoln, a commander from Massachusetts who showed both courage and caution, had taken charge of the Continental Army's Southern Department in 1778. He attempted to drive British forces from Georgia early in 1779, but without success. During the spring of 1780, Lincoln, with 3,000 Continentals and 2,500 militia, prepared Charleston for defense. When one British sortie cut off his escape route to the North, Lincoln had two undesirable choices: fight to the death or surrender his army. Local citizens at first insisted that the South's major seaport should be defended at all costs, but a furious bombardment from Clinton's fleet changed their minds. When local support collapsed, Lincoln surrendered. For the first time in the war an American army—virtually the whole Southern Department of the Continental forces—had been captured.

Leaving the strong-willed, petulant General Lord Cornwallis behind, Clinton sailed back to New York in triumph. Before embarking, he insisted that Cornwallis proceed slowly and cautiously, making sure that loyalists had full control of the ground behind his army. Clinton also urged that supply lines into the interior be made secure, so that Cornwallis would not find himself cut off from the sea. But the latter did not listen very carefully. Cornwallis, filled with contempt for American fighting prowess, made the chronic high command error of overestimating his army's ability. Partisan resistance, kept alive by "Swamp Fox" Francis Marion and others, cowed local loyalist bands; small-scale skirmishes often pitted former friends, relatives, and neighbors against one another and were vengeful, bloody affairs. Conditions such as these helped to undermine Cornwallis's efforts over the long run.

But the delusion continued during the short run. In mid August 1780, Cornwallis routed a hastily reorganized southern army under General Horatio Gates at Camden, South Carolina. Gates's army—largely untrained, raw militia with virtually no experience in field maneuvers and battle—seemed destined for defeat. They marched toward Camden in the dead of night. Having no rum supplies, traditionally served in liberal quantities before impending battles, the men received molasses as a substitute. One American officer reported that "the troops . . . had frequently felt the bad consequences of eating bad provisions; but at this time, a hasty meal of quick baked bread and fresh beef, with a dessert of molasses, mixed with mush or dumplings, operated so cathartically as to disorder many of the men."²⁷ An untrained and sick army had no chance against Cornwallis's regulars. The British army completely routed them early in the morning with Gates, the "hero of Saratoga," fleeing for his life into North Carolina.

By the late summer of 1780 very little seemed to be going well for Americans in the South. One Southern Department army had been captured and another nearly wiped out. Despite the invaluable alliance with France and the formal entry of Spain (1779) and the Netherlands (1780) into the war, American fortunes still looked quite bleak. In the North, Washington found it impossible to mount a joint Franco-American land campaign. Soldiers everywhere grew more restless as Continental currency plummeted in value. New recruits received ever greater bonuses, many now in specie. Anger over improved bonuses and promises of up to two hundred acres of land to new recruits helped to provoke the mutinies of the Pennsylvania and New Jersey lines in early 1781. These uprisings frightened civilian authorities enormously because they saw that Washington's army might turn violently against the population and inaugurate a phase of internal social revolution, such as forced property redistribution, directed against the middle and upper classes. For his part, Washington wondered whether he would have an army left. His effective manpower dropped to about 6,000 troops in late 1780, the lowest point since recruiting and drafting had begun. For the determined Commander, the situation seemed so grave that he virtually gave up making plans for the campaign season of 1781.

Even before the Pennsylvania and New Jersey soldiers mutinied, angry Continental officers added their voices to the din of threatening words. As men of property, standing, and financial means before the war, they had been expected to absorb personal expenses while in the field and to provide their own personal supplies, uniforms, horses, and even requirements for their military aides. For many officers, the personal financial burden of command had become too heavy, especially when many civilians appeared to be growing wealthy from war profiteering. Typical of these suffering officers was Major General Alexander McDougall of New York, the prewar popular leader whose personal fortune from privateering during the Seven Years' War and peacetime mercantile activity had dwindled precipitately. McDougall and other veteran officers wanted two concessions from Congress: higher short-term salaries and half-pay pensions for life at the war's end. A memorial to that effect fell on deaf ears in Congress during the fall of 1779. Justifying themselves in theoretical terms, the delegates claimed that they did not want to create a privileged military caste through pensions. A second petition from the general officers confronted Congress in July 1780. It was extremely blunt. "Exposed as" they were "to the rapacity of almost every class of the community," the angry officers insisted upon a promise of pensions, or they "should be obliged by necessity to quit the service." If "ill consequences should arise to their country," they concluded, "they [would] leave to the world to determine who ought to be responsible for them."[28]

Still the stubborn Congress refused to budge. It was only the news of the disastrous defeat at Camden (August 16), combined with the shocking revelation of Benedict Arnold's treason (September 25)—Arnold had been a masterful Continental field general whose shaky financial status helped to cause his political apostasy—that brought Congress around. In late October it approved in principle half pay for life, should funds become available. The discontented officers were assuaged, at least momentarily. But the promised pensions continued to stir up more trouble in the months ahead.

Battlefield reverses in the South, declining manpower, angry officers and common soldiers, ongoing problems in supply, and citizen indifference threatened to overwhelm the American war effort at the very time that it should have been enjoying its greatest success. But just as everything seemed at its darkest, the fortunes of war suddenly brightened for the Americans. Cornwallis's aggressive southern forces now overextended themselves. His left wing, under Major Patrick Ferguson, a daring, resourceful officer, pushed toward frontier North Carolina into the Piedmont region late in the summer of 1780. Ferguson's troops were by and large loyalists, many of whom had shown no mercy in dealing with rebels. Soon Ferguson found himself being stalked by enraged "over-the-mountain men," coming together as militia in virtually leaderless fashion. Ferguson began a retreat, then found a mountain jutting up from the Piedmont. With 1,100 men, he prepared to defend that promontory. As Ferguson, perhaps apocryphally, announced: "He was on King's Mountain, and . . . he was king of that mountain and God Almighty could not drive him from it."[29] But he was wrong. On October 7, 1780, the frontiersmen surrounded him and moved up from all sides. They avenged the deaths of loved ones and friends and cut the loyalists to shreds. Major Ferguson died in the midst of battle from several wounds; before the over-the-mountain men were done, 157 loyalists were dead, another

163 wounded, and 698 were prisoners. The mountain men, nearly 1,000 in number, suffered only 80 casualties.

Not only did the Battle of King's Mountain amputate Cornwallis's left wing, but its bloody removal also greatly weakened southern loyalist support for the British cause. Colonel William Campbell, nominally leading the King's Mountain victors, permitted hasty trials of the most obnoxious Ferguson loyalists. Charges ranged from entering homes and stealing to destroying property and mercilessly killing individual rebels and their families. Eventually nine loyalists were hanged; others received gallows reprieves. King's Mountain and its aftermath was a telling blow to the British southern strategy. Again loyalists learned that British soldiers could not guarantee them protection. Fewer were willing to give aid to an overextended Cornwallis.

Cornwallis, with loyalist support faltering, should have retrenched. But the disdainful general refused to heed the danger signals. He kept trying to accomplish too much too rapidly. Moreover, Cornwallis rejected the notion that any regular American general could stand up against him. In particular, he underestimated the ingenuity of Nathanael Greene, a Rhode Island Quaker of gifted military talent, who replaced the demoralized Gates upon Washington's recommendation. Accepting the southern command the day before King's Mountain, Greene faced an overwhelming assignment: to create an army out of Gates's remaining troops and, then, to maneuver Cornwallis into oblivion. Greene, taking command from Gates in December 1780 with fewer than 2,000 effectives, mostly militia, boldly divided his army. He placed one group under the crafty Virginia rifleman, Daniel Morgan. Greene's plan was to run Cornwallis in circles and harass his army while avoiding full engagements. Twice the American forces brushed against the British. In January 1781, Morgan's soldiers drew a British regiment into a fight at Hannah's Cowpens in northern South Carolina. The British fled with heavy casualties. Then Greene, whose forces increased daily, squared off against Cornwallis in March 1781 at Guilford Court House in North Carolina. He again inflicted heavy casualties. Cornwallis, backing off, retreated south. Greene's strategy of hit-and-run was succeeding handsomely.

But the reckless Cornwallis refused to regroup carefully and re-pacify South Carolina districts which had once been under his firm control. He would leave that task to subordinates. In May 1781, he marched the bulk of his forces toward Virginia. His immediate goal was the support of marauding British units under turncoat Benedict Arnold and Major General William Phillips. The youthful Marquis de Lafayette, less than twenty-five years old but a seasoned veteran under Washington's tutelage, was challenging these two skilled officers. Washington adored Lafayette as though he were a son; and he had given the Frenchman command of a detachment of Continentals in Virginia. The game of cat-and-mouse maneuvering was on, with Lafayette particularly eager to catch Phillips, whom the French nobleman believed had been responsible for his father's battlefield death during the Seven Years' War. However, Lafayette did not have enough troops to risk a major battle, a problem only compounded by Cornwallis's arrival.

Factors beyond Cornwallis's control, however, were pushing him into a trap. For some inexplicable reason, Sir Henry Clinton, back in New York, put renewed emphasis in the campaign of 1781 on recapturing Philadelphia. Thinking about that foolhardy venture, as well as about thrusts into New England, Clinton also feared—and with good reason—that a Franco-American sortie against New York City might be coming soon. It looked as if Washington, working with recently arrived French land forces under the Count de Rochambeau, was near launching the long-awaited attack. But an opportunity at Yorktown was soon to intervene—and decisively so for the rebels.

Clinton, convinced that Cornwallis had turned the British southern campaign into a fiasco, ordered his subordinate to prepare to embark his troops so that they might join the putative expedition against Philadelphia. In late June 1781, a stunned Cornwallis began angling toward an acceptable point on Chesapeake Bay. He chose Yorktown, located where the York River flows into Chesapeake Bay.

What Cornwallis did not know was that a large French naval fleet under Admiral de Grasse was coming up from the West Indies. It ultimately blocked off the Bay, fended off a British naval squadron in September, and sealed off the escape route by sea. Meanwhile, Lafayette's and Greene's soldiers began moving in from the West and the South. Washington and Rochambeau decided to forego New York City for the moment in favor of springing the trap in Virginia. French and American soldiers started moving south *en masse*, leaving behind just enough troops and false signals to confuse Clinton. Combined armies of 7,000 Frenchmen, 5,700 Continentals, and 3,100 militia had surrounded Cornwallis on the land side by the end of September. Encircled by land and sea, the 8,000-man British army girded itself for the siege. But its position was hopeless, and the Americans knew it. Perhaps the excitement in anticipation of such a decisive victory at long last was best captured by an overly enthusiastic militiaman "possessed of more bravery than prudence" during the siege. One comrade recalled that the man "stood constantly on the parapet and d———d his soul if he would dodge for the buggers. He had escaped longer than could have been expected, and growing foolhardy, brandished his spade at every ball that was fired till, unfortunately a ball came and put an end to his capers."[30]

If the militiaman died foolishly, so did the British cause in America. Cornwallis, mainly because of Clinton's order, had placed his army in an impossible position. Under steady pressure as the allies moved closer and closer (they increased the volume of cannonading at almost every step), Cornwallis struggled against overwhelming odds. A second British army was about to be captured, and it was happening in a year when French and Spanish forces were ravaging British possessions in the Caribbean. West Florida had already fallen to the Spanish. De Grasse's fleet was about to leave the Chesapeake Bay and set a southern course in an attempted offensive against valued British Jamaica. Combined Franco-Spanish forces were preparing for another siege against Gibraltar. There were too many enemies, and they were threatening to take too heavy a toll. It appeared to many leaders in England that persevering against so many enemies on so many fronts would completely destroy the Empire. The British disaster at Yorktown helped to increase the volume of the cry among England's antiwar leaders that the war must stop before the Empire was cut to shreds.[31]

Cornwallis must have sensed the impact that losing his army would have on opinion in England. He planned one last desperate effort to escape under cover of night across the York River to Gloucester Point. But a howling storm beat his lead parties back. The proud British general, rather than see hundreds die needlessly, asked for terms of surrender. With the details of capitulation in final form, the British army moved out into a large field between American and French soldiers on the autumn afternoon of October 19, 1781. The "indisposed" Cornwallis was not there. His second in command turned over his superior's sword to Benjamin Lincoln, the second of the elated Washington, who was standing by.

As the British columns began the traditional parade upon surrender, their musicians struck up a melancholy song, "The World Turned Upside Down." No tune could have been more poignant. The proud and mighty had fallen. An American rabble in arms, with inestimable French aid, had survived the days of despair following those of sunshine patriotism. Washington's soldiers at last had hurdled all obstacles. For its part, Great Britain had nothing to celebrate that day. His Majesty's forces had never found the vital American center. Militarily, it had not existed. British armies had not followed through on easy advantages during the critical 1776 campaign, and they had blundered miserably in 1777. All along Washington, his generals, and his men were gaining valuable experience, and then they had been bolstered by direct French support. All the necessary elements had finally meshed together. One celebrating American officer wrote to a friend from Yorktown: "I think I may with propriety now congratulate you . . . and the country in general with certain Independence and the pleasing approach of Peace."[32] A distraught British corporal in another location near the battlefield bellowed in utter disgust: "May you never get so good a master again!"[33]

Both men, the winner and the loser, expressed matters clearly. Looming large after Yorktown were not only the problems of separating completely from the parent state and of negotiating final independence, but also the problem of how independent the new nation could be when it consisted of thirteen quarreling, self-interested states rapidly losing the common bond of the struggle for independence. Those problems needed both rapid and sure solutions, especially when forces capable of destroying the nascent experiment in republicanism lurked in more than one hidden corner.

Notes

1. John Ross quoted in Alexander Graydon, *Memoirs of a Life Chiefly Passed in Pennsylvania* (Edinburgh, 1822), 115. For an intriguing assessment of the war's impact upon neutrals and the building of a sense of nationhood, among other matters, see John Shy, "The Military Conflict Considered as a Revolutionary War," *A People Numerous and Armed: Reflections on the Military Struggle for American Independence* (New York, 1976), 195–224.

2. Excellent brief summaries of the war, especially in relation to battlefield action, include John R. Alden, *The American Revolution, 1775–1783* (New York, 1954); Howard H. Peckham, *The War for Independence: A Military History* (Chicago, 1958); and Willard M. Wallace, *Appeal to Arms: A Military History of the American Revolution* (New York, 1951).

3. Quoted in *Rebels and Redcoats* (ed. G. F. Scheer and H. F. Rankin, Cleveland, 1957), 60.

4. On the British fear of using up available troop manpower, see Eric Robson, *The American Revolution in its Political and Military Aspects, 1763–1783* (New York, 1955), 93–199. Robson usefully formulated the questions of why the British lost and the Americans won. Also indispensable for understanding the British side is Piers Mackesy, *The War for America, 1775–1783* (Cambridge, 1965), *passim.*

5. General Murray to George Germain, September 6, 1777, quoted in Robson, *Revolution in its Political and Military Aspects*, 127.

6. Quoted in Wallace, *Appeal to Arms*, 32.

7. Robert Biddulph to [?], New York, September 4, 1779, *American Historical Review*, 29 (1923–1924), 90.

8. Ira D. Gruber, *The Howe Brothers and the American Revolution* (New York, 1972), 72–157, stresses the Howes' conciliatory role in not pushing through to total victory. For an excellent overview of preparations for the 1776 campaign, see David Syrett, "The Fleet that Failed," United States Naval Institute *Proceedings*, 101 (1975), 66–77.

9. Captain John Bowater to the Earl of Denbigh, New York, May 22, 1777, *The Lost War: Letters from British Officers during the American Revolution* (ed. M. Balderston and D. Syrett, New York, 1975), 126.

10. Mackesy, *War for America*, 46–60, contains a positive assessment of Germain, unlike many earlier studies. Typical of the scholarly controversy over Germain and his vital role are Alan Valentine, *Lord George Germain* (New York, 1962), and Gerald Saxon Brown, *The American Secretary: The Colonial Policy of Lord George Germain, 1775–1778* (Ann Arbor, Mich., 1963).

11. Lieutenant William Digby, quoted in Scheer and Rankin, eds., *Rebels and Redcoats*, 284.

12. *Histoire philosophique et politique*, VI (Amsterdam, 1770), 376, quoted in Durand Echeverria, *Mirage in the West: A History of the French Image of American Society to 1815* (Princeton, N.J., 1957), 14.

13. *Ibid.*, 39–78. See also R. R. Palmer, *The Age of the Democratic Revolution, Vol. I: The Challenge* (Princeton, N.J., 1959), 3–139; and William C. Stinchcombe, *The American Revolution and the French Alliance* (Syracuse, N.Y., 1969), *passim*.

14. Report by Achard de Bonvouloir, dated December 28, 1775, quoted in Cecil B. Currey, *Code Number 72: Ben Franklin, Patriot or Spy?* (Englewood Cliffs, N.J., 1972), 64.

15. Samuel Flagg Bemis, *The Diplomacy of the American Revolution* (New York, 1935), 36–38.

16. Echeverria, *Mirage in the West*, 45–61.

17. Passy, April 3, 1778, *The Writings of Benjamin Franklin* (10 vols., ed. A. H. Smyth, New York, 1905–1907), VII, 132.

18. To [?], May 26, 1778, James T. Austin, *The Life of Elbridge Gerry* (2 vols., Boston, 1828–1829), I, 276.

19. Dave R. Palmer, *The Way of the Fox: American Strategy in the War for America, 1775–1783* (Westport, Conn., 1975), argues that Washington favored a strategy of offense throughout the war, contrary to others who place the Commander squarely in the "Fabian" category. No doubt the offensive or defensive reality of Washington's actions depended upon circumstances.

20. Conway, ed., *Writings of Paine*, I, 170.

21. To James Warren, January 7, 1776, *Warren-Adams Letters*, I, 197–198.

22. An excellent case study on the creation of an American standing army is Mark Edward Lender, "The Enlisted Line: The Continental Soldiers of New Jersey" (doctoral dissertation, Rutgers University, 1975), *passim*. For somewhat different conclusions, see Don Higginbotham, *The War of American Independence: Military Attitudes, Policies, and Practice, 1763–1789* (New York, 1971), esp. 1–80, 389–419.

23. Quoted in Higginbotham, *War of American Independence*, 395.

24. Quantitative studies verifying lower-class socioeconomic characteristics of the Continentals include Lender, "The Enlisted Line," 110–139, and Edward C. Papenfuse and Gregory A. Stiverson, "General Smallwood's Recruits: The Peacetime Career of the Revolutionary War Private," *William and Mary Quarterly*, 3rd Ser., 30 (1973), 117–132.

25. Quoted in Lender, "The Enlisted Line," 153–154. See also John Shy's comments on "Long Bill" Scott in *A People Numerous and Armed*, 163–179.

26. Different approaches to women in the armies may be found by comparing Walter Hart Blumenthal, *Women Camp Followers of the American Revolution* (Philadelphia, 1952), and John Todd White, "The Truth about Molly Pitcher," *The American Revolution: Whose Revolution?* (ed. J. K. Martin and K. R. Stubaus, New York, 1977), 99–105.

27. Colonel Otho Williams, "Southern Army: Narrative of the Campaign of 1780," Scheer and Rankin, eds., *Rebels and Redcoats*, 407.

28. Memorial of General Officers, July 11, 1780, quoted in Champagne, *Alexander McDougall and the American Revolution*, 160. For infighting among the American officers, as opposed to united action, see Jonathan G. Rossie, *The Politics of Command in the American Revolution* (Syracuse, N.Y., 1975), *passim*.

29. Quoted in Scheer and Rankin, eds., *Rebels and Redcoats*, 416.

30. Captain James Duncan, "Diary," *ibid.*, 480.

31. Mackesy, *War for America*, 367–445.

32. Richard Butler to William Irvine, October 22, 1781, Scheer and Rankin, eds., *Rebels and Redcoats*, 495.

33. Quoted in *ibid.*, 495.

VII

The Potential for Revolution

The most extreme form of human resistance, organized warfare in full-scale rebellion, set the erratic course in motion that led to Yorktown and the final severing of political ties with the British Empire. Yorktown was the beginning of the military end, but it by no means guaranteed the success of the American cause. Even before the war had reached its crescendo in the late summer and fall of 1776, erstwhile provincials were debating questions central to the future character and organization of American social and political institutions. No more important question was being asked than how "revolutionary" the rebellion should be permitted to become. Should there be a real revolution, a movement that was more than a mere uprising against the constituted authority of the King in Parliament? It would take years to formulate an answer.

The term revolution implied, then as now, profound alterations in economic, social, and political relationships. Although it did not necessarily denote a total rejection of past traditions and habits, it did suggest the creation of something new, uplifting, and beneficial for humanity. The most vexing and challenging question confronting rebellious Americans was how much change should be permitted. On that point there was wide disagreement.

While the war raged in the foreground, an awesome, if not potentially destructive, gap opened among those who were deciding how far the Revolution should proceed in reordering human relationships, that is, whether there should more than a mere transfer of power and authority from the ruling elite in Britain to one in America. In the end, that bitter internal controversy caused as much confusion and instability in the republic as did the war itself or the problems of international diplomacy. War-related problems dominated at first after 1776, because everyone knew that all other questions were academic unless the military struggle resulted in favorable peace terms. But always alongside pressing military and diplomatic questions of the day stood the most disruptive issue of all—that of the potential form and character of the nascent republic.

The Battle of Yorktown set in motion the train of events that resulted in peace terms. Official news of Cornwallis's debacle reached London on Sunday, November 25, 1781. Germain, the intractable colonial secretary, carried the ominous report to the usually affable Lord North at Ten Downing Street. North was stunned. He received the news "as he would have taken a ball in the breast." "Oh God, it is all over! Oh God, it is all over!" the astonished cabinet head exclaimed over and over again.[1] North knew that his government, already on the verge of a serious parliamentary crisis, might not be able to withstand the repercussions of so significant a military setback at the very time that allied powers seemed to be overwhelming the Empire everywhere. The moment to face facts had come. The government might have to recognize American independence in order to extricate Britain from what appeared at the end of 1781 to be a hopeless military situation.

King George, however, was obdurate. He agreed with Lord Germain, who stated flatly that the English "can never continue to exist as a great or powerful nation after we have lost or renounced the sovereignty of America."[2] Lord North, having quickly regained his composure, accepted his fate more willingly. Sentiment for continuing the war was losing ground rapidly in and out of Parliament. It reached low ebb in early March 1782, when Parliament reconvened from its winter recess. On March 4 the House of Commons resolved that any person wanting to continue the war against America was to be considered an enemy of Great Britain.

North and the King acknowledged that verdict, even if they did not like it. At one point George III even talked about abdicating, but it was North who surrendered on March 20, concluding his twelve-year tenure with these words as he left the Commons: "Goodnight, gentlemen. You see what it is to be in the secret!"[3] North thus paved the way for the formation of a new cabinet charged with negotiating a peace settlement. The former government head was not altogether disappointed about relinquishing his authority; he had talked about doing so on and off during the war. Rather, he felt the burden of having tried, even through the extreme measure of warfare, to recon-cile differences with America—and of having failed. North had brought stability to the British ministry, but he had come to office too late. The destruction sown by others would forever be his harvest.

In the spring of 1782 the focus of concerns rapidly turned to the formulation of a satisfactory peace settlement. Throughout the war, American leaders had debated diplomatic stands heatedly. Congres-sional delegates rancorously argued over the details of a favorable peace settlement; and those details directly reflected regional inter-ests. New Englanders, such as John Adams and the outspoken mer-chant Elbridge Gerry, were uncompromising on the matter of free access to prime fishing grounds off the coasts of Nova Scotia and Newfoundland. New Englanders also persisted in talk about taking Canada, as did other delegates outside of New England who dreamed about a vast republican phoenix rising in the West out of the ashes of the British Empire in North America. Some middle states delegates, like the wealthy and influential Philadelphia merchant Robert Morris, sought a whole new array of international trading connections. Mor-ris and his friends wanted full access to the markets of France, Spain, and the Netherlands, indeed any country where handsome trading profits could be made. If France wanted to bar New England from competition in the fisheries, then the middle states merchants were willing to give that northeastern interest away so that the door to new trading connections could swing wide open.

Southerners, in contrast, put primary emphasis on western de-velopment. With support from New Englanders, southern leaders insisted that the Mississippi River should be the western boundary of the new nation, contiguous to the Spanish domain. They also de-manded that western settlers enjoy free navigation of the Mississippi River as an outlet for agricultural products. Moreover, Southerners desired a southern boundary no farther north than 31° of north latitude, the line separating British-controlled East Florida from Georgia, presuming of course that the Floridas themselves could not be had. Richard Henry Lee explained in 1778 how it should happen: "Should Great Britain be engaged in war with the Bourbon family it furnishes us an opportunity of pushing the former quite off the Northern continent, which will secure us peace for a Century, instead of war in seven years, which British possession of Canada, Nova Scotia, and the Floridas will inevitably produce."[4]

On the other hand, middle states leaders had few compunctions about conceding western and southern territories, if that would ap-pease France and Spain, while encouraging new opportunities for trading with Europe. The commercial-minded gentlemen around

Robert Morris were not particularly eager to see the West emerge as an identifiable economic or political region. Given their interests, the middle states men looked eastward for postwar opportunity while those around them gazed in all other directions.

Interests overlay interests, compounded by regional differences. Vituperativeness generally epitomized the behavior of congressional delegates as they debated the issues after 1776. And the pattern of turmoil was exacerbated by the conflicting goals of America's allies. Initially, Vergennes's primary objective had been the humiliation of Great Britain, but he had also sought Spain's explicit involvement in support of that war aim from the start. Even though the King of Spain, Charles III, was a Bourbon and related to Louis XVI, Spain remained diffident about entering the controversy. Spain could be interested only if France guaranteed Charles support for his territorial ambitions (mainly to regain the Floridas and the Rock of Gibraltar, commanding the gateway to the Mediterranean).

The brilliant, calculating Count Floridablanca took charge of Spain's foreign policy for Charles III in 1777. The new Spanish Minister intended to mold the allied war effort exclusively for Spanish purposes, giving as little and gaining as much as possible. Floridablanca had no interest in developing close commercial ties with the United States. He felt no urgency about lending money to a republican cause. His price for entering the war was, basically, two shopping items: Gibraltar and a new American nation so territorially circumscribed that it could never become a threat to far-flung Spanish holdings in the western hemisphere. Most of all, Floridablanca feared the development of a thriving republican nation which could serve as a model for disaffected Spanish colonists in the New World. The Spanish Minister clearly reveled in the thought of seeing British power broken; but, mercantilist and absolutist that he was, he did not want to help create something that might prove fatal to Spain's long-term interests.

Vergennes, no fool, did not question the Spaniard's logic. The French Minister well understood that the creation of a strong republican state could threaten monarchical, imperial systems everywhere. Vergennes also believed that Spain's direct involvement as an ally against Great Britain was vital to crushing the hated English foe. Sacrificing American interests could accomplish this goal and, as Floridablanca made clear, more or less create an American state permanently dependent, particularly commercially, upon France and Spain. By fusing short- and long-term objectives, France and Spain thus imagined that they were going to be the winners in the game of diplomatic intrigue. Great Britain and the thirteen states would be the losers. The monarchical-imperial status quo was to be preserved, yet with the balance of power tilted dramatically in the Bourbons' favor.

The ink on the Franco-American treaties of 1778 was hardly dry before Vergennes, while pursuing an allied military buildup against Britain, was undercutting specified American objectives by playing on regional differences among American leaders. In July 1778, Conrad Alexandre Gérard arrived in Philadelphia as the first French Minister to the United States. He immediately went to work, hinting here, suggesting there, meddling everywhere among congressional delegates. His instructions contained warnings about American territorial pretensions to Canada, Nova Scotia, and the Floridas, which appeared to be "of the utmost importance to Congress." Gérard should never forget, warned Vergennes, that "the King feels that the possession of these three countries, or at least that of Canada by England, would be a serviceable principle for keeping the Americans *uneasy and cautious;* that it will make them feel to an even greater extent *the need which they have* for friendship and alliance with the King; and that it is not in his interest to destroy this principle."[5]

Understandably, Gérard ingratiated himself with the middle states group. He urged Morris and his associates to persuade Congress to disclaim all rights to the trans-Appalachian West. He also tactlessly involved himself in the Silas Deane-Arthur Lee controversy, upsetting New Englanders and Virginians who mistrusted Robert Morris and his "private" commercial correspondents like Deane. (No one at the time knew that Deane had been spying for the British while in France.) At the same time, Gérard set out to undermine the reputation of John Adams, who had replaced Deane as an American Minister to France. Vergennes disliked Adams intensely, considering him too boring for court and, worse yet, too independent, too committed to the fisheries, and just too peevish in general. He wanted someone else in the delegation—someone more sociable, less independent, and more to the liking of the preferred middle states interests. When Congress in 1779 debated terms for an acceptable peace settlement, which included full navigation rights on the Mississippi, with that river as the western boundary, Gérard urged that John Jay of New York (whom he considered favorable to his purposes) be designated as the primary peace commissioner. But Congress, less dominated by middle states interests than it would be during the early 1780s, named the uncompromising Adams instead and selected Jay as the first American Minister to Spain.

Sending Jay to Madrid turned out to be a fortunate choice for the new republic. Jay, who consistently favored the formation of strong Old World commercial ties, got absolutely nowhere in his dealings with Floridablanca. The New Yorker quickly became wary of European diplomats and their machinations. Instinctively, he sensed that the Spanish court wanted everything for nothing. Spain had entered the war in 1779 many months before Jay arrived, but only after signing the Convention of Aranjuez with France. This secret agreement, unknown to the Americans, committed France to continue the war with England until Spain had recovered Gibraltar. What the Aranjuez Convention meant was that France, having been assured by the Franco-American alliance that the Americans would not pull out of the war without France's permission, had locked the United States into continuing the war effort until Spain had regained Gibraltar. It is little wonder that Jay, although in the dark about the Convention, found himself repeatedly rebuffed in his efforts to gain commercial concessions or cash loans from the other Bourbon ally. His mounting suspicions about duplicity and intrigue helped in the negotiations leading to a peace settlement.

Thus Spain entered the war in 1779 ostensibly in support of the American cause, but in reality she worked with contradictory purposes. As with France, the Spanish dangled the prospect of postwar commercial agreements. But in actuality, Floridablanca had a keen sense of national purpose. This encouraged Vergennes to modify his objectives. Vergennes began imagining a weak republic, squeezed into constraining boundaries, a republic lacking in fishing rights and increasingly dependent upon French commerce. He envisioned the formation of an informal commercial empire, with French merchants supplying credit and manufactured goods to Americans in return for raw materials and staples. France would simply take up where Britain had left off. Because some powerful middle states merchants were hungry for commercial opportunities (although they certainly did not want to fall back into a quasi-colonial status) and were willing to sacrifice western territories and the fisheries to obtain favorable trading privileges, the new nation was getting itself into deep trouble. It is one of the ironies of the period that French loans and military support were critical in winning the war when, in the diplomatic sector, this vital support was actually expended for the creation of a nonnation in the New World. Only blatant national self-interest could explain such a paradox.

Indeed, by 1781 the traps being laid by European diplomatic leaders were potentially deadly. And by that time middle states commercial interests were becoming more prominent in the dealings of the Continental Congress. France had replaced the incautious Gérard with the more polished Chevalier de La Luzerne. One of his prime assignments was to divest John Adams of his sole responsibilities for peacemaking. The middle states group supported Luzerne, but rather than dump Adams outright (which the New Englanders never would have tolerated), they surrounded the sage of Braintree with four additional peace commissioners—Benjamin Franklin, John Jay, Henry Laurens, and Thomas Jefferson. Revised instructions also inhibited the commissioners' ability to negotiate freely. Beyond the issue of the recognition of American independence, the commissioners were to do nothing about peace terms without France's approval. This included the settlement of boundary lines. Luzerne, it appeared, had boxed in Adams, and it looked as if Vergennes could dictate a settlement completely favorable to France and Spain. In fact, a nervous Congress had given more than the Franco-American alliance called for; the peace treaty was to be the product of mutual consent, not the dictate of a single party.

If Vergennes thought that he was in control, thanks to Luzerne's efforts, he was in for some enlightening days. In the first place, John Jay's suspicions had turned to outright mistrust. In September 1781, Jay protested to Congress "that this instruction, besides breathing a degree of complacency not quite republican, puts it out of the power of your ministers to improve those chances and opportunities which in the course of human affairs happens more or less frequently to all men." "Nor is it clear," the agitated New Yorker continued, "that America, thus casting herself into the arms of the King of France, will advance either her interest or reputation with that of other nations."[6] A worried Jay soon was traveling to France to join Franklin in working out peace terms with Britain. There was little danger of his buckling under to any European diplomat.

Secondly, Benjamin Franklin did not feel constrained by the instructions. (Thomas Jefferson was unable to serve. Henry Laurens was captured at sea on his way to the Netherlands and cast into the Tower of London. His involvement in the final peace negotiations came very late. John Adams, working in other courts, kept in constant communication and came to Versailles for the most crucial deliberations.) Outwardly pleasant if not obsequious around Vergennes, Franklin took every opportunity to construct a peace settlement in private without keeping Vergennes informed about details. Before initial meetings during the spring of 1782 with Richard Oswald, an aging Scottish slave trader who was England's emissary to the American delegation, Franklin and Vergennes agreed explicitly that preliminary peace terms required France's blessing. Then Vergennes, trusting too much in Franklin's republican countenance, encouraged the preparation of the negotiated details for his review. By the time that Vergennes saw the details, the French Minister had his own reasons for not wanting to abort what others had created.

Confusion in the higher circles of the British government after North's departure also abetted the American position. The new coalition cabinet headed by Rockingham (he had also been in charge of the short-lived ministry that rescinded the Stamp Act), soon was fighting openly about proper peace terms. Rockingham wanted to recognize American independence and let the former colonists go their own way. Lord Shelburne, who had succeeded Germain as colonial secretary, subscribed to independence in name only. He insisted that proper peace terms should keep American commerce firmly locked in the imperial box. Just to confuse everyone, Rockingham died suddenly in July 1782, clearing the way for Shelburne's orchestration of the negotiations through Oswald. The hard-nosed Shelburne was predisposed to offer as little as possible, but just enough to make sure that France and Spain did not so weaken Britain's children that they could be used by the Bourbon powers against their former parent. Furthermore, Shelburne believed that Britain could still control American commerce if it did not permit France and Spain to emasculate the new nation at the peace table. Thus the British made many concessions to the American negotiators that otherwise might never have materialized.

In the preliminary articles of peace signed at Paris by Richard Oswald and the American commissioners on November 30, 1782, Great Britain did much more than acknowledge American independence. The articles established the Mississippi River as the western boundary, proclaimed free navigation of that inland waterway for British and American subjects, and (in a secret provision) settled 31° of north latitude as the southern boundary. The articles recognized American fishing rights, though as a "liberty"; it also stipulated that confiscations of loyalist property would stop; and it obligated Congress to recommend to the states that loyalist property be returned. The British agreed not to carry away slaves when their armies evacuated American soil, but they absolutely refused to concede Canada. On that point the American commissioners made no headway whatsoever.[7]

John Adams had feared for years that the attempt to create a new nation would not be destroyed on the battlefield but at the peace table. "America has been long enough involved in the wars of Europe. She has been a football between contending nations from the beginning," Adams mused, "and it is easy to foresee, that France and England both will endeavor to involve us in their future wars. It is our interest and duty . . . to be completely independent, and to have nothing to do with either of them, but in commerce."[8] Generally, the peace settlement satisfied Adams. It was certainly enough of a foundation upon which to construct a worthy edifice. And it was a double irony that Great Britain, the enemy, was helping to lay that foundation (admittedly in its own self-interest) while the allies, France and Spain, were not.

It fell to Franklin to inform Vergennes about the commissioners' duplicity in not keeping the French minister fully informed. Vergennes accepted the news passively. In fact, the signing of the preliminary accords was not that badly timed, given his plight. By late 1782, the international war had suddenly turned against France and Spain. A major Franco-Spanish expedition had just failed in a massive assault on Gibraltar. The cost of continuing the war with such disasters was putting intolerable burdens on Louis XVI's treasury. Benjamin Franklin meekly opined in communicating the news to Vergennes that *"the English, I just now learn, flatter themselves that they have already divided us."* "I hope that this little misunderstanding will therefore be kept secret," added the disingenuous Franklin, "and that they will find themselves totally mistaken."[9] Vergennes must have chuckled to himself more than once over Franklin's words. Not to be completely outmaneuvered, the French Minister used the preliminary Anglo-American articles as an excuse for renouncing his Spanish commitments.

The other belligerents worked out draft peace terms in early 1783, preparatory to formal reviews by their governments. The preliminary articles between Britain and America stood as written and, on September 3, 1783, all parties signed the definitive peace settlement at Versailles. At last the war, grown more complex and enervating through the years, was over. At least for a short time the western world ceased its incessant militarism—until the holocaust of the French Revolution engulfed Europe. The new American nation, having survived the pitfalls of international diplomatic intrigue through its determined peace commissioners, gained everything that realistically could have been won in the circumstances.

The rebellion had been successful in its military and diplomatic phases, yet the kinds of internal institutions and socioeconomic and political values and practices that would pervade the new nation were very much in the process of being determined. That process, involving the potential for real revolution, still threatened to tear apart from within what had triumphed from without.

The act of full-scale rebellion meant that the former colonists had to decide for themselves whether they would alter significantly political and social relationships. Thomas Jefferson made the issue paramount in the Declaration of Independence. In writing about "self-evident truths," and in envisioning governmental institutions that would protect and defend each citizen's right to life, liberty, and happiness, the Virginian had asked, circumspectly, about how revolutionary the American Revolution was to be. Earlier in 1776 John Adams had touched upon the same issue somewhat differently in discussing the nature of republics. He stressed that republican governments in past ages had been of "an inexhaustible variety, because possible combinations of the powers of society are capable of innumerable variations." But all republican governments had common characteristics. They based their authority in the people and drew sovereign life from them. In principle, Adams explained, "the very definition of a republic is 'an empire of laws and not of men'."[10] Representative governments, above all else, reflected and served popular needs; and they were wise and just in legislating for the best interests of all citizens.

Americans in 1776 were thus setting themselves apart from Britain's "corrupted" practices. The call for republicanism and the rule of law was a logical extension of perceptions about a conspiracy from above in the form of political tyranny. It was also the beginning of a definition of what the Revolution should seek to create—an experiment in republicanism in which all fit persons had access to authority; in which no one would be favored for the artificial reasons of family bloodline, social standing, personal wealth, or formal education; and in which all citizens who behaved virtuously and acted meritoriously in service to the community would have the actual responsibility for governing their peers through representative institutions. As the rebellion turned to full-scale warfare, then, it was necessary to institutionalize in reality what was at that moment a group of half-tested and half-tried political theories. For some insurgents, the assignment carried with it a larger mission as the redeemers and defenders of human liberty in a darkened world in which tyranny had all but snuffed out liberty and the light of human reason.

To make words come alive and have meaning in practice would not be easy for the former colonists. Theirs was a world that was becoming less rather than more equalitarian in the distribution of wealth and property. Theirs was a society in which the fashionable were becoming ever more imitative of English life-styles. Theirs was a society in which a burgeoning native elite was putting greater stress upon a formal hierarchy of privileges and distinctions according to artificial measures, a society in which the concept of deference still held exalted meaning. And it was a society in which black slaves, all women, indentured servants, and the propertyless poor—as much as

80 percent of the adult population—had neither *de jure* nor *de facto* political or social rights. In 1776 a citizen had to be a white adult male, with at least modest property holdings, to be eligible even to vote. It was a narrow base, although not necessarily narrow for its time. An important question was whether the base could or would be broadened by a generation dedicated to the institutionalization of human liberty.[11]

It may have been gratifying to the insurgent leaders to speak of republicanism, sovereignty of the people, and the rule of law. But very few of these leaders were fully prepared to accept all of the implications of their words—and very few were willing to apply them to slaves, women, or indentured servants. Even those who considered the implications seriously thought primarily in political rather than in social terms. What the most radical among them sought were structures of government that excluded the possibility of monarchy and placed decision-making authority as close as possible to the people.

Indeed, what the small number of *radical* Revolutionary insurgents of 1776 had in common was an unbounded abstract faith in the people. In their personal social origins, many of these men were quite common; others had worked very closely with the colonial citizenry as popular leaders during the years of protest and resistance. Thomas Paine had not been a popular leader, but the commitment to sweeping change had been strongly evidenced in his writings. In *Common Sense* he stressed that the people were inherently *virtuous* and imbued with a capacity for self-sacrifice when it came to serving the greater good of the republican community. Monarchs had been the real source of bad behavior, the true corruptors: "It is easy to see that when Republican virtue fails, slavery ensues. Why is the constitution of England sickly, but because monarchy hath poisoned the Republic, the Crown hath engrossed the Commons?" Declare independence, leave behind the tainted monarchical past, Paine vehemently urged, and watch the people glorify the new nation by virtuously ruling themselves.[12]

The transplanted British staymaker bluntly urged his readers to renounce their British political heritage (many Americans believed that the English government had inherent republican qualities because the monarch was not all-powerful) and to cast aside notions about balanced government. Monarchy in the personage of the king or queen, and aristocracy in the form of the House of Lords, were nothing more than "the base remains of two ancient tyrannies, compounded with new Republican materials . . . in the persons of the Commons, on whose virtue depends the freedom of England." Seize upon these materials, Paine insisted, and create simple governments without constraining structural checks upon the popular will. Form governments close to and in the hands of the people and their elected representatives. Have annually elected state assemblies, with only a national congress above these popularly based bodies charged with bringing the states together in realizing the nation's republican strength. Emphasize structural simplicity and popular sovereignty; place full trust in the virtuous citizenry. Paine's was clearly a radical vision in 1776.[13]

Inherent in Paine's program was the idea of the regeneration of mankind through the model of a republican government. It would wean citizens from the lure of offices, titles, honors, power, and property accumulation as ends unto themselves and lead them toward what Jefferson, five months later would describe as the pursuit of happiness.

Other radical Revolutionaries, using less emphatic terminology, agreed with Paine during the turbulent months when the question of independence was resolved. Not unexpectedly, Samuel Adams was one of them. John Adams reported in the summer of 1775 that his older cousin "was perfectly unsettled in any Plan to be recommended to a State, always inclining to the most democratical forms, and even to single Sovereign Assembly."[14] Having worked so closely with the citizenry of Boston in bringing about the fall of the Hutchinson-Oliver faction, Samuel Adams was not about to become a hypocrite and turn against those very people in the streets who had supported him loyally in the past. In 1776 he did not mistrust the commonalty or fear its possible abuse of power. As he explained to a close friend: "Public bodies of men legally constituted are too prone to covet more power than the public had judged it safe to entrust them with. It is happy when their power is not only subject to control while it is exercised, but frequently reverts into the hands of the people, from whom it is derived, and to whom men in power ought forever to be accountable."[15]

There were many others among the most articulate insurgent leaders who spoke out in favor of the full implementation of popular sovereignty. A New York editorialist expounded in June 1776 that "we should always keep in mind that great truth, viz.: that the good of the people is the ultimate end of civil government." The sure strategy for seeing that "America bids fair to be the most glorious state that has ever been on earth" was through properly arranged governments: "There can be no doubt that a well regulated Democracy is most equitable."[16] Another anonymous writer from Pennsylvania voiced the same feelings: "Popular government—sometimes termed Democracy, Republic, or Commonwealth—is the plan of civil society wherein the community at large takes care of its own welfare, and manages its concerns by representatives elected by the people out of their own body."[17]

As the radical Revolutionaries of their day, these individuals insisted that the new American governments be stripped to the bone to prevent corrupting influences. They rejected complex tripartite structures promising the protection of liberties by checking and balancing the interests of the traditional social orders. The people could be their own best governors, as one pamphleteer optimistically summarized it.[18] With fully popular governments and with decision-making authority residing in the commonalty and its elected representatives, everything else needed for uplifting the lot of mankind, they believed, would soon fall into place, that is, within the inhibiting constraints of the social, racial, and cultural attitudes of the times.

In juxtaposition to the radical Revolutionaries of 1776 were those leaders who may be classified as *reluctant* Revolutionaries. For purposes of comparative analysis, it seems appropriate to conceptualize differences in thoughts and attitudes among radical and reluctant Revolutionaries along a continuum of possibilities starting at one end with those who fully trusted in the people's virtue. At the other end were those who did not in any way trust the people and who believed that the democracy of citizens was as fully capable of abusing power and despoiling liberty as were willful monarchs. Reluctant Revolutionaries were generally more attached to traditional forms and practices; they had faith in institutions which balanced societal interests and social orders and encouraged orderliness and deference from the "common herd," as they continually thought of the people well after 1776. They viewed structural restraints as vital for protecting men of property and high standing from popular convulsions from below. They often characterized the latter by the phrase "democratic licentiousness"—the obverse of public virtue in government and society. One New Yorker summarized these attitudes as well as anyone: "No one loves Liberty more than I do, but of all Tyranny I most dread that of the Multitude."[19]

Wedded in varying degrees to the conception of hierarchical and balanced government, the reluctant Revolutionaries of 1776 found themselves suspended in time and space between the British monarchy and its corrupting minions above them and the American people below them. Unlike their loyalist counterparts, with whom they shared many attitudes, the reluctant Revolutionaries could envision an American society surviving the transfer of power from a corrupted Britain to an uncorrupted America. Moreover, they could countenance concepts of republicanism and the rule of law. Yet like their loyalist counterparts, they could not approve of vesting power fully in the people. That conjured up to them visions of social and political chaos and doom.

Thus the reluctant Revolutionaries, a number of whom had been reconciliationists in the second Continental Congress, insisted that new American governments of the balanced variety had to be well established before the independence movement deteriorated into a state of anarchy. While some acts of anti-imperial violence had been condoned by them as necessary for checking tyranny, the reluctant Revolutionaries fretted incessantly about popular disturbances that had not been anti-imperial but rather had been directed against men like themselves—of property and of cautiously Whiggish persuasion. For instance, there had been the Paxton Boy uprising in central Pennsylvania during 1763, when Scots-Irish frontiersmen had got out of hand by first killing innocent Indians in mindless retaliation for tribal depredations associated with Pontiac's Rebellion. Then, in early 1764, the Boys marched toward Philadelphia with sinister threats about attacking the city unless the provincial government did something for the protection of western settlers.

Another example was the Regulator movement in North Carolina, in which backcountry settlers had risen up in defiance of excessive governmental taxes and legal and court fees. The Regulators challenged the Whig leadership in the eastern part of the province, and they had to be put down by an army of volunteers in what amounted to a civil war that culminated during 1771 in the Battle of Alamance Creek. To take yet a third example, northcentral Pennsylvania in 1775 was locked in a state of civil turmoil (the Yankee-Pennamite Wars) between Connecticut and Pennsylvania settlers over conflicting land claims to the Wyoming Valley region. If someone wanted to find proof of popular turmoil that was unstabilizing and unrelated to threats of imperial tyranny, the reluctant Revolutionaries had these and other examples to draw upon.[20]

Even stouthearted independence men like John Adams and Richard Henry Lee feared the specter of democratic licentiousness. In late April 1776, Lee, while pushing for national independence, wrote pointedly: "Do you not see the indispensable necessity of establishing a government [during] this convention [in Virginia]? How long popular commotions may be suppressed without it, and anarchy be prevented, deserves intense consideration." "A wise and free government," Lee reminded his correspondent, "will, added to the magistrate's authority, effectually prevent the numerous evils to be apprehended from popular rage and license whenever they find the bonds of government removed."[21] To Lee, returning to a full state of nature and casually creating less complex governments, as some of the most radical of the Revolutionaries advocated, was naive as well as dangerous; governmental systems and "proper" magistrates were mandatory for social stability.

John Adams in 1776, like Lee, would have fallen only slightly toward the popular rights end of the attitudinal continuum separating radical and reluctant Revolutionaries. Even though an early and strong advocate of independence, Adams was not prepared to turn everything over to the people in a frenzied rush. Writing from Philadelphia in the same month as Lee, Adams spelled out his "fear, that in every Assembly, Members will obtain an Influence, by Noise not Sense, by Meanness not Greatness, by Ignorance not Learning, by contracted Hearts not large Souls." "There is one Thing," Adams warned, "that must be attempted and most Sacredly observed, or We are all undone. There must be a Decency, and Respect, and Veneration introduced for Persons in Authority, of every Rank, or We are undone."[22] The repetition of "undone" underscored Adams's concern. Even some men fully committed to independence did not foresee much of a future for a separately constituted republican nation devoid of respect for enlightened leadership and proper decision making. Lee and Adams had revealed less than full faith in the concept of a virtuous citizenry.

It might appear that men like Adams and Lee were being inconsistent—favoring independence, on the one hand, but worried about popular excesses, on the other hand. Yet that was not the case. The bulk of insurgent leaders, even those who pushed early and hard for independence in the second Continental Congress, would have been horrified to be classified as social levelers. Trained from their youths in the wisdom of balanced governments and the deferential norm, these men wanted to make sure that control of the Revolution did not get out of their hands and go to licentious extremes. They worked for new state governments that assured a linear transfer of *de facto* decision making authority from the humbled British lion to themselves as appropriate stewards of the American people. They were not afraid of the concept of popular sovereignty in the *de jure* sense. Yet they felt that the people could not sustain virtuous behavior and would be quickly corrupted by power, if given too much actual authority. The only chance for an enduring republic, then, was to make sure that they held power in trusteeship for the people, as befitting men with established records of ability, talent, and "disinterested" community service.

Great numbers of insurgent leaders in the years of the dawning rebellion before 1776 were men who had held important local and elective provincial offices. But they were also men who had not been favored with Crown appointments to the highest and most prestigious offices—governorships, councilorships, and colony-wide judgeships. Many of them were men of great personal accomplishments, given their rather humble origins. Some of them were prominent local leaders who viewed the British Empire as constraining their range of socioeconomic and political opportunities in almost every sector, especially after 1763. As local and assembly leaders of proved "talent and merit," they had come to fear the diminution of their range of authority and opportunities, especially with the new outpouring of imperial programs during the 1760s. But their defense of liberty did not mean that they also thought that the concepts of enlightened leadership, deference, or good order should be abandoned. On the contrary, they argued that such concepts should be applied correctly in the science of government.[23]

John Adams, always probing the issues, explained in his *Thoughts on Government* during early 1776: "In a large society, inhabiting an extensive country, it is impossible that the whole should assemble to make laws. The first necessary step, then, is to depute power from the many to *a few of the most wise and good.*"[24] Out of his concern for stable government, Adams preferred that the wise and the good be vested with power. Men like Adams, not disclaiming the prospect of replacing old enemies like Hutchinson and the Olivers, put greater faith in their own virtue than in the people's. They simply did not trust the people as much as the radical Revolutionaries did. That restrained them from constructing governments that were too popularly based in actual practice.

Advocating independence and favoring significant Revolutionary change simply did not follow parallel lines. Almost all reconciliationists were reluctant Revolutionaries. But radical Revolutionaries who were not intense independence advocates did not exist. And there were quite a number of independence men who were reluctant Revolutionaries. The primary issue was how much the people could be trusted in a republican polity with *de facto* power. Thomas Paine had no doubts, but there were many others who felt that they had compelling evidence that tyranny and the destruction of liberties could come as easily from below as from above.

During the spring of 1776, a number of anxious and cautious insurgent leaders expressed concerns about Paine's full-blown endorsement of popular rule. None reacted more vigorously against the "leveling spirit" than Carter Braxton, a wealthy and politically influential Virginia planter-merchant, who suspected that "the author [of *Common Sense*], with what design I know not, seems to have cautiously blended private and public virtue, as if for the purpose of confounding the two, and thereby recommending his plan under the amiable appearance of courting virtue." Writing as "A Native" to delegates who were meeting in Williamsburg to draft a new state constitution, Braxton underscored that "it is well known that private and public virtue are materially different." While an individual practiced private virtue "with a view of promoting his own particular welfare," public virtue reflected "a disinterested attachment to the public good, exclusive and independent of all private and selfish interest, and which, though sometimes possessed by a few individuals, never characterized the mass of people of any state." "And this is said," Braxton added as an afterthought, "to be the principle of democratical Governments." What particularly upset the Virginian was that "advocates for popular Governments" were becoming too influential in the state constitutional convention and were blinding the delegates to the limitations of public virtue. Specifically, he referred to men who were taking advantage of "the temper of the times," men who might have something personal to gain from "the tumult and riot incident to simple Democracy."

The "Native," presuming that leveling propagators of anarchy were poisoning the Virginia convention, presented an alternative plan of government based upon the best precepts of English tradition. "What has been the Government of *Virginia*, and in a revolutionary situation how is its spirit to be preserved, are important questions," insisted Braxton. He urged that the delegates "take a view of the Constitution of *England.*" "Our ancestors, the *English*, after contemplating the various forms of Government, and experiencing . . . the defects of each, wisely refused to resign their liberties either to the single man, the few, or the many. They determined to make a compound of each the foundation of their Government," one that had functioned effectively for all parties until "national degeneracy and corruption" made life under the British regime intolerable for Americans.

Thus Braxton proposed a governmental structure for Virginia modeled fully on the English original, but guarding more carefully against some of the sources of tyranny. The government of Virginia, Braxton explained, should have a popularly elected lower house, but it should be balanced with an upper house of twenty-four persons selected from the lower house and serving lifetime terms ("They will acquire firmness from their independency, . . . wisdom from their reflection and experience, . . . [and] Being secluded from offices of profit, they will not be seduced from their duty by pecuniary considerations"). In turn, there should be a governor chosen by the full Assembly "to continue in authority during his good behavior" (to keep that person beyond the reach of public opinion and away from the perils of electoral influence). The only elective branch of government, the lower house, was to consist of representatives facing new elections every three years. Braxton would have preferred a longer term, but there was no guarantee that the people would be discriminating in their selection of representatives. Since the commonalty was likely as not to elect men with "improper motives," willing to abuse power for personal gain, triennial elections at least gave "their constituents an opportunity of depriving them of power to do injury."[25]

Braxton's plan stood in glaring juxtaposition to Thomas Paine's proposals. The Virginian urged his fellow Revolutionaries not to repudiate the past but to learn from it and build carefully upon it. He stressed the importance of a balanced range of structural checks on authority rather than trust in public virtue as the most appropriate check upon tyranny. He minimized the role of the people by permitting them to vote only once every three years—and only for members of the lower house. And he proposed an upper legislative branch to serve for life, almost as if it was to act as a titled political nobility in restraining the self-interested excesses of others. Indeed, if Braxton's plan had been universally adopted by state constitution makers, the term revolution would have been a complete misnomer in describing the events of 1776 and afterward. The Revolution would have amounted to little more than a transfer of power and attendant privileges from an English to an American based ruling elite.

In the end, neither Braxton's nor Paine's suggestions prevailed in state constitution making, a process that was well under way before July 1776. Between 1774 and the end of 1777, ten of the thirteen rebellious American colonies—Massachusetts, Rhode Island, and Connecticut were the exceptions—adopted new constitutions. The Massachusetts insurgents, facing a fully developed military conflict in 1775, kept their charter of 1691 as the foundation of government, while dropping all trappings of British authority. In 1780 the citizenry adopted, although by a slim margin, a new constitution stressing balanced relationships. Rhode Island and Connecticut retained their liberal seventeenth-century charters—even governors and councilors had been popularly elected—while deleting all references to British sovereignty. Everywhere else insurgent leaders, meeting at first in extralegal congresses and conventions, eventually drafted constitutions, as the Virginians were doing in the spring of 1776. The provisions of the new state constitutions in turn became one expression of the extent of Revolutionary sentiment. They represented universally a commitment to the abstract principle of popular sovereignty, but, structurally, a weaker commitment to full-blown popular rule.

The state constitutions, in fact, exhibited the vast range of possibilities which can be distributed along the continuum suggested by the differences separating Thomas Paine (democratic republicanism) and Carter Braxton (republicanism by stewardship of the talented, the proved, and the wise). Pennsylvania came closest to writing Paine's democratic sentiments into basic law. Its constitution of 1776 provided for an all-powerful, annually elected unicameral assembly. Pennsylvanians thus gained the right to govern themselves without traditional upper-hierarchy structural checks, except that there was an elected executive council which provided for the daily administration of government—it had no legislative functions. To ensure that decision making was as open as possible, citizens were given the right to attend legislative sessions; also, all proposed legislation had to be published in the newspapers before the final vote by the assembly. The constitution also provided for a council of censors to meet once every seven years for a full-range review of legislation. The censors had the authority to declare null and void any piece of legislation inconsistent with the constitution. All adult males could vote, provided they had resided in the state for at least a year; representation was to be according to the geographic distribution of population; and no representative could hold an assembly seat for more than four years out of seven. This precluded the possibility, according to the "rotation-in-office" principle, of "the danger of establishing an inconvenient [elected] aristocracy" with the ability to abuse power and flout the popular will endlessly through manipulation of the enfranchised at election time. If one believed in balanced government, the Pennsylvania constitution was radical. And reluctant Revolutionaries in and out of the state disliked it intensely.[26]

The constitution of neighboring Maryland represented the other end of the continuum. Not only did reluctant Revolutionaries there retain the three traditional branches, but they also adopted ascending levels of property requirements for officeholding in each. Delegates to the lower house had to own at least a fifty-acre freehold; senators had to possess real and personal property worth a minimum of £1,000 current money; and the governor had to hold a minimum of £5,000 in real and personal property, £1,000 of which was to be in a freehold estate. To vote for delegates, white male citizens had to own property valued at a minimum of £30 current money, less than had been the case in the old regime. The constitution provided that these same freeholders also were to name senatorial electors (men with at least £500 in property), who in turn were to meet separately and elect the upper house. The governor was to be elected by a joint ballot of the lower and upper houses. While the governor and delegates to the lower house served annual terms, senators were to hold office for five years. As men of more than modest property holdings, they were to be the stabilizing influence against popular excesses. Moreover, only the governor was limited in tenure by the rotation-in-office rule (he was able to serve only three in every seven years consecutively). The constitution also constrained the full range of prerogatives which governors under the Baltimore family had enjoyed, such as extensive patronage privileges and the power to adjourn assemblies and veto legislation.

Even though the Maryland constitution of 1776 circumscribed executive powers—a logical extension of perceptions of the Crown's abuse of power—it retained many vestiges of Britain's balanced government. The intent of the Maryland constitution makers was to have government by stewardship of the propertied elite, untrammeled by royal and proprietary authority. The Maryland constitution makers, unlike the Pennsylvanians, could not bring themselves to trust the people fully. It was the other way around. The propertied elite put full faith in themselves.

The other state constitutions generally fell on the continuum somewhere between Maryland's elitist and Pennsylvania's democratic models. New Hampshire, North Carolina, and Georgia came closest to Pennsylvania, demonstrating the least concern for balance and stewardship, while New York, Virginia, and South Carolina shared more in common with Maryland. New Jersey and Delaware were somewhere in the middle. Important general trends included a sharp reduction in gubernatorial powers and the lodging of extensive decision-making authority in the lower houses of assemblies. In a few cases, the executive branch ceased to exist or only had ceremonial functions. There was a general lowering of property requirements for voting as well as for holding statewide offices, and many more positions than ever before became directly or indirectly elective. Many constitutions specifically prohibited the kind of plural officeholding that some prerevolutionary Crown appointees had fed upon. Certainly these trends represented significant gains for the people, especially in the sense that no constitution rejected the principle of popular sovereignty. As embodied in the state constitutions, the first Revolutionary settlement was surprisingly enlightened for its time, though certainly tempered in some states by the restraining influence of the reluctant Revolutionaries.

The sum and substance of the written state constitutions, however, did not represent a linear victory for the Revolutionary citizenry.

Property qualifications did not cease to exist, nor did all offices be-come directly elective. The old notion that citizens should have a propertied stake in society before they could participate in political matters did not die out; nor did the concepts of hierarchy, deference, and stewardship. All told, the constitutions may be viewed as going further toward popular rule than the reluctant Revolutionaries would have liked but certainly not as far (except perhaps for Pennsylvania) as the radical Revolutionaries would have preferred. Whatever the structural arrangements, community elite leaders rushed into the void created by the downfall of British leadership. The Patrick Henrys replaced the Lord Dunmores everywhere. Frustrated insurgent lead-ers maximized their political aspirations in the process—and they were doing so in support of liberty and the people.[27]

Whether or not the process of state constitution making in the Revolutionary settlement of 1776 represented a democratizing trend was less important in shaping the future course of events than con-temporary individual perceptions about that process. Thomas Jeffer-son believed that it was a satisfactory settlement: "The people seemed to have deposited the monarchical and taken up the republican gov-ernment with as much ease as would have attended their throwing off an old and putting on a new suit of clothes. . . . A half dozen aristocratical gentlemen agonizing under the loss of preeminence have sometime ventured their sarcasms on our political metamor-phosis. They have been thought fitter objects for pity than punish-ment."[28] Another Virginian, who took "a view of our new Assembly, now sitting—under the happy auspices of the People only," declared excitedly that "though it is composed of men not quite so well dressed, nor so politely educated, nor so highly born as some As-semblies I have formerly seen—yet upon the whole I like their Pro-ceedings—and upon the whole rather better than formerly." What endeared the spectacle to him was that the assembly now consisted of "the People's men (and the People in general are right.)" The new delegates were more "plain and of consequence less disguised, but I believe to be full[y] as honest, less intriguing, more sincere."[29]

The evidence about the new leadership does not, however, dem-onstrate such a sharp break with past habits. None of the new state legislators came from the propertyless poor. In New Hampshire, New York, and New Jersey, 38 percent of the Revolutionary legislators held at least £200 in property, placing them comfortably in the prop-ertied class. In Maryland, Virginia, and South Carolina, 70 percent of the new legislators were at least at that level. All the others held more property. More men of less personal wealth did appear in statewide elective positions after 1776, but the vast bulk of these individuals were established leaders in their local communities. They were men out of the people, and they had already proved their worth and talent.[30]

Appearances of a radical break with prerevolutionary leadership traditions were thus as deceptive as they were real. But that did not matter to the reluctant Revolutionaries. They did not count, measure, and quantify before they formed their conclusions. As one of them stated: "A pure democracy may possibly do, when patriotism is the ruling passion but when the state abounds in rascals, as is the case with too many this day, you must suppress a little of that popular spirit."[31] Many reluctant Revolutionaries simply never accepted the first Revolutionary settlement. Rather, they shared their dire predictions of impending doom with one another and looked for opportunities after 1776 to readjust it.

It was not only fear about the inevitability of convulsions from an unchecked democracy of citizens that bothered these men. They also resisted the settlement because it did not involve the creation of a powerful central government to replace Britain's. They wanted a central government that clearly would bind the states together while guiding the establishment of a new nation of vigor and strength. They wanted to promote and protect their commercial and propertied interests, while acting as a counterweight to the popular turmoil that was sure to build in the states. The reluctant Revolutionaries of 1776, having failed to bottle up leanings toward popular rule in the states, lost a second time from their perspective in national constitution making. Out of that double defeat may be traced the beginnings of the powerful *nationalist* coalition, a group of determined men who formulated a second Revolutionary settlement in the years ahead.

In June 1776, when Congress set up a committee on a declaration of independence, it also established a committee to draft a plan of national union. Trying to assuage John Dickinson, Congress named him as head of the group that produced the first draft of the Articles of Confederation in mid July. Dominated by reluctant Revolutionaries, the committee members sought to place as much power as possible in the central government—and mostly at the expense of the states. The draft, although it embodied compromises limiting uncontrolled national authority far removed from the people, stated that "the name of this Confederacy shall be 'THE UNITED STATES OF AMERICA'," described in turn as "a firm League of Friendship" among the states "for their common Defense, the Security of their Liberties, and their mutual and general Welfare." In practice, Dickinson's committee wanted the proposed government to be superior to the states in its full range of authority. Each state was to retain "as much of its present Laws, Rights and Customs, as it may think fit . . . in all matters that shall not interfere with the Articles of this Confederation."[32]

The Dickinson draft satisfied almost no one. Even men of potential nationalist persuasion, such as the wealthy Edward Rutledge of South Carolina (he had also been a member of Dickinson's committee), were not pleased with the document's centralizing thrust. Rutledge in particular feared that any national government, whether strong or weak, would be dominated by the scheming and power-hungry New Englanders. "The Force of their Arms I hold exceeding cheap, but I confess I dread their overruling Influence in Council." "I dread their low Cunning," he went on, "and those leveling Principles which Men without Character and without Fortune in general possess, which are so captivating to the lower class of Mankind." Thus Rutledge was "resolved to vest Congress with no more Power than that is absolutely necessary, and to use a familiar Expression, to keep the Staff in our own hands."[33] He was referring to the hands of the South Carolina socioeconomic elite, which had just written one of the least democratic of the new state constitutions.

Only the force of events after 1776 persuaded potential nationalists like Rutledge to overcome their sectional fears and prejudices. Rutledge's response of that year, however, was symptomatic of the reasons why Dickinson's draft got nowhere. It was caught between localists of radical Revolutionary sentiment and fearful potential nationalists. Almost everyone started picking away at the carcass. On and off over the next year and a half, Congress, when not focusing on pressing problems related to the war effort, stripped the flesh from the bones of the Dickinson draft.

The final version of the Articles of Confederation, endorsed by Congress in November 1777, was explicitly anticentralist: "Each State retains its sovereignty, freedom and independence, and every power, jurisdiction and right, which is not by this confederation expressly delegated to the United States, in Congress assembled." The central government was to be a coordinating agency for a loose confederation of sovereign states, neither the kind of a government upon which a powerful nation could be built nor the kind that could act as an effective counterweight to democratic licentiousness. The central government was to be fully dependent upon the goodwill of the states for tax monies as well as for nearly everything else. It was the shell of a government that turned out to be virtually penniless and powerless—a government that the nationalists, beginning to pull themselves together as an identifiable intersectional political alliance

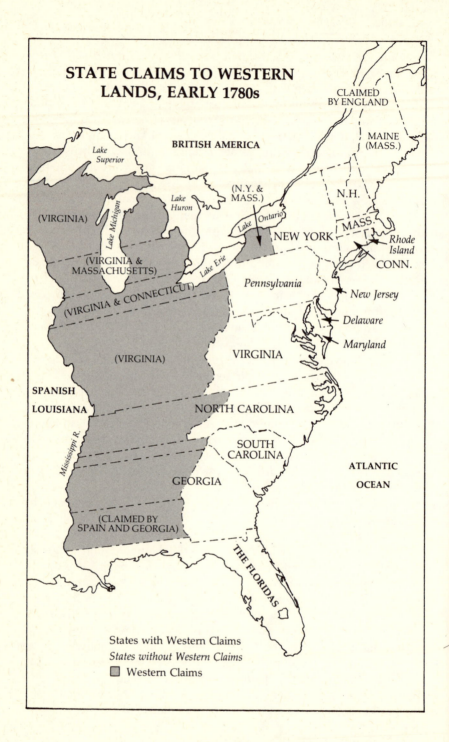

STATE CLAIMS TO WESTERN LANDS, EARLY 1780s

CLAIMED BY ENGLAND

BRITISH AMERICA

Lake Superior

MAINE (MASS.)

Lake Huron

(N.Y. & MASS.)

N.H.

Lake Ontario

(VIRGINIA)

Lake Michigan

MASS.

NEW YORK

Rhode Island

CONN.

(VIRGINIA & MASSACHUSETTS)

Lake Erie

(VIRGINIA & CONNECTICUT)

Pennsylvania

New Jersey

Delaware

(VIRGINIA)

Maryland

VIRGINIA

SPANISH

LOUISIANA

NORTH CAROLINA

Mississippi R.

SOUTH CAROLINA

ATLANTIC

GEORGIA

OCEAN

(CLAIMED BY SPAIN AND GEORGIA)

THE FLORIDAS

States with Western Claims
States without Western Claims
☐ Western Claims

during the later war years, would desperately try to strengthen before, from their angle of vision, the new nation collapsed under the weight of its unbalanced and ill-conceived beginnings.[34]

Given its innocuous character, the final version of the Articles of Confederation should have taken no time to gain ratification by the states. That is exactly what most congressional delegates assumed when they asked for final ratification by March 10, 1778. But those who hoped for some expression of national unity in the face of a common enemy were to be sorely disappointed. A few states approved the document with dispatch, as Congress had asked. A few others, totally indifferent, kept putting off the issue because of more pressing business. By January 1779 (nine months behind schedule) twelve states had finally instructed their congressional delegates to ratify. Only Maryland stood outside. William Whipple, a seafaring merchant from New Hampshire, whimsically pointed out that "there now only remains Maryland who you know has seldom done anything with a good Grace. She has always been a froward Hussey."[35]

Whipple's was only one explanation. In more precise terminology, Maryland was a "landless" state. It had a fixed western boundary and thus held no claim to western lands. Rhode Island, New Jersey, Pennsylvania, and Delaware also lacked colonial charter claims to western lands. The other eight states had at least some type of claim upon sea-to-sea clauses in their colonial charters or upon other documents dating back to the days when the Crown first issued patents to North American lands. Virginia's claim, encompassing the vast territory not only due westward but also northwestward of its eastern settlements was by far the largest—including today states as far east as Ohio and as far north as Minnesota. Several parts of the "Old Northwest" had been a hotbed of prewar land speculation involving several groups, some of them outside Virginia; but all vied for full legal title to vast portions of the region. Leading Maryland elite leaders had been involved in these get-rich-quick schemes. They were not going to give up their claims, no matter what, even if the war effort's success depended upon fully establishing a modicum of national unity through the Articles of Confederation.

Land speculation focusing on the trans-Appalachian region east of the Mississippi River had been an avocation for a number of prominent provincial elite leaders since the 1740s. Men like George Washington, Patrick Henry, and Benjamin Franklin instinctively understood that the overcrowding plaguing the older seaboard settlements made the trans-Appalachian west a region ripe for expansion. They wanted to engross as much territory as possible and sell the land at easy profits to overcrowded Easterners fleeing westward. However, valid land company titles depended upon gaining a charter from the Crown and extinguishing Indian claims. There always seemed to be an Indian sachem or two willing to sign away tribal rights—they rarely had authority to do so—in return for stupefying amounts of liquor and other "gifts" from whites. On the other hand, gaining the Crown's approval was virtually impossible, especially after the Proclamation of 1763 and the imperial determination to limit westward expansion.

Once imperial authority ceased to exist, the question of whether the state governments or Congress controlled the western lands took on new significance. In fact, there were many disquieting debates on that subject associated with the emasculation of Dickinson's draft of the Articles. Land-speculating interests from the landless states insisted that the region must become a national domain for all Americans. Beneath such "enlightened" thinking was pure self-interest. If the national government controlled the West, then speculators from the landless states would have as good a chance as those from the landed states in validating their dubious Indian purchases.

Simple mathematics dictated congressional voting. The landed states conceded nothing to their landless counterparts. In the final draft of the Articles, a clause specified "that no state shall be deprived of territory for the benefit of the United States." Speculators from the landless states, it appeared, had been deprived of any share of the western treasure. It now looked as if only landed state governments would have the right to dispose of western territory, and everyone knew that they would favor their own jobbers.

Maryland's speculators, well-established men who wanted even more wealth, dominated that state's senate. Refusing to give up the fight, they blocked favorable action on the Articles by the Maryland legislature, thereby subverting the whole ratification process. The Marylanders, holding their heads high, acted as disinterested patriots. Western lands should be for all, not for some of the people, they argued. In reality they were thinking as much about some of the people (themselves) as anyone else. In what may be described as political blackmail, the Maryland speculators suggested that the transfer of state western land claims to the central government would make good cement for the union. Once the landed states acted virtuously and conveyed their sea-to-sea claims to Congress, the Marylanders would be the most enthusiastic ratifiers. It was not the last time that self-interested behavior would embarrass the fledgling confederation.[36]

After months of wrangling, Virginia finally caved in, largely because local land speculators did not dominate that state's assembly and because the war was shifting into the Old Dominion. The completed union, however feeble, might help to prevent a local holocaust. In January 1781 the Virginia assembly announced its intention to cede the Old Northwest to the Continental Congress, but with several qualifications, including a mandatory disallowance of all claims based on Indian deeds. That condition infuriated the Marylanders, whose titles came from negotiations with Indians. Their first instinct was to demur once again in ratification, but they, too, had been trapped. Fearing a British land and naval invasion from the South, the Marylanders suddenly needed military assistance. The suggestion came back from Philadelphia that help would be forthcoming, once Maryland had given its congressional delegates authority to ratify the Articles. Suddenly the Maryland assembly saw the light. The final barrier to creating a central government had fallen.

Thus it took nearly three and a half years to get all thirteen states to agree about a matter of great importance to them all—the matter of formal union. The Confederation finally came into being on March 1, 1781, amidst a mixture of jubilation and doubt. One Philadelphia newspaper reported the celebration in the capital city that day, noting that "this great event . . . will confound our enemies, fortify us against their arts of seduction, and frustrate their plans of division." In describing the local festivities, the report predicted that "the union, begun by necessity, [has] been indissolubly cemented. Thus America, like a well constructed arch, whose parts, harmonizing and mutually supporting each other, . . . is growing up in war into greatness and consequence among the nations."[37]

This editorialist, who ignored recent events, may have viewed the ratification of the Articles as the key to national greatness. There were many others, however, who shook their heads. By 1781 the nationalists were beginning to mold themselves into an effective political coalition. They were not happy with the first Revolutionary settlement. They feared that a monster, rather than a nation, had been created, one that would devour their interests and the republican experiment unless they attacked and destroyed it first. By 1781 the only point that was not clear in their minds was how to react.

Notes

1. Sir Nathaniel Wraxall, *Historical Memoirs of My Own Time, 1772–1784*, II (Philadelphia, 1837), 263–264.

2. Quoted in Mackesy, *War for America*, 460–461. Germain, who desperately wanted to keep the war effort going, or at least to keep fighting until a

truce assured Great Britain of some territory in the rebellious provinces as a permanent wedge into American affairs, became one of the cabinet scapegoats and left office in early February 1782. For further details, consult *ibid.*, 460–470.

3. Wraxall, *Memoirs*, II, 282–284. See also Ian R. Christie, *The End of North's Ministry, 1780–1782* (London, 1958), and Alan Valentine, *Lord North* (2 vols., Norman, Okla., 1967), esp. II, 258–316.

4. To George Washington, June 24, 1778, *The Letters of Richard Henry Lee* (2 vols., ed. J. C. Ballagh, New York, 1911–1914), I, 419–420. On the importance of sectional disagreements, see Joseph L. Davis, *Sectionalism in American Politics, 1774–1787* (Madison, Wisc., 1977), *passim*.

5. March 29, 1778, *Despatches and Instructions of Conrad Alexandre Gérard* (ed. J. J. Meng, Baltimore, 1939), 129. (Italics mine)

6. To Thomas McKean, September 20, 1781, *The Revolutionary Diplomatic Correspondence of the United States* (6 vols., ed. Francis Wharton, Washington, 1889), IV, 716–717.

7. The text of the preliminary articles may be found in *ibid.*, VI, 96–100.

8. To Robert R. Livingston, November 11, 1782, *The Works of John Adams* (10 vols., ed. C. F. Adams, Boston, 1850–1856), VIII, 9.

9. To Count de Vergennes, December 17, 1782, Wharton, ed., *Revolutionary Diplomatic Correspondence*, VI, 143–144. Valuable secondary studies include Bemis, *Diplomacy of the American Revolution;* Lawrence S. Kaplan, *Colonies into Nation: American Diplomacy, 1763–1801* (New York, 1972), 73–144; Richard B. Morris, *The Peacemakers: The Great Powers and American Independence* (New York, 1965); and Stinchcombe, *American Revolution and French Alliance*.

10. "Thoughts on Government," Adams, ed., *Works of John Adams*, IV, 194. See also Bailyn, *Ideological Origins*, 281–301, and Gordon S. Wood, *The Creation of the American Republic, 1776–1787* (Chapel Hill, N.C., 1969), 46–90.

11. De Pauw, "Land of the Unfree," *Maryland Historical Magazine*, 355–368; Wilson, "The Illusion of Change," Young, ed., *The American Revolution*, 385–445; and Martin, ed., *The American Revolution, Whose Revolution?*, *passim*.

12. Conway, ed., *Writings of Paine*, I, 83.

13. *Ibid.*, I, 72–73.

14. Autobiography, June 9, 1775, Butterfield, ed., *Diary and Autobiography of John Adams*, III, 353–354.

15. To James Warren, December 27, 1775, *Warren-Adams Letters*, I, 196.

16. "Spartanus," Letter II, *New York Journal*, June 13, 1776.

17. "Salus Populi," Number V, *Pennsylvania Journal*, March 13, 1776.

18. [Anonymous], *The People the Best Governors, Or a Plan on the Just Principles of Natural Freedom* (1776), contained in Frederick Chase, *A History of Dartmouth College and the Town of Hanover New Hampshire (to 1815)* (2nd ed., ed. J. K. Lord, Brattleboro, Vt., 1928), 654–663.

19. John Vardill to Peter Van Schaack, September 15, 1774, quoted in David C. Humphrey, *From King's College to Columbia, 1746–1800* (New York, 1976), 215.

20. Brooke Hindle, "The March of the Paxton Boys," *William and Mary Quarterly*, 3rd Ser., 3 (1946), 461–486; John S. Bassett, "The Regulators of North Carolina, 1765–1771," American Historical Association, *Annual Report, 1894* (Washington, 1895), 141–212; Marvin L. Michael Kay, "The North Carolina Regulation, 1766–1776: A Class Conflict," Young, ed., *The American*

Revolution, 73–123; James Kirby Martin, "The Return of the Paxton Boys and the *Historical* State of the Pennsylvania Frontier, 1764–1774," *Pennsylvania History*, 38 (1971), 117–133. See also Richard M. Brown, *The South Carolina Regulators* (Cambridge, Mass., 1963); Irving Mark, *Agrarian Conflicts in Colonial New York* (New York, 1940); and Edward Countryman, " 'Out of the Bounds of the Law': Northern Land Rioters in the Eighteenth Century," Young, ed., *The American Revolution*, 39–69.

21. To Robert Carter Nicholas, April 30, 1776, Ballagh, ed., *Letters of Richard Henry Lee*, I, 184.

22. To James Warren, April 22, 1776, *Warren-Adams Letters*, I, 234.

23. Martin, *Men in Rebellion, passim.*

24. Adams, ed., *Works of John Adams*, IV, 194. (Italics mine)

25. Force, ed., *American Archives*, 4th Ser., VI, 748–754.

26. All the constitutions are contained in *The Federal and State Constitutions, Colonial Charters, and Other Organic Laws of the States, Territories, and Colonies . . . Forming the United States of America* (7 vols., ed. F. N. Thorpe, Washington, 1909), as follows: New Hampshire (1776), IV, 2451–2453; Massachusetts (1691 charter), III, 1870–1886; Rhode Island (1663 charter), VI, 3211–3222; Connecticut (1662 charter), I, 529–536; New York (1777), V, 2623–2638; New Jersey (1776), V, 2594–2598; Pennsylvania (1776), V, 3081–3092; Delaware (1776), I, 562–568; Maryland (1776), III, 1686–1701; Virginia (1776), VII, 3812–3819; North Carolina (1776), V, 2787–2794; South Carolina (1776), VI, 3241–3248; and Georgia (1777), II, 777–785.

27. Martin, *Men in Rebellion*, esp. 173–201.

28. To Benjamin Franklin, August 13, 1777, *The Papers of Thomas Jefferson* (ed. J. P. Boyd *et al.*, Princeton, N.J., 1950 to date), II, 26.

29. Roger Atkinson to Samuel Pleasants, November 23, 1776, *Virginia Magazine of History and Biography*, 15 (1908), 357–358.

30. Jackson T. Main, "Government by the People: The American Revolution and the Democratization of the Legislatures," *William and Mary Quarterly*, 3rd Ser., 23 (1966), 391–407. See also Jackson T. Main, *The Upper House in Revolutionary America, 1763–1788* (Madison, Wisc., 1967), Martin, *Men in Rebellion*, esp. 61–126, and Edward M. Cook, Jr., *The Fathers of the Towns: Leadership and Community Structure in Eighteenth-Century New England* (Baltimore, Md., 1976), *passim.*

31. Philip Schuyler to John Jay, late 1776, quoted in Rossie, *Politics of Command*, 133.

32. Dickinson draft, dated July 12, 1776, Ford, ed., *Journals of the Continental Congress*, V, 546–554. See also Jensen, *Articles of Confederation*, 107–139, and H. James Henderson, *Party Politics in the Continental Congress* (New York, 1974), 130–156.

33. To John Jay, June 29, 1776, *Letters of Members of the Continental Congress* (8 vols., ed. E. C. Burnett, Washington, 1921–1936), I, 517–518.

34. Final version, dated November 15, 1777, Ford, ed., *Journals of the Continental Congress*, IX, 907–925. See also Jensen, *Articles of Confederation*, 140–184, and Henderson, *Party Politics*, 70–186, for the broad view of congressional differences.

35. To Josiah Bartlett, February 7, 1779, Burnett, ed., *Letters*, IV, 60.

36. Jensen, *Articles of Confederation*, 150–160, 185–245.

37. *Pennsylvania Packet*, March 3, 1781.

VIII

The Nationalists in the Confederation Period, 1781–1787

Young and brash Alexander Hamilton, in 1780 the leading member of General Washington's personal military staff, thought that the Confederation was a disgrace to humanity. Writing at the very nadir of the war effort, he lashed out at the current state of American affairs. "'Tis an universal sentiment that our present system [of government] is a bad one, and that things do not go right on that account," Hamilton insisted. The dilemma was not that the Articles of Confederation had not been ratified. It ran much deeper than that. It was, as Hamilton reported, that Congress did not have the authority necessary to solve national problems, whether related to the war effort or anything else. Ratifying the Articles would not change that fact or improve conditions, even if the central government became legitimate at last. Hamilton believed that there was no hope for the new nation unless "the confederation . . . should give Congress complete sovereignty."[1]

The young officer, who had known adversity in childhood and had overcome it, was increasingly dubious whether the republican experiment could succeed as he had personally done. He had risen out of obscure parentage in the British Virgin Islands to attend King's

College (now Columbia University) and to become one of Washington's most trusted aides-de-camp. He would soon marry into the wealthy Schuyler family of New York. Hamilton's personal ambitions were unlimited and, in his mind, they were already tied to the fate of the new nation. From his vantage point in the Continental army, it looked as though the nation-making struggle was about to expire in the last travails of its own birth.

The most pressing issue was the inability of Congress to support its men in arms. The result, explained Hamilton, was that "we [in the army] begin to hate the country for its neglect of us; the country begins to hate us. . . . Congress has long been jealous of us; we have now lost all confidence in them, and give the worst construction to all they do. Held together by the slenderest ties we are ripening for a dissolution." The only solution, he argued, was a national constitutional convention "with full authority to conclude finally upon a general confederation, stating . . . beforehand explicitly the evils arising from a want of power in Congress." Only the creation of a strong national government, which could stand behind its army and support it effectively with men and materiel, could save the floundering nation.[2]

Hamilton composed his thoughts at a time when congressional leadership seemed hopelessly inept, a whole campaign season in the North had been lost for lack of troops and supplies, and the central government was all but bankrupt. He wrote at a time when a political clash was deepening between Continental officers and Congress over the issue of postwar pensions. He framed his words just a few weeks before Benedict Arnold went over to the British and within a few months of the mutinies of the Pennsylvania and New Jersey lines. Hamilton had good reasons for his despondency about the future.

Indeed, men of Hamilton's maturing nationalist persuasion fairly bristled at those who did not accept the reality of wartime conditions with the same sense of foreboding. He and other nationalists could not understand why some leaders remained so doctrinaire about the distribution of power and authority in the republic. To the nationalists, protecting liberty by emasculating Congress and keeping decision making close to the people through the state governments had set the country on a sure course to ruin. By saving Americans from centralizing British tyranny, the radical Revolutionaries had in reality formed "partial combinations subversive to the general one," argued Hamilton. They had not remembered their history, or they would have recalled that "the leagues among the old Grecian republics . . . were continually at war with each other, and for want of union fell a prey to their neighbors."[3] If the republican experiment was to have a chance, let alone become the basis for a respectable new nation, someone had to redress the imbalance in authority—and with great haste.

Hamilton's short-term solution was a constitutional convention with binding instructions. In demanding a convention, he was well ahead of the more prominent nationalist leaders of the later war years, most of whom preferred less extreme measures. In fact, the civilian nationalists, although worried, were not as pessimistic as Hamilton and many other officers. In 1780 and early 1781, they were moving into Congress in ever greater numbers. The radical Revolutionaries were losing their grip on that body. It was more than fatigue or frustration that caused the change in personnel; the rotation-in-office principle barred congressmen from serving more than three consecutive years out of six. As the radical Revolutionaries succumbed to the rotation rule and went home, a number of strong-willed nationalists entered the ranks of Congress.

Further facilitating the shift in congressional leadership was the decision of the nationalists to form three cabinetlike departments—foreign affairs, war, and finance—each headed by one official. Early in 1781, Congress offered the post of "Superintendent of Finance" to Robert Morris, the wealthy Philadelphia merchant who was also at the center of the middle states bloc and the nationalist coalition. Rotund, florid Morris had reluctantly signed the Declaration of Independence before proceeding to build a new set of non-British trading ties stretching throughout the states and into Europe. His personal wealth, certainly extensive before the war, had grown accordingly, so much so that many radical Revolutionaries despised him as the master war-profiteer of his generation. Yet they did not fight his election to the superintendency. Morris was a known financial genius. If anyone could solve the grave fiscal problems besetting the all but bankrupt nation, it was this man who has since been called the "financier" of the Revolution.[4]

In 1781 Morris was preeminent among the group of middle states nationalists. Among their goals were strong commercial ties with Europe. These had resulted in the constraining instructions which Franklin, Jay, and Adams ultimately ignored at Paris. The related issue of servicing the national debt was perhaps even more important to them. Morris's most notable ally in all such matters was Gouverneur Morris, a witty and urbane New Yorker turned Pennsylvanian, who rarely thought of the people in more flattering terms than the "rabble." No relation to Robert, Gouverneur Morris served as the former's assistant superintendent. In Congress, among the nationalists were young James Madison of Virginia, outwardly dour and gloomy and almost always dressed in black, yet a man who possessed a creative intellect, especially in political theory; James Wilson, the Scottish-born lawyer of Pennsylvania, myopic in eyesight and always capable of shrewd legal insights; James Duane, a wealthy New York lawyer-aristocrat who could be even more dismayed by the anarchical tendencies of the "common herd" than Gouverneur Morris; and Alexander Hamilton, who left the army after Yorktown, studied law, and first appeared in Congress during 1782 as a representative from New York.[5]

Duane expressed some of the nationalists' objectives early in 1781 when he explained to George Washington that "the day is at length arrived when dangers and distresses have opened the Eyes of the People and they perceive the Want of a common head to draw forth in some Just proportion the Resources of the several Branches of the federal Union." He added: "There are some political Regulations . . . I have exceedingly at heart. . . . The Principal Measures to which I allude are the Establishment of Executives . . . in the departments of Finance, War, the Marine and foreign affairs, the accomplishment of the Confederation: the procuring to Congress an augmentation of power and permanent Revenues for carrying on the War."[6]

Unlike Hamilton, Duane believed that the new nation's ills could be corrected short of a full-blown constitutional convention. Duane understood that such a convention was politically unfeasible because leaders from the sovereign states would block it, no matter how grave war-related problems were. Centralization of authority was too threatening for those fully committed to the localist protection of liberty. Like Hamilton, however, Duane knew that a national government without full and permanent powers of taxation was not worth very much fuss. Hamilton had stated the proposition this way: "The confederation too gives the power of the purse too entirely to the state legislatures. . . . That power, which holds the purse strings absolutely, must rule."[7]

Actually, Duane was prematurely optimistic in hoping that Congress might be vested with an independent source of revenue. Leading nationalists of the 1781–1783 period wanted, above all else, permanent fiscal powers lodged in Congress. They saw fixed revenues as the first element in a program designed to construct a powerful new nation, which in turn was essential from their perspective in healing the republic's many ills.

Even before Robert Morris took office, Congress had approved the Impost Plan of 1781, in the form of a constitutional amendment awarding the central government revenues from import duties of 5 percent *ad valorem* on all imports. It was a modest proposal, one that would have given Congress enough revenue to fund the national debt properly. Yet, like all proposed alterations in the Articles, the Impost Plan needed ratification by all thirteen state legislatures. Optimism should have been carefully restrained because of this fact alone.[8]

For the nationalists of 1781, permanent revenue for Congress was the essential panacea for all sorts of ills. It would end financial dependency on the less than dependable states while building up power at the center. Since Congress had only requisition rights, states facing their own financial burdens had not been enthusiastic about filling national tax quotas. Between 1777 and 1779, for instance, Congress had asked the states for nearly $100,000,000 in paper money, but had received only about half that sum. The record was even more dismal when it came to requisitions for gold and silver. During late 1780 and early 1781—the very time when the nationalists were pulling themselves together—Congress requested slightly over $10,000,000 in specie but received less than one tenth of that amount. The central government could not depend upon the states, so long as it lacked constitutional authority and political coercion.

An independent and permanent source of revenue represented more than just rebalancing power and authority between the states and the central government. As the nationalists saw it, fixed revenues would permit Congress to solve many related problems, such as supplying the Continental army properly, paying soldiers back salaries, providing the officer corps with promised postwar pensions, and meeting other civilian and foreign obligations. Such groups as the army had been faithful creditors. Loyalty to the cause was a valuable asset, but creditors on all fronts were growing more restless.

Permanent sources of revenue would also enhance prospects for securing further foreign and domestic loans, deemed essential by the nationalists in creating a stable national currency and in providing for orderly economic growth. Indeed, many nationalists envisioned the day when America would rise as an economic empire in the West, fully capable of competing with European powers. The nationalists, as men of ambition and wealth, had dreams of economic grandeur for the republic, dreams which men like Robert Morris already had started realizing in their own personal business affairs.

An alliance of men of wealth and high standing tied to and supporting the central government was essential to the achievement of these grand schemes. Personal economic involvement with the nation, instead of the states, would build an interested constituency at the core. As citizens of influence reaffirmed old or developed new financial links with the national government, they would become an effective coalition underpinning the nationalist desire for the creation of a republican nation of internal stability and international stature. "The political existence of America depends on the accomplishment of this [Impost] plan," stated Robert Morris flatly.[9]

The national government's debt—it was a product of heroic efforts to finance the war effort—took many forms, not all of equal significance to the Morris coterie. Not that important were the interest bearing notes, which Congress had circulated in 1780 to replace worthless Continental dollars at an exchange ratio of forty to one. Nor were so-called commissary or quartermaster notes, issued by army officers in the field as a form of payment for on the spot "contributions" of food and related supplies. Farmers in the path of moving armies rarely accepted these notes with grace. In some states, however, the notes, some of which bore interest, could be used for tax payments. Still, that was often little consolation for the loss of prime farm goods in exchange for fiat currency of rapidly depreciating value.

Far more central to the concerns of the nationalists were foreign and domestic loans. Specie loans from France and Dutch bankers (Spanish credit had been quite limited) had been essential in sustaining the war effort. In fact, foreign credit in hard money was vital to the republic's specie-short economy. But the prospects of foreign allies making additional loans to the postwar republic seemed slim, unless Congress met its current obligations. The nationalists did not want these future sources of hard money to dry up, and that depended upon funding foreign wartime obligations properly.

Of equal importance to the nationalists were loan-office certificates, or interest-bearing government bonds. Congress had borrowed several million dollars worth of goods and supplies during the war by issuing loan-office certificates to American merchants. These notes carried an interest rate of 6 percent. Congress lacked the means to meet these obligations, yet the certificates circulated among large merchants as a form of trading currency, although at a constantly declining value. If the central government had a permanent source of revenue and could pay interest as well as principal at face value, then businessmen controlling large quantities of the certificates stood to make a financial killing through the instant rise in market value of these notes.

Robert Morris, who was one among many nationalists buying up loan-office certificates cheaply, wanted more than bulging profits for little effort. (Obviously, he wanted profits too.) In fact, he hoped that the loan-office certificates, having an estimated market value of $11,000,000 in 1781, would stay in circulation, but at a much higher market value. The notes could then become one form of a national currency. All in all, the goal was to establish the national credit and to form a centralizing financial link with persons of wealth. Business leaders, assured of full faith in the payment of principal and interest, would be eager to invest in the republic's future. They would thus abet economic growth and the expansion of personal wealth.

The Morris coterie, while committed to national development, worried about localist responses in the states. If the localists blocked their Impost Plan, then the nationalists fully expected public creditors to turn to the states for the settlement of debts. If the states assumed national wartime obligations (a notion with considerable appeal in some circles), then the nationalists knew that their hopes for a strong union were dead—and with them any prospect for a stable social, economic, or political future. They knew that the radical Revolutionaries would argue that central governments, far removed from popular control, remained susceptible to the abuse of power, often manifested through heavy taxes favoring the few at the expense of the many. They knew that the localists would remind their constituents that the issue of taxation had widened the breach between the far distant British government and the American people. They knew that their Impost Plan was flying in the face of the first Revolutionary settlement, because the taxing power usually dictated the real location of authority among competing governments. The first Revolutionary settlement had denied the central government significant fiscal power as a logical reaction against the imperial system. But the Impost, in seeking to reverse that pattern, would "give stability to Government by combining together the interests of moneyed men for its support," as Robert Morris informed a correspondent in 1782. He went on to explain: "And consequently in this Country, a domestic debt would greatly contribute to that Union, which seems not to have been sufficiently attended to, or provided for, in forming the national compact."[10]

Morris toyed with and pushed other economic plans during his superintendency. One proposal resulted in the creation of a national bank (the Bank of North America), while another called for the assumption of all state debts by Congress. However, the most important item in the nationalist program of the early 1780s was the Impost Plan. And in the autumn of 1782 it appeared as if the nationalists were on the verge of success. Twelve states had ratified, largely on the grounds that the republic was in serious financial trouble. Only Rhode Island stood between the nationalists and their linchpin legislation. All eyes riveted on the smallest state, and optimism was running high.

Rhode Island, like the other states, had its own war debt which needed servicing. Given its shortage of land and heavy mercantile orientation, Rhode Island's leaders correctly perceived that the one prospect for meeting state obligations was through local import duties on foreign commerce. Surrendering these duties to the central government meant that Rhode Islanders would find it nearly impossible to make any significant headway against their own state debt.

The elevation of state over national interests was only one aspect of the problem. Beneath the surface were the dealings of a small band of speculating Providence merchants who were making the most of every opportunity to increase their wealth. Holding large amounts of loan-office certificates, the Providence merchants let word leak out that they would push in the state assembly for ratification of the Impost Plan (hence the wave of optimism). Their assurances carried weight because some of them were powerful assembly leaders. The effect on the securities market in Rhode Island and elsewhere was a steady rise in the value of loan-office certificates. At the same time, the market value of Rhode Island securities, as well as those of other mercantile-oriented states, began a precipitate decline as investors began to dump them at almost any price. The Providence merchants held on to their rapidly inflating national certificates to the last moment. Then in early November 1782, they sold their federal notes at the highest market value they had reached in years and quickly bought an immense number of state securities at heavily deflated prices. Next they went to the assembly and helped to insure defeat of the Impost Plan. The defeat of the Impost sent the market value of state securities soaring, securities which they now owned in excess. It was an inglorious moment in statesmanship, although glorious for the Providence speculators because they had made a double financial killing.[11]

The speaker of the Rhode Island house, rationalizing the assembly's action, pointed out, perhaps disingenuously, that the congressional plan tended to make the central government "independent of their constituents; and so the proposed impost is repugnant to the liberty of the United States."[12] But the nationalists derided such words as mere political sham. From their point of view, self-interested individuals from one state had blocked much needed financial reform; the incident seemed to be comparable to the selfish behavior of the Maryland land speculators in delaying ratification of the Articles. The beneficiaries had been self-serving localists, while the loser had been the nation (and the nationalists). For the Morris coterie, the moment had arrived for heightened confrontation. The critical question at the end of 1782 was how far the nationalists would dare to go in challenging state sovereignty and the first Revolutionary settlement.

News of Rhode Island's rejection of the Impost Plan coincided with the decision of Washington's pensive field officers at the Newburgh cantonment to pursue their drive for half-pay pensions more vigorously. Some officers had decided that new threats, perhaps even military action, might be necessary. Before the year was out, a delegation of officers carried the petition to Congress with those threatening words: "Any further experiments on their patience may have fatal effects."

The disgruntled officers and the Morris nationalists in Congress had many interests in common. The army was a national creditor, and Congress owed it back pay and pensions. The Morris group desperately wanted to build an alliance with all creditors, not permitting any creditor to become dependent upon the states. The strategy that emerged was simple. The alliance of congressional nationalists, army dissidents, and civilian public creditors would threaten the states with military coercion. The officers' petition was at the center of the scheme. If necessary, the officers would have to turn the army out into the field for a show of force. For Robert Morris, Gouverneur Morris, and Alexander Hamilton, the main congressional plotters, it was a dangerous gambit. They had decided to use intimidating words and deeds from the military, if necessary, to influence civilian decision making. As Hamilton discreetly explained the idea to Washington: "The great *desideratum* . . . is the establishment of general funds, which alone can do justice to the Creditors of the United States. . . . In this the influence of the army, properly directed, may cooperate."[13]

Hamilton directed these calculated hints of advice from Philadelphia to Newburgh in February 1783. He did so because the plot was fast thickening. A final peace settlement was just beginning to become a real possibility. If peace came and the Continental army disbanded without incident, then the leverage of military threats would be lost forever.

The greatest obstacle to the machinating Morris nationalists was Washington, who clearly understood the destructive potential of his quasi-standing army. He realized that decision making by military force was antithetical to rule by civilian law and human reason, and that the ideal of a republic would become a chimera if civilian authority succumbed to military force. Washington was clearly sympathetic to the plight of his men and personally desirous of an accretion of national authority, but he refused to countenance the plotters on ideological grounds. Rather, he waited and prepared for the crisis that he knew was coming.

For lack of alternatives, the Morris nationalists appealed to General Horatio Gates, second in command at Newburgh. Gates detested Washington, having felt for years that he deserved to be the army's head. Since earning glory as the "hero of Saratoga," Gates had fallen on evil days. His disastrous defeat at Camden in 1780, followed by his precipitate retreat from the scene of action, had resulted in his removal from command. Gates, sent home in disgrace, harbored resentment against Washington and pestered Congress about clearing his name. He also demanded a full restoration of command privileges. The beleaguered delegates, beset by so many more pressing concerns, restored Gates to active duty in 1782 and sent him to Newburgh. It was Gates, with urging from the Morris coterie, who sought to supplant Washington in March 1783.

Ostensibly, the Morris nationalists were strongly behind Gates. In reality, they were exploiting him for their own political purposes, which did not center on a military takeover but upon the threat of force against the states in favor of congressional powers of taxation. By early March, the nationalist plan was for Gates to seize command for a moment and to lead dissident units into the field. (Gates, however, was unaware of the momentary character of his assignment.) At the same time, the nationalists expected Washington, whose prestige was higher than that of any other citizen, to regain control of the army and to subdue Gates. Meantime, the mutiny, carried out in the name of financial justice to the army, would bring the states into line on the issue of a permanent revenue. It was a complex plot, and that was its real danger. No one knew where the script might end with a mutinous army in the field. If Washington failed to regain control of the army, then the prospect of a full military *coup d'état* against the very institutions which the army had been created to establish was a distinct possibility—with all sorts of unknown implications.

Washington, amply warned by the double-dealing Hamilton, personally despised Gates and carefully prepared for the attempted takeover. He brought the plot up short at the contentious officers' meeting on March 15, 1783. Washington, realizing that his officers and soldiers were "plunging themselves into a gulph of Civil horror from which there might be no receding," forced them to remember the glory of the cause.[14] A year after the conspiracy came to its climax, Thomas Jefferson reflected about Washington "that the moderation and virtue of a single character has probably prevented this revolution from being closed as most others have been by a subversion of that liberty it was intended to establish."[15]

The Newburgh Conspiracy thus passed into oblivion. Playing dangerously with the threat of military coercion, the Morris nationalists ended with virtually nothing. In the aftermath, the officers got their half-pay pensions converted into lump sum payments equivalent to five years of full salary, but there was still no federal revenue source back of that promise. The threatened congressional delegates did frame a new impost plan with a twenty-five year limit on the congressional right to levy import duties. Forwarded to the states in 1783 with little optimism, the new plan was still languishing in 1786 for lack of unanimous state support.

The nationalists, frustrated on almost all fronts and having exceeded what little congressional power there was, began drifting even among themselves before the end of 1783. The most realistic alternative seemed to be to let events lead where they might and to hope for a change in attitudes that would result in a respectable national funding and economic program at some future date. Meantime, the rotation-in-office principle began to take its toll. Even before their terms were up, Hamilton and Madison went home in disgust. Having resigned earlier, Robert Morris left the Superintendency of Finance in 1784. All that the nationalists could do for the moment was to persist in their predictions of impending disaster.

The message that lingered in 1783 was the one conveyed by George Washington. In early June, the Commander in Chief, reflecting upon his desire for a strong national edifice and for a just financial settlement for the army, sent a circular letter to the states. Washington insisted that localist-minded leaders, while defending liberty by keeping power close to the people, consider carefully whether they wanted to "be respectable and prosperous, or contemptible and miserable, as a nation." That, above everything else, remained the critical issue. The former condition, the Commander insisted, depended upon the establishment of "a Supreme Power to regulate and govern the general concerns of the Confederated republic, without which the Union cannot be of long duration." Washington begged the states to support Congress in finding a plan for discharging the national public debt honorably. He added, poignantly, that he had personally pledged himself "to the Army, that their Country would finally do them complete and ample Justice."[16]

In actual fact, the Continental army never received full compensation for services rendered in creating the nation. The down and outers in Washington's army did not fare well in the end. In 1783, however, none of them knew that matters would end that way, or the lot of virtuous civilians might have been quite different.

Events dragged on in the months surrounding Washington's circular letter. In April news of the signing of the preliminary peace articles became a matter of widespread public knowledge. Washington's soldiers, especially those who had enlisted for the duration, demanded release. Demands turned into threats of reprisals against restraining officers. Congress wanted the army fully mobilized until final peace terms were signed and all British troops had been withdrawn from American soil. Washington urged Congress to get the "duration" regulars out of camp before discipline completely broke down. Meantime, the officers insisted that the full army remain together until Congress (or anyone else for that matter) settled their financial accounts. Finally, at Washington's urgent plea, Congress furloughed the army without formal demobilization, in case the Continentals had to reassemble for action against unexpected British forays.

To add a note of symbolic confusion, an angry group of Pennsylvania Continentals marched on Philadelphia in June after being furloughed from the army. They surrounded the State House and demanded immediate financial satisfaction from Pennsylvania and from Congress. The frightened delegates, warned of the approaching columns, begged the Pennsylvania government for protection by the state militia. State officials refused. The congressional delegates, embarrassed and humiliated, filed out of the State House and walked past the armed and jeering men. The irate congressmen relocated themselves in Princeton; later they moved to Annapolis, and finally to New York City.

The national government was so powerless in June 1783 that it could not even protect itself against a small band of hostile regulars—at a time when thousands of British regulars were still on American soil. The incident said something about the national union, specifically that it was apparently so fragile and seemingly unimportant that state leaders in Pennsylvania did not even attempt to stand up against a crowd of angry soldiers for Congress's protection or survival. [17]

With the nationalists being rotated out of Congress and the central government floundering, the problems of the day blended into a kaleidoscopic array of blurring colors. No one issue dominated, but all seemed to forebode doom to leaders of nationalist temperament. They wanted to make Americans honor the terms of the Treaty of Paris; they were also deeply concerned about international relations and the search for commercial treaties. Sectional disagreements were a third worry. After 1783 it increasingly appeared as if the union was collapsing for lack of care or concern. To the nationalists, that meant that society was moving closer to total anarchy, especially since the unifying external enemy was gone.

To take one example, an important test case developed in New York over the authority of the Treaty of Paris. New York had been a gathering place for loyalists during the war because of the continued presence of the British army there. In retaliation, insurgent New York legislators confiscated huge amounts of loyalist property (as did governing bodies in other states), selling them gladly for ready cash. (Rarely did the propertyless poor benefit from these sales. The states sought quick money for funding their mounting war debts; the result was that speculators with cash bought large tracts and then sold them off at neat profits to middle-class citizens with good credit.) But Article V of the Paris treaty stipulated that Congress should recommend to the states the return of confiscated property to loyalists who had not borne arms against the United States. Article VI exempted loyalists from further prosecution and loss of property.

Alexander Hamilton and other New York nationalists supported loyalist claimants. From their perspective, they had more in common with wealthy supporters of the Crown who disdained the "rabble" than with everyday citizens of the city streets and countryside. For future social stability, it seemed more important to reconstruct an alliance of the "better sort" than to see the best families, regardless of political persuasion, overrun in the popular surge toward power and property.

It was in this setting that the case of Rutgers *v.* Waddington was litigated. New York had a Trespass Act which allowed its citizens to sue loyalists who had used rebel property during wartime. The good widow Elizabeth Rutgers had operated a brewery before the war. The loyalist Joshua Waddington took over the building and supplied His Majesty's soldiers with a steady stream of liquid refreshments. In February 1784 Widow Rutgers sought damages under the Trespass Act. Alexander Hamilton, defying popular opinion, defended Waddington. He argued that the Treaty of Paris, standing as international law and accepted as such by the Continental Congress, effectively nullified the state trespass statute. The state courts finally upheld the Treaty and recognized it as superior to New York law, but most local leaders scoffed at the decision. They were not going to let an international agreement compromise the sovereignty of New York or their right to prosecute or disenfranchise enemies of the people. [18] Rutgers *v.* Waddington had serious implications, for the Articles of Confederation stipulated that treaties were legally binding on the states. It also brought into question the new nation's good faith in implementing other portions of the Treaty.

A second point of contention was the question of prewar debts, owed largely by southern planters to English and Scottish merchants. Virginians and Marylanders may have owed their creditors as much as £2,000,000, and the Treaty of Paris called for the full settlement of all accounts—and with interest. A few honorable Virginians, such as the gentleman-lawyer George Mason, insisted that debts be paid in full. "The ministry in Great Britain and the Tories here have indeed constantly accused us of engaging in the war to avoid the payment of our just debts," wrote the displeased Mason, when all thinking people knew that the war had come, "not to avoid our just debts or to cheat our creditors; but to rescue our country from the . . . tyranny of the British government, and to secure the rights and liberties of ourselves and of our posterity." Mason forwarded his sentiments to Governor Patrick Henry in May 1783, along with the sharp warning that some Virginians were saying: " 'If we are now to pay the debts due British merchants, what have we been fighting for all this while?' " [19] Yet Henry, well-known for his many pronouncements on liberty, allied with leaders who fought the repayment of prewar debts as a matter of high principle.

Postwar discrimination against loyalists and efforts to avoid payment of prewar debts were not the only festering sores in Anglo-

American relations. Even though King and cabinet agreed to remove all troops from American soil, they maintained several regiments after 1783 in a string of forts running along the northern frontier, from central New York through the Old Northwest to the Mississippi River. According to the ministry's public statements, the troops would stay there until Americans lived up to their treaty obligations. Actually, the regiments were supporting lucrative fur-trading operations centered in Quebec. They were also protecting wartime Indian allies with whom the British had signed convenants of protection. British officials knew that the Indians were deathly afraid of the continuing wave of white encroachments upon tribal lands. The British feared that if they peremptorily closed forts and pulled the redcoats back into Canada the disgruntled northwestern Indian tribes might fall prey to American expansion, which in itself could threaten the British hold on Canada.

The presence of British troops in the Northwest, even if far removed from the western edge of white settlements, became another cause for slurs against the powerless Congress. With the Continental army permanently furloughed, there was no way that the central government could challenge Britain. All that could be hoped for was a diplomatic miracle.

Congress anxiously wanted the West cleared of all obstructions north of the Ohio River, not only because of the blatant violation of American sovereignty, but also because the West represented a possible source of permanent revenue from land sales. There were millions of fertile virgin acres between the Appalachians and the Mississippi River. That land was already in the process of becoming a national domain. During the 1780s, many of the landed states followed Virginia's lead and turned over western land claims to the central government. The western region thus represented one area in which Congress had some clear-cut authority, and it moved ahead successfully in legislating for the orderly development of the national land reserve. It was one great accomplishment of the decade which the nationalists later called the "critical period."

Congress enacted three ordinances for the West. Thomas Jefferson headed the committee that drafted the first, the Ordinance of 1784 to provide for governments in new territories. Crucial in this measure was the decision not to hold the West in perpetual colonial status but to allow future settlers the privilege of writing their own state constitutions and earning full statehood status once the population had become sufficient. The idealistic Jefferson, envisioning a new American frontier filled with prospering freehold farming families living in simple republican virtue, also fought for the inclusion of a clause forever banning chattel slavery north of the Ohio River. But that clause offended too many Southerners. Rejecting perpetual colonial status was as far as the delegates would go in 1784.

The Land Ordinance of 1785, implementing the act of the year before, provided for the orderly survey and design of settlement lines through townships of 6 miles square divided into 36 sections of 640 acres each. The smallest unit any one purchaser could buy was 640 acres, priced at $1.00 an acre. Furthermore, to help fill empty congressional coffers quickly, there were to be no purchases on credit. Since the average overcrowded eastern family did not need that much acreage for a working farm and had little hope of purchasing new land on anything but credit, the terms were not altogether advantageous, even though families could pay in depreciated public securities. Indeed, the minimum acreage provision worked against Jefferson's bucolic vision. But he was now in Europe representing Congress as its Minister to France. Congress needed revenue, something well-healed speculators could provide. Before long the central government was selling thousands of acres to influential speculators—and on credit at that. Downwardly mobile citizens once again had to wait their turn, as so many of them had done all through the period of resistance and rebellion.

Once eastern land speculators began their "purchases," they demanded that Congress tighten up provisions for popular rule in the western territories. Thus the highly acclaimed Northwest Ordinance of 1787, the last important act of a dying Congress, reversed some of the provisions in the Ordinance of 1784. Henceforth, Congress and its agents were to have greater control over local decisions through appointed territorial governors, secretaries, and judges. These officials would govern districts until enough adult male inhabitants were present for the calling of popular assemblies. Territorial assemblies were also to be subject to the vetoes of governors, which meant that speculators would have to control only the highest appointive officials.

In other provisions, Congress reduced the maximum number of states to be carved out of the Northwest from ten to five. The fear was that too many western states might someday dominate national affairs and siphon off eastern resources. However, the Ordinance of 1787 contained one clause which has given the act its celebrated stature. It specifically banned the spread of chattel slavery into the Northwest. It is possible that this provision, out of character with the antipopular tone of the document, was part of a larger northern-southern compromise being worked out at virtually the same time in the Constitutional Convention in Philadelphia. Whatever its origin, it was the most important limitation placed on the spread of the peculiar institution by the Revolutionary generation.[20]

The ordinances, despite their rejection of the concept of free or inexpensive land for a growing population of poorer people (federal western land policy changed dramatically on this point in the nineteenth century), may have been the most significant legislation emanating from the Confederation Congress. Besides erecting a barrier against the expansion of slavery, the ordinances guaranteed that Westerners would not be trapped in the bondage of permanent colonial status, as the thirteen provinces had once been in the British Empire. The right to full statehood status may have been the critical element in avoiding future repetitions of the clash that had finally befallen the British parent state and its American colonies. But the reality of the 1780s, even with the land ordinances, was that British troops controlled the Old Northwest and continued to do so well into the 1790s.

Diplomatic talks with the former parent state were leading nowhere on that aggravating point. John Adams, appointed in 1785 as the first Minister Plenipotentiary from the United States to Great Britain, gave highest priority to the resolution of the removal issue. One of his many letters to Jefferson encapsulated Adams's dilemma. He explained that "they [the ministers] rely upon our Disunion" as an excuse for avoiding serious negotiations.[21] Disunion among the thirteen sovereign states remained an undermining element everywhere.

John Adams also hoped to negotiate a general commercial treaty at the Court of St. James. His assignment was especially difficult, if not hopeless, because the states retained the right under the Articles to govern their own commercial relations. Any commercial treaty with a foreign power could not violate the prerogatives of the states to impose their own import duties and control the goods flowing in and out of their ports. Yet Adams desperately tried to fulfill his charge, specifically because of postwar trade restrictions that Great Britain had placed on the flow of American commerce. These restrictions were aggravating what in 1785 was a deepening postwar depression.

At the war's end, the new nation's economy went into a spiraling tailspin. The depression drew its biting strength from many sources. For one, the euphoria associated with the return of peace encouraged American merchants to reestablish prewar trading connections. British export houses, eagerly garnering as much of the old American trade as possible, sold their goods on extremely favorable terms.

American merchants responded with buoyant optimism, but they overestimated demand and soon found themselves overloaded with goods and with few customers.

Southern planters made poor customers because they had to settle their prewar accounts in specie. In addition they had been hard hit by losses in slave property. Some 60,000 blacks had disappeared from Virginia and South Carolina alone during the war, most carried off as confiscated property by the British army. To complicate matters, the rice and indigo crops in South Carolina were a virtual loss in 1784 and 1785 because of bad weather. Farther north, renewed tobacco production did not begin to approach prewar levels. The planter class lacked the money to buy many necessities, let alone fineries.

In the northern states, and especially in New England, the deepening depression was the result in large measure of a hotly debated decision by the British ministry, supported by Parliament, which gave the former provinces a good taste of what it was like to be outside the Navigation System. Rejecting Adam Smith's call for free trade, the ministry in 1783 issued a new set of standing Orders in Council discriminating against American trade and traders. The orders specified that American goods shipped to the English West Indies would have to be carried in British vessels. By one stroke of the pen, the Orders in Council wreaked havoc on the major New England shipbuilding industry. The orders, moreover, made it illegal for much needed imports, such as rum, molasses, and sugar, to be transported to the United States in anything but British vessels. Finally, American dairy products, cured meats, and fish were excluded from the British West Indies.

Economic chaos quickly befell New England, at least until ingenious American smugglers recaptured some of the West Indian trade. Meantime, the prices of farm products and fish fell precipitately as the market became glutted. Yeomen and fishermen, in desperate economic straits because they could not sell their products, had no money to buy the piles of British goods on the shelves of eastern merchants.

John Adams thus had been sent to England with a critical assignment. Congress wanted an end to trade discrimination, but the gritty New Englander lacked bargaining weapons. The British cabinet, as Adams explained, fully believed "the Doctrine . . . that this Country and her Commerce are so essential to the U[nited] States that they cannot exist without them, and that the States can never unite in any measures of Retaliation, nor in any Plan to encourage their own Navigation Acts."[22] At a loss for meaningful alternatives, Adams wrote home urging a concerted campaign of home manufacturing in the absence of a commercial alliance; he also called for retaliatory legislation against Great Britain and commercial treaties with other powers.

Yet the British, disdaining Adam Smith's free trade doctrines, remained good imperialists. And they did not seem worried. They had the Americans in a trap, and they were not going to let them out, especially when 75 percent of all American foreign commerce in the postwar decade was with the Empire (the total market value of British goods flowing to America in the 1783–1786 period was £8,000,000 sterling). It may have been galling, but informal economic imperialism had replaced formal political ties, at least for the time being.

The American response to the economic tailspin took a number of forms. One was to try to build up trade with other nations, particularly France. However, relations with that country had worn thin, and trade had not blossomed to the extent that wartime boosters had predicted, despite the continuing commercial alliance. American exports to France far exceeded imports in value (about $2,000,000 per year), which helped to balance the serious deficit with Great Britain. The Dutch trade also took on added significance, and there were the first outward thrusts toward China in 1784. Even though a few gained enormous personal profits from these efforts, they did not have broad-ranging economic significance or help to loosen the British grip.

To make matters worse, Spain, the unfriendly wartime ally, was still at work trying to undermine the new republic. The Spanish planned to use the lure of a commercial treaty to stifle American growth in the West, a development which the Spaniards correctly perceived as a long-run threat to their trans-Mississippi empire. The Spanish were particularly nervous about the hordes of Americans spilling over into the future states of Kentucky and Tennessee. The rough-hewn frontiersman, Daniel Boone, had opened up the "Wilderness Road" to Kentucky in 1775. By 1790, two years before statehood was gained, Kentucky's population was almost 74,000. The Tennessee territory, likewise, had started its boom with a recorded population of 36,000 in 1790.

The desire to shut off the tide of southwestward migration gave the Spaniards something in common with middle states mercantilists of the Robert Morris persuasion, who feared that the West in time would become directly competitive with the East. Also, the westward exodus could drain the reservoir of cheap and exploitable labor in eastern cities. The Spaniards tried to take full advantage of lingering

sectional mistrust by offering the middle states group trading concessions in return for a congressional agreement to closure of the Mississippi River to all American commercial traffic, a policy that the Spanish government actually put into effect in 1784.

It was this ominous controversy over sectional interests that en-
veloped John Jay after he returned from Europe and accepted appointment as Secretary of Foreign Affairs in 1784. Like many well-
bred Easterners of nationalist temperament, Jay had many prejudices
against the rude Westerners. At the same time, his extensive experience with wily European diplomats caused him to keep his guard up.
He did not want to provoke an irreconcilable division between eastern and western interests, if for no other reason than that the West
remained a potential source of permanent congressional revenue.
Within a short time, Jay was being courted by Don Diego de Gardoqui, the first Spanish Minister to the United States. The dapper,
aging Gardoqui arrived in New York fully armed with instructions to
get the American government to give up all claims to the Mississippi
River for a minimum of twenty to thirty years.

The Spanish ministry did not depend exclusively on Gardoqui's
bargaining skills. Spanish agents, circulating through the western
settlements, offered the frontiersmen of Kentucky and Tennessee access to the Mississippi as an outlet for farm products in return for
renouncing political allegiance to the republic and allying with Spain.
Indeed, some Westerners actually plotted with the Spanish agents,
but they could not get the bulk of the population to support a Catholic
regime. The western settlers feared being sold out by eastern mercantile interests, to be sure, but their prejudices against "popish" religion
counterbalanced those fears and in the end nullified the threat of an
alliance.

While the Spanish agents traveled and tempted, Gardoqui ban-
tered with Jay. The Spanish Minister finally convinced the New
Yorker that he should present a *quid pro quo* to Congress—a commercial treaty in exchange for the renunciation of navigation rights on the
Mississippi for several years. Jay did so in the summer of 1786. After a
vituperative debate, Congress, in a clearly sectional vote, agreed by a
margin of seven northern against five southern states that the negotiations should continue. Since it took the approval of nine states for
the adoption of a commercial treaty, the South held the trump card.
Jay had no choice but to break off negotiations with Gardoqui. There
was no hope for a commercial treaty with Spain on such terms.[23]

The Jay-Gardoqui negotiations infuriated Southerners and Westerners. Charles Pinckney, a wealthy South Carolinian who was

normally a nationalist-minded leader, warned his congressional colleagues in the midst of the storm that "there is one consideration, . . . that is, the impropriety of the United States ever acting
under the influence of that kind of policy which is calculated to acquire benefits for one part of the confederacy at the expense of the
other." Selling out to Spain was a dangerous threat to the union's
survival. At that very juncture, Pinckney was one among those
urging Congress to go to the states with a series of specific proposals
for strengthening the central government. But Jay's audacity, remarked the Southerner, surely would "be the means of souring the
states, and indispose them to grant us those additional powers of
government, without which we cannot exist as a nation." Pinckney
also warned that some states, so incensed by the negotiations,
might push for the total dissolution of the "feeble and inoperable"
republic.[24]

Indeed, the Jay-Gardoqui negotiations encouraged many hot-tem-
pered leaders, especially from the South, to speak lightly about the
union's future. In the mid 1780s, it was the "Old Southwest" that was
filling up with population. It seemed certain that new southwestern
states would ally themselves with the older southern states in the
future. They would be invaluable in defending the minority region,
especially if a full-scale assault on slavery ever developed. The Jay-
Gardoqui negotiations clearly threatened the South—and for commercial advantages that would benefit only the North. Yet, as one
agitated New Englander put it: "It well becomes the eastern and
middle States, who are in interest one, seriously to consider what
advantages result to them from their connection with the Southern
States. They can give us nothing, as an equivalent for the protection
which they derive from us but a participation in their commerce. . . .
Even the appearance of a union cannot in the way we now are long be
preserved."[25] A worried Virginian summarized the fears of more
cool-tempered persons by saying that he was increasingly nervous
about "gentlemen [who] talk so lightly of a separation and dissolution
of the Confederation."[26]

If the year 1780 represented the nadir of the war effort, then 1786
was the low point of the Confederation period. Disagreement, contention, and rancorousness were coming to a head. The experiment in
republicanism, in the minds of the nationalists at least, seemed to be
on the verge of death. The West was in an uproar. British troops still
occupied American territory. The government had not gained any
commercial concessions. The postwar depression had only started to
ease. Worst of all, there was serious talk about dismembering the

union, which included one plan for creating three regional confederations.

Yet all this was not enough to galvanize the nationalists into a full-scale drive for constitutional change. What brought all the nationalistic elements together, while effectively neutralizing localist opposition, was an outburst of what the nationalists described as popular convulsions from below. There were serious riots in New Hampshire, Connecticut, and Maryland during 1786, largely over straitened economic conditions. In Rhode Island, the feared specter of democratic licentiousness produced a legal popular takeover of the state and a plan of debtor relief that horrified the better sort throughout the land. Before the year was out, backcountry citizens in Massachusetts topped everyone else through an outpouring of protest and violence later known as Shays's Rebellion. The nationalists in particular, and men of property in general, speculated that the new nation's collapse was at hand, largely because the people seemed drunk with the "intoxicating Draughts of Liberty run mad."[27] The question for them now was whether the republic could be saved from itself before it was too late.

Rhode Island's financial manipulations were one pivotal instance of the turmoil. Mired in depression, debtors there naturally wanted to make paper money legal tender in the payment of debts; to creditors, it was of course anathema. The paper-money radicals swept into power in an election during the spring of 1786 and passed legislation calling for a large issue of state currency, backed only by the faith of the government—currency that was good for all personal debts. The courts were to prosecute creditors who refused to accept the new state money. For the people, burdened by depressed economic conditions and threats of property seizures, the ready supply of fiat currency was a boon. Now they could meet personal obligations by insisting that their creditors accept the rapidly depreciating state currency—and at its face value. Moreover, the Rhode Island state government could do the same to liquidate its war debt.

Creditors (many of whom were overstocked merchants heavily pressed by British mercantile firms demanding specie) were caught in the middle. They no longer could attach property with some market value as a source of hard money. Instead, they were buried by unusable paper currency.

The paper money faction knew exactly what it was doing. It was shifting the debt burden from the poor to the rich and leaving the rich high and dry. In fact, the popular faction's program represented sophisticated monetary manipulation with the social purpose of unburdening the poor. More than one desperate merchant, in panic, fled "Rogue Island," as many of them had come to call the state.

Men of property and standing throughout the country were mortified. Rhode Island's paper money law was "the most extraordinary that ever disgraced the annals of democratical tyranny," wrote an apoplectic Connecticut man. Only "the depravity of human nature" could explain "such palpable fraud and dishonesty, by a solemn Act of legislation."[28] In Rhode Island one editorialist sardonically suggested that the paper money faction should take matters to their logical extreme. He proposed the following assembly resolutions:

> And whereas, the continuation of a republican government depends upon supporting the principles of equality: Be it therefore further Enacted, That forever hereafter, at the end of thirteen years respectively there be a general abolition of debts, and an equal distribution of property.
>
> And whereas there may be some so bold and daring as to attempt the payment of debts, notwithstanding the good intentions of this General Assembly: Be it therefore Enacted, That every person offending herein, shall for every offense receive thirty-nine lashes, and be closely confined in jail for the space of six months . . . and shall moreover forfeit his proportion of property to be distributed as aforesaid.[29]

Implied in this stinging commentary was the perception that the Revolution was going to absurd democratizing extremes, that the people were abusing the power entrusted to them. They were destroying all standards and distinctions for their own selfish benefit. They lacked the stabilizing quality of virtue. The commentator did not point out, however, that the Rhode Island paper money faction may have avoided the extralegal violence and bloodshed that characterized other popular responses to the depression in other regions.

The fact that the depression was beginning to ease in 1786 did not instantaneously relieve those who had been suffering from it for more than two years. Western Massachusetts had been perhaps most severely hit. There, in the bleak year of 1786, people turned from protest to violence and rebellion in Shays's Rebellion—a second event that shook the country.

Various problems galled the farmers and laborers of western Massachusetts. In particular, the everyday folk despised being dominated politically by Easterners, whom they suspected, with some validity, of always favoring mercantile over agrarian interests. They also detested wealthy and aggrandizing creditors and their ever-present agents in their own region. By the middle of 1786 they had had enough. The immediate cause of their anger was that merchants and creditors from Boston and other seaboard communities had success-fully warded off all proposals for paper money. These same busi-nessmen also held the bulk of state wartime securities; they wanted funding at face value, and the assembly accommodated them. The effect was a virtual doubling of the state debt, since securities had been circulating in the market at little more than 50 percent of face value. It was a windfall for the speculators, many of whom were overextended merchants, but the result was higher taxes for common people in the midst of depression.

To facilitate rapid redemption of the state debt, the legislature also imposed a poll tax. Every male over the age of sixteen had to pay an equal sum into state coffers, regardless of personal financial cir-cumstances. The final straw was the stipulation that the tax had to be paid in hard money, virtually nonexistent outside commercial cen-ters. The sum total effect was to force farmers and day laborers to pay increased taxes in specie for the benefit of the mercantile class as the depression was hitting bottom.

Backcountry merchants and lawyers, seemingly out looking for trouble, only exacerbated matters by following the traditional practice of having real and personal property attached by county courts when citizens desperately in debt could not satisfy public or private obliga-tions. Many of them hoped to profit in buying up attached property at court-ordered auctions. When sales of property did not cover debts or court fees, some judges adhered to the witless custom of throwing debtors in prison until they could find the money to settle ac-counts—certainly difficult to do from jail cells By mid 1786, more and more sturdy yeomen had lost their holdings and taken on the appear-ance of "sturdy beggars"; sheriffs and tax collectors held an increas-ing number of public auctions and let property go for ridiculously low prices. The poor struggled while the well-to-do solidified their finan-cial standing.

Conditions had reached the diametric opposite from those prevail-ing in Rhode Island. In Massachusetts there was no prospect of a large legal tender paper money issue; nor was there any likelihood of a "stay law," suspending the payment of outstanding personal debts until economic conditions improved. Connecticut, Delaware, and Virginia already had stay laws on the books, significantly lessening the threat of political turmoil. But Massachusetts was not dem-onstrating any more imagination in meeting urgent problems than the British government had shown two decades before.

At first, western Bay State freemen responded by working through regular channels and by employing legitimate forms of protest. Pleas for tax relief, stay laws, and an end to property foreclosures and the practice of sending debtors to prison filled petitions sent to Boston by special county conventions. The conventioneers also complained bitterly about the excessive legal fees of pettifogging attorneys, as well as about heavy court costs. The backcountry settlers made their position ominously clear in their petitions to the assembly. As one exasperated petitioner put it, "the placemen, the pensioners, and above all that aristocratical people too generally prevalent among the wealthy men of the state" had plotted among themselves to force honest, plain people to "follow the example of the oppressed Irish and live wholly on potatoes and skimmed milk."[30]

Some hotheaded Westerners, sensing that petitioning was a waste of time, helped to heighten the mood of confrontation by resorting to direct intimidation and selective acts of violence. At the end of August 1786, over a thousand angry farmers descended upon the town of Northampton on the Connecticut River and prevented judges from holding court. For a time the county courts—the symbols of governmental oppression—remained the primary targets of organized crowd resistance in defense of local community and personal economic needs.

State leaders in Boston, following phlegmatic Governor James Bowdoin, at first sought to check what they perceived as a dangerous pattern of potential insurgency by legislation bringing tax relief; but the word did not spread fast enough. Farmers and laborers kept ravaging the courts, and the gentlemen of Boston began to suspect that British agents were stirring up the trouble. Bowdoin and others had nightmares of roving hordes of bumpkins sweeping down upon Boston, destroying property, raping wives, and mutilating children. Fears of anarchy produced virtual panic and a public subscription of £5,000 for the formation of an "eastern" army commissioned to give the "rebels" a strong dose of military medicine.

The insurrection came to a head when an estimated 1,200 backcountry settlers under Captain Daniel Shays, a Continental army officer who had returned to his farm only to fall heavily into debt, tried to seize a cache of arms at the federal arsenal in Springfield during late January 1787. The besieged defenders attempted to scare off Shays's followers without bloodshed. Not dissuaded, the Shaysites, who had few arms, kept closing in until the pressed commander opened up with cannon fire; four insurgents fell to the ground mortally wounded while the remainder retreated in complete disarray. Two weeks later, the eastern army under the former Continental general, Benjamin Lincoln, caught up with the bedraggled, hungry

Shaysite forces at Petersham. Hardly a shot was fired as the insurgents fled into the woods with the subscription army in hot pursuit. Popular resistance all but collapsed at that point. It ultimately ended with promises of amnesty and further tax relief.

Shays's Rebellion did not result in much destruction of property or loss of life. Backcountry citizens were simply defending their property, personal possessions, and human integrity. Intimidating violence had a clear social purpose—the protection of local community interests. As events mushroomed, the movement became better organized, only to be shattered by superior military force. It was ultimately an extralegal and anti-institutional movement, to be sure, but its legitimacy rested on the issues that the rebels had tried to redress. Most of the grievances had lost their force by the summer of 1787 with the improvement of economic conditions and extended tax relief from the assembly. In the end, the insurrection had finite and fixed limits—in Massachusetts. The most important result was its impact on the country at large.

For leaders of radical Revolutionary persuasion, Shays's Rebellion was not dangerously foreboding. Thomas Jefferson, receiving numerous reports in France, concluded: "The commotions which have taken place in America . . . offer nothing threatening. They are a proof that the people have liberty enough, and I would not wish them less than they have." Jefferson further elaborated: "If the happiness of the mass of the people can be secured at the expense of a little tempest now and then, or even of a little blood, it will be a precious purchase. . . . Let common sense and common honesty have fair play and they will soon set things to rights."[31] Indeed, many of the Shaysites saw themselves as continuing the defense of liberty against tyranny, but this time against their own government corrupted by eastern monied interests. The scenario was essentially the same as it had been two decades before; only the characters had changed. If the government was hopelessly oppressive, then the people had the right to replace it—if such an extreme act was necessary.

While some radical Revolutionaries may have accepted such tenets with philosophical detachment, revealing their continued faith in the virtue of the people, events in Massachusetts appalled and frightened the nationalists. From their point of view, it was not a question of protecting liberty, rather of abusing it in attacking not only property rights, but the very foundations of a stable society. To them, the Shaysites and their kind were desperadoes, certainly worse than the filching Rhode Island paper money faction. What it all boiled down to was that virtue had succumbed to democratic licentiousness. If some nationalists seemed certain about anything late in 1786, it was the belief that all of their dire predictions seemed at last to be coming true.

Henry Knox, Washington's former chief of artillery, who became Secretary of War in 1785, was in Massachusetts during the fall of 1786 and reported details in apoplectic language to some of his former army associates. Knox wrote to Washington that "their creed is, that the property of the United States has been protected from the confiscation of Britain by the joint exertions of *all,* and therefore ought to be the *common property* of all." Knox seemed to be overcome by trepidation about the future. "We imagined . . . that we were not as other nations requiring brutal force to support the laws," he confided to Washington, "but we find that we are men, actual men, possessing all the turbulent passions belonging to that animal and that we must have a government proper and adequate for them."[32]

Knox's commentary arrived at Mount Vernon like a thunderbolt. "Good God! Who, besides a tory could have foreseen, or a Briton predicted" such a state of affairs, Washington replied. "There are combustibles in every State, which a spark might set fire to." All the former commander could pray for was "a prompt disposition to support, and give energy to the federal System . . . if the unlucky stirring of the dispute respecting the navigation of the Mississippi does not become a leaven that will ferment, and sour the mind of it." After musing on a whole host of agonizing problems, Washington summarized his feelings pointedly: "If the [national] powers are inadequate, amend or alter them but do not let us sink into the lowest state of humiliation and contempt, and become a byword in all the earth."[33]

Washington's and Knox's commentaries, reflecting visions of anarchy which spurred their desire to strengthen the central government, are representative samples of nationalist perceptions at the end of 1786. To the nationalists, the republican world had lost its sense of reason. "A spirit of licentiousness" was ravaging the land, claimed John Jay, as he described the disease that had "infected Massachusetts."[34] The people, unchecked by proper governmental structures, had turned into agents of chaos. While monarchs were always capable of tyranny from above, the people now were convulsing society from below. Liberty was once again at stake. "Anarchy, if I may use the term, or rather worse than anarchy . . . pure democracy" was enervating the experiment in republicanism, stated Charles Pinckney.[35] The ultimate danger was that demagogues would emerge out of the chaos, seize all power for themselves, and force everyone into a state of abject political slavery. As John Jay noted: "If faction should long bear down law and government, tyranny may raise its head, or the more sober part of the people may even think of a king."[36]

The nationalists had always been doubtful about virtue as a possible stabilizing force in government and society. They preferred structural restraints more characteristic of the abandoned British political order. The first Revolutionary settlement had not provided for balanced governments, they had often insisted. To compound problems, the central government lacked the means to check licentiousness from below, should the state governments fail to appease popular fury. Henry Knox, for example, had pushed Congress to raise a national military force for use against the Shaysites on the assumption that the Massachusetts government might not be able to protect itself. But the shortage of revenue to pay soldiers had aborted that plan. Congress even lacked the ability to support the sovereign states when they were in deep trouble and wanted assistance. A government so helpless was useless, the nationalists reasoned. It had to be strengthened or the republican experiment would have to be abandoned as hopeless.

Thus the nationalists, unable for several years to unite successfully in achieving their ends, began to prepare for their final assault on the first Revolutionary settlement. The new drive carried forward out of old fears and ideas sparked by the turmoil of Shays's Rebellion. It was fueled by the weight of so many other nagging problems. The goal was still the creation of a central government with authority to govern and to provide for a stable future—a government that would tie together the worthy and the wealthy, the wise and the talented, and protect the people from themselves through enlightened public policy. The "worthy," as the nationalists described themselves and their efforts, had to regain the right to rule in stewardship over the "licentious."[37]

Even before Shays's Rebellion had reached its crescendo, a convention of delegates from the middle states—all the states were invited but only representatives from New York, New Jersey, Pennsylvania, Delaware, and Virginia attended—gathered at Annapolis, in mid September 1786. Their charge was to consider a number of pressing interstate commercial issues. But the delegates, among them Alexander Hamilton, John Dickinson, and James Madison, did not proceed with the agenda since the turnout was so small. Rather, they fell to complaining about the times. Hamilton accepted the task of writing a report which went far beyond particular commercial disputes. It referred to "important defects in the system of the Federal Government" and called for "a Convention of deputies from the different States, for the special and sole purpose of . . . digesting a plan for supplying such defects as may be discovered to exist" in the Articles of Confederation.[38] The Annapolis delegates quickly disbanded after endorsing Hamilton's words and urging Congress and the state governments to implement their recommendations.

Had it not been for all of the turmoil that autumn and winter, the Annapolis Convention's proposals might simply have collected dust. But there were now even many antinationalists who, still wanting to preserve authority close to the people, had been temporarily thrown off balance by the course of events. Samuel Adams was so upset about the Shaysites that he viewed the attack upon Massachusetts government as fully treasonable. "In monarchies the crime of treason and rebellion may admit of being pardoned or lightly punished," penned the aging radical, "but the man who dares to rebel against the laws of a republic ought to suffer death."[39] Richard Henry Lee, like his northern counterpart, a known defender of popular rule so long as it was in good order, said even before Shays's uprising that liberty always hung in the balance "without *virtue* in the people."[40]

The dismay and temporary doubt in the antinationalist camp was crucial. Localist-minded leaders had for years battled against the nationalists and their desire for a stronger central government. Now the full impact of the turmoil had raised some doubts which, however temporary, gave the initiative to their opponents. The nationalists vigorously pursued the goal of a national constitutional convention as the winter of 1786–1787 turned into spring. The antinationalists, later labeled Antifederalists, did slowly regain their equilibrium. Within time they tried to halt the nationalist surge, but they never recaptured the initiative.

In late 1786, a Vermonter, Samuel Ellsworth, prepared a pamphlet entitled *There Shall be Wars and Rumors of War before the Last Day Cometh: Solemn Predictions of Future Events Plainly Manifested by the Planets.* Ellsworth claimed that 1787 would be "troubled by intestine jars, and domestic quarrels, and contentions of every kind" because of "the malign influence of these eclipses" of the moon. The eclipse in January 1787 was to be the worst: "It will have much influence on men's tempers and dispositions. . . . Great tumults and contentions will arise [and] . . . several parts of America will suffer great disorders."[41] Dire prognostications indeed!

Many took Ellsworth's predictions seriously. We may accept them as a metaphor for the times. The nationalists had for years been forecasting doom, although not because of the movements of the planets. Rather, they insisted that the first Revolutionary settlement had been too trusting of the masses. For them, at least, their prophecies now had a self-fulfilling quality. They were already preparing for further change when the moribund Congress finally reacted affirmatively to the recommendations from Annapolis. Even before Congress acted, some states had started naming delegates to the proposed constitutional convention. Although dominated by men of localistic feelings in early 1787, Congress gave in during late February and admitted that "experience has evinced that there are defects in the present confederation." Accordingly, the delegates conceded that a convention should assemble in Philadelphia beginning in May "for *the sole and express purpose* of revising the Articles of Confederation" and to "render the federal Constitution adequate to the exigencies of Government and the preservation of the Union."[42] Not to be outdone by their opponents this time, the nationalists were already hard at work to make certain that men of their persuasion would dominate the convention. To them, it was the last chance to restabilize the republican universe.

Notes

1. To James Duane, September 3, 1780, *The Papers of Alexander Hamilton* (ed. H. C. Syrett *et al.*, New York, 1961 to date), II, 407, 417.

2. *Ibid.*, II, 406–407.

3. *Ibid.*, 403. On Hamilton's life, consult John C. Miller, *Alexander Hamilton: Portrait in Paradox* (New York, 1959); Broadus Mitchell, *Alexander Hamilton* (3 vols., New York, 1957–1970); Gerald Stourzh, *Alexander Hamilton and the Idea of Republican Government* (Stanford, Cal., 1970); and James Thomas Flexner, *The Young Hamilton: A Biography* (Boston, 1978).

4. E. James Ferguson, "The Nationalists of 1781–1783 and the Economic Interpretation of the Constitution," *Journal of American History*, 56 (1969), 241–261; Jensen, *The New Nation*, 54–67; and Clarence L. Ver Steeg, *Robert Morris: Revolutionary Financier* (Philadelphia, 1954), *passim*.

5. Ferguson, *Power of the Purse*, 109–124; McDonald, *E Pluribus Unum*, 1–32; and Henderson, *Party Politics*, 246–317. See also the materials cited in note four above.

6. January 29, 1781, Burnett, ed., *Letters*, V, 551.

7. To James Duane, September 3, 1780, Syrett, ed., *Papers of Hamilton*, II, 404.

8. For the draft text of the Impost Plan, presented in Congress on January 31, 1781, Ford, ed., *Journals of the Continental Congress*, XIX, 102–103.

9. To Nathaniel Appleton, April 16, 1782, Wharton, ed., *Revolutionary Diplomatic Correspondence*, V, 311.

10. A Report to the President of Congress, July 29, 1782, Ford, ed., *Journals*

of the Continental Congress, XXII, 432. On the debt, see Ferguson, *Power of the Purse,* 25–69.

11. For a description of this incident, see McDonald, *E Pluribus Unum,* 20–22. Emphasizing the states rights' thrust is Irwin H. Polishook, *Rhode Island and the Union, 1774–1795* (Evanston, Ill., 1969), 53–80.

12. From William Bradford, November 30, 1782, Ford, ed., *Journals of the Continental Congress,* XXIII, 788–789.

13. February 13, 1783, Syrett, ed., *Papers of Hamilton,* III, 253–255.

14. Washington to Alexander Hamilton, March 12, 1783, *ibid.,* III, 287.

15. To Washington, April 16, 1784, Boyd, ed., *Papers of Jefferson,* VII, 106–107. See also note one in Chapter V, for important secondary sources.

16. Dated June 8, 1783, *The Writings of George Washington* (39 vols., ed. J. C. Fitzpatrick, Washington, 1931–1944), XXVI, 483–496.

17. See Hamilton to George Clinton, June 29, 1783, and Hamilton to James Madison, June 29, 1783, Syrett, ed., *Papers of Hamilton,* III, 407–409. For the broader context, consult Davis, *Sectionalism in American Politics,* 49–75. On postwar politics in New York, see Jackson Turner Main, *Political Parties before the Constitution* (Chapel Hill, N.C., 1973), 120–155.

18. Jensen, *The New Nation,* 265–277. See also Hamilton's two letters from "Phocion," dated January and April 1784, Syrett, ed., *Papers of Hamilton,* III 483–497, and 530–558.

19. May 6, 1783, Kate Mason Rowland, *The Life of George Mason, 1725–1792* (2 vols., New York, 1892), II, 44–47. On Virginia politics, consult Main, *Political Parties,* 244–267.

20. For the 1784 Ordinance, see minutes of April 23, 1784, Ford, ed., *Journals of the Continental Congress,* XXVI, 275–279; 1785 Ordinance, minutes of May 20, 1785, *ibid.,* XXVIII, 375–386; 1787 Ordinance, minutes July 13, 1787, *ibid.,* XXXII, 334–343. See also Jensen, *The New Nation,* 350–359. On the Virginia cession, consult Peter Onuf, "Toward Federalism: Virginia, Congress, and the Western Lands," *William and Mary Quarterly,* 3rd Ser., 34 (1977), 353–374. For possible links between the national constitution makers and those in Congress preparing the 1787 Ordinance, see Staughton Lynd, "The Compromise of 1787," *Class Conflict,* 185–213.

21. November 5, 1785, *The Adams-Jefferson Letters: The Complete Correspondence between Thomas Jefferson and Abigail and John Adams* (2 vols., ed. L. J. Cappon, Chapel Hill, N.C., 1959), I, 93.

22. To Thomas Jefferson, November 1, 1785, *ibid.,* I, 88. For more details, see Frederick W. Marks III, *Independence on Trial: Foreign Affairs and the Making of the Constitution* (Baton Rouge, La., 1973), 52–95.

23. Jensen, *The New Nation,* 154–176; Henderson, *Party Politics,* 387–400; Davis, *Sectionalism in American Politics,* 109–126.

24. Speech before Congress, August 16, 1786, *Colonies to Nation, 1763–1789: A Documentary History of the American Revolution* (ed. J. P. Greene, New York, 1967), 475–480.

25. Theodore Sedgwick to Caleb Strong, August 6, 1786, Burnett, ed., *Letters,* VIII, 415–416.

26. Henry Lee in debates, minutes of August 18, 1786, *ibid.,* VIII, 439.

27. Charles Pettit to Jeremiah Wadsworth, May 27, 1786, Burnett, ed., *Letters,* VIII, 330.

28. *United States Chronicle,* June 1, 1786, quoted in John P. Kaminski, "Democracy Run Rampant: Rhode Island in the Confederation," Martin, ed., *The Human Dimensions of Nation Making,* 253.

29. *Providence Gazette,* January 6, 1787, quoted in *ibid.,* 261–262. Besides Kaminski's essay, see also Polishook, *Rhode Island and the Union,* 103–162.

30. George Brock, "Address to the Yeomanry of Massachusetts," quoted in Marion L. Starkey, *A Little Rebellion* (New York, 1955), 18. On Massachusetts politics, see Van Beck Hall, *Politics Without Parties: Massachusetts, 1780–1791* (Pittsburgh, Pa., 1972), 190–255, and Main, *Political Parties,* 83–119. An overview of continuing backcountry turmoil, even predating the war years, is contained in Robert J. Taylor, *Western Massachusetts in the Revolution* (Providence, R.I., 1954), *passim.*

31. To Ezra Stiles, December 24, 1786, Boyd, ed., *Papers of Jefferson,* X, 629.

32. October 23, 1786, quoted in Robert Arnold Feer, "Shays's Rebellion" (doctoral dissertation, Harvard University, 1958), 102, 472.

33. December 26, 1786, Fitzpatrick, ed., *Writings of Washington,* XXIX, 121–125.

34. To Thomas Jefferson, October 27, 1786, *The Correspondence and Public Papers of John Jay* (4 vols., ed. H. P. Johnston, 1890–1893), III, 212.

35. Speech before the New Jersey Assembly, March 13, 1786, Burnett, ed., *Letters,* VIII, 328.

36. To Thomas Jefferson, October 27, 1786, Johnston, ed., *Correspondence of Jay,* III, 213.

37. John Dickinson, "Letters of Fabius," V, published in 1788, reduced the struggle to these terms. See *Pamphlets on the Constitution of the United States* (ed. P. L. Ford, Brooklyn, N.Y., 1888), 188. Consult also Wood, *Creation of the American Republic,* 471–518.

38. Annapolis Convention report, dated September 14, 1786, Ford, ed., *Journals of the Continental Congress,* XXXI, 677–680.

39. Quoted in William V. Wells, *The Life and Public Services of Samuel Adams,* III (Boston, 1865), 246.

40. To Martin Pickett, March 5, 1786, Ballagh, ed., *Letters of Richard Henry Lee,* II, 411.

41. Pamphlet published in Bennington, 1787. I am indebted to David Szatmary for this citation.

42. February 21, 1787, Ford, ed., *Journals of the Continental Congress,* XXXII, 73–74. (Italics mine)

IX

A Final Revolutionary Settlement

"The evils we experience flow from the excess of democracy," stated a disturbed Elbridge Gerry of Massachusetts. "The people do not want virtue; but are the dupes of pretended patriots," he explained to his fellow delegates at an early session of the Constitutional Convention in Philadelphia.[1] The merchant from Massachusetts had conveyed two essential thoughts. First, the convention had to find the means to check popular influences in government. Second, the people, although not necessarily at fault for disturbances like Shays's Rebellion, were inherently virtuous but still could be led astray by self-serving demagogues. Indeed, Gerry had suggested that the republican experiment could survive and flourish for ages to come, if only his fellow delegates could find the proper formula for reconciling liberty with authority.

The vast majority of the leaders who assembled in Philadelphia during May 1787 agreed with Gerry. They looked back over recent events with horror; they wanted to look forward with hope. On the surface these national constitution makers were a diverse lot. A few were quite young, such as James Madison and Alexander Hamilton, both in their thirties; some were aged, such as the octogenerian Benjamin Franklin; most were passing beyond their middle years, such as George Washington, Robert Morris, and John Dickinson. They were not sent from heaven, as some commentators have implied; rather, they ostensibly came as representatives from the states. Only a hand-ful of them were localists. Of the fifty-five men who attended the convention during its three and a half months of deliberations, thirty-nine had at one time or another served in Congress; twenty-one were former Continental army officers. Their focus on problems no doubt reflected the national orientation of their previous office-holding experiences.[2]

Initially, twelve state legislatures (Rhode Island ignored the call of Congress) selected a total of seventy-four delegates to go to Philadel-phia. Some begged off. A few like Patrick Henry smelled a rat, as he put it, and refused appointment. During the spring of 1787, Samuel Adams lacked the political weight in Massachusetts that was neces-sary for election. Richard Henry Lee, although named to the Virginia delegation, did not attend because he was already serving in Con-gress, which was then meeting in New York. Participating in both bodies at once, he believed, could result in a direct conflict of interest. Thomas Jefferson and John Adams were on diplomatic assignments. (One wonders how Jefferson would have acted had he been there, given his unfailing defense of the people's liberties.)

As it turned out, then, the nationalists were clearly dominant. Among those in attendance were Washington, Franklin, Madison, Hamilton, Robert Morris, Gouverneur Morris, John Dickinson, Charles Pinckney, and James Wilson. Most of them played critical roles. Washington, as the convention's president, sat patiently through agonizing hours of debate. He rarely participated but lent an aura of legitimacy by his presence. The former Commander had al-ready been virtually deified by the populace as the Revolution's single hero. Franklin, the shrewd diplomatic tactician, also avoided exten-sive debating; he accepted his status as elder statesman and delicately smoothed over vexing disagreements among haggard and quarrel-some delegates. Madison, the diligent student of history and political theory, carefully prepared himself ahead of time. While waiting in Philadelphia for the convention's formal opening, he worked with other members of the Virginia delegation, particularly Governor Ed-mund Randolph, to frame a plan calling for fundamental change. This effort assured that the delegates would not drift or lose interest at the outset for lack of alternatives. Gouverneur Morris, although erratic and raucous, contributed his facile language skills and prepared many of the Constitution's final passages.

Of those who attended, there were a few dissidents, clearly out of step with the dominating nationalists. Typical was Luther Martin of

Maryland, a schoolteacher turned lawyer who had developed a reputation for his large drinking capacity. Martin spoke rarely, but when
he did his words came out as huge gusts of wind. Few objected when
Martin gave up and left the convention in complete disgust over the
proceedings. Less noisome were John Lansing and Robert Yates of
New York, antinationalists of local political standing. They expected
the worst, especially from the other New York representative, Alexander Hamilton, and soon saw that their fears were confirmed. They
eventually left the convention, but that did not enhance Hamilton's
influence as the remaining New York delegate. He even questioned
his own standing as a spokesman for his state, since his political
views were directly opposed to those of the localist faction then
dominating New York. Hamilton, thinking that he was cutting a poor
figure, came and went and contributed little to the discussions.

Generally, the delegates, whether nationalists or antinationalists,
were not representative of the people, socially or economically. There
were no freehold farmers, artisans, or day laborers among their numbers. On the contrary, the delegates were by and large men of wealth,
high social standing, and extensive formal education. A few had
moved far beyond humble family economic origins. As merchants,
lawyers, and slaveholding planters, they owned vast amounts of personal property. Many were public creditors. Of the fifty-five delegates, some thirty held significant amounts of federal public securities. Thus the creation of a fiscally solvent national government capable of paying off the national debt could potentially reward these
men with handsome monetary profits.[3]

Personal economic gain, however, represents far too narrow a basis
to explain why these delegates gathered in Philadelphia. That factor
may have lurked in the background, as did the question of protecting
property against paper money, legal tender, and debt stay laws,
comprehended by the nationalists in images of anarchy associated
with convulsive incidents like Shays's Rebellion. The desire to protect
property was an important motivating factor, but only in the context
of frustrations caused by the imbalance of authority between the
states and the central government. Through the years, the nationalists had been hampered at every turn, whether in funding the national debt, securing commercial treaties, honoring the peace treaty,
or removing British troops from American soil. Everything seemed to
be destroying the union—and their personal property and standing
with it. Constitution making gave them an opportunity to release
pent-up frustrations because they now had the opportunity to redis-
tribute power and authority in the republic.[4]

Recent events, threatening on so many fronts, epitomized what was wrong. But events alone do not fully explain why the nationalists often thought that the Confederation was on the brink of ruin. Elbridge Gerry captured the essence of the answer when he exclaimed about an "excess of democracy" and the people as "dupes of pretended patriots." An essential tenet of the political theory of the time was that liberty could be destroyed from below as well as from above, by self-serving commoners as well as by willful monarchs. The mixed government of the British constitution balanced social orders in the branches of government. In contrast, the first Revolutionary settlement (at least as the nationalists viewed it) had been unstabilizing because it placed too much trust in a virtuous citizenry. The nationalists were not surprised when they found evidence that public virtue had failed as a substitute balancing mechanism. They were simply collecting materials which proved what many of them (at least among the reluctant Revolutionaries) had believed even before 1776. From the outset, they had been afraid of overbearing popular influences and potential "democratic licentiousness," now fully manifested in social anarchy. For them, events preceding 1776 had been repeated, but this time liberty was threatened from within the republic by petty demagogues and from the people instead of the king and his ministerial sycophants. "We have been guarding against an evil that old States are most liable to, *excess of power* in the rulers," Benjamin Franklin pointed out after the convention, "but our present danger seems to be *defect of obedience* in the subjects."[5]

Even before the rumblings that erupted into Shays's Rebellion, George Washington had written anxiously: *"We have, probably, had too good an opinion of human nature in forming our confederation.* Experience has taught us, that men will not adopt, and carry into execution, measures the best calculated for their own good, without the intervention of a coercive power." The sage of Mount Vernon did not "conceive" how the country could "exist long as a nation, without having lodged somewhere a power which will pervade the whole Union."[6] Despite his repeated reluctance to leave his beloved plantation again, Washington went to Philadelphia to help create a structural edifice with stabilizing authority, one capable of checking the people and their excesses.

The republican Commander was responding to the pessimistic prophecies of John Jay, who had written him that "the mass of men are neither wise nor good, and the virtue like the resources of a country, can only be drawn to a point and exerted by strong circumstances ably managed, or a strong government ably administered."[7] In his choice of words, Jay had plucked the two major strings in the nationalist bow. But one string was less taut than the other. Whether or not citizens were virtuous was less critical a question than whether able, disinterested leaders controlled decision making on all levels of government. Without high-minded leadership, it was folly to hope for enlightened public policy or political stability, since self-interested leaders could always find the means to incite the commonalty for petty ends.

Jay's assumptions related to the central maxim about the corrupting influence of power. The nationalists never doubted that power had the most debilitating effect upon human behavior. They thought that the radical Revolutionaries had been hopelessly naive in placing so much legislative faith in the people. Their opponents had erred in trusting popular judgments without providing for appropriate structural restraints. In 1778, for example, the South Carolina physician David Ramsay had asserted: "It is the happiness of our present [state] constitution, that all offices lie open to *men of merit*, of whatever rank or condition; and that even the reins of state may be held by the *son of the poorest man*, if *possessed of abilities* equal to the important station."[8] Ramsay's qualifying words were the most significant ones. It was not only that Revolutionary offices were to be open to a wider range; it was also necessary that officeholders had to have the appropriate qualifications. Regardless of origin, they had to be men of demonstrated ability and talent.

But the Revolutionary spirit had led to extremes. The people had not been careful enough. Men of proved wisdom and merit had not maintained control in the state governments. Rather, designing demagogues had risen to power, men who had irresponsibly "duped" the people for the sake of personal gain. "A set of unprincipled men, who sacrifice everything to their popularity and private views," claimed a concerned North Carolinian in 1783, "seem to have acquired too much influence in all our Assemblies."[9] John Dickinson expressed it as bluntly a few years later: "For the *government will partake of the qualities of those whose authority is prevalent*," he explained. Governments were intended not only for "the happiness of the people," but also for "the protection of the worthy against those of contrary characters," Dickinson elaborated, the sum total of which added up to "the general welfare." The vexing problem remained that governments had to be "secured, as well as can be, from the undue influence of passions either in the people or their servants."[10]

The first Revolutionary settlement, nationalist partisans asserted, had unleashed a torrent of uncontrollable passions. The only hope lay in circumventing the Confederation's misguided emphasis upon state sovereignty. The future of the republic depended upon bold action, since the democratic hedonism of the masses would inexorably swing in cyclical fashion toward tyranny. The ultimate legacy of chaos and anarchy, stated John Jay, was that "the charms of liberty will daily fade," even in "the minds of the rational and well-intended."[11] For the sake of stability, then, citizens would deliver up their rights to a tyrant—and all that the Revolution had tried to achieve would be lost.

Thus the nationalists who gathered in Philadelphia viewed their task as much broader than the protection or expansion of their property. They were trying to contain popular anarchy (admittedly a threat to their property), which could so easily spill over into tyranny, whether in demagogic or monarchical forms. They viewed their task as finding the constitutional means for saving the people from *themselves*. That depended upon establishing a structure of government capable, among other things, of sustaining enlightened leadership by men of wisdom and talent who, once in office, would have the untrammeled authority necessary for constructing intelligent public policy.

At its core the nationalist world view was both hierarchical and deferential. It was fully rooted in the premodern attitudes of the age, although it was certainly modified by the ingredients of republicanism, which reflected the decreasing willingness of citizens, as the rebellion had flowered, to defer in matters of state to their socioeconomic "superiors." The nationalists viewed themselves as natural rather than artificial aristocrats, as men who had proved themselves rather than having been born into a hereditary leadership caste. Yet they had the feeling that they had been pushed aside, and their frustrations had been immense, arising logically from their bifurcated placement in the Revolutionary order of things. Although men of exalted socioeconomic standing, they lacked comparable political power, which they assumed was their natural heritage as established socioeconomic stewards. They continued presuming that social stability depended upon an indivisible relationship between the leaders and the led in state and society, whether in monarchical or republican systems. The problem, they believed, was that the first Revolutionary settlement had weakened that relationship, leaving confusion and a harvest of anarchy in its wake. The wrong men had got into power, and the republican order was suffering its death throes because of democratic and demagogic excesses.

The convention was supposed to open on May 14, 1787, yet not enough delegates had appeared by the appointed date. The convention finally got started on May 25, and George Washington modestly accepted a unanimous invitation to take the president's chair. Next, a committee mapped out rules of procedure, including a decision to keep all deliberations secret. The delegates did not want to confuse the public with contradictory daily reports, especially if they altered early decisions later on in their proceedings. Moreover, they wanted complete frankness in debates. Some nationalist delegates preferred the veil of secrecy to prevent public pressure against their plan to go far beyond their instructions and to create a new government.

The crucial moment arrived once procedural questions were disposed of and it was agreed that each state delegation should have one vote (the states were to remain equal at least through the convention). On Tuesday, May 29, energetic Edmund Randolph rose from his chair and explained the outline of a new plan of government. Although a few delegates murmured in surprise, the presentation was not totally unexpected. James Madison and other members of the Virginia delegation had not hidden their preconvention caucusing. Madison was the principal author of the so-called "Virginia Plan," which Randolph was now presenting. As the Governor spoke, those who had thoughts of a brief series of meetings devoted to strengthening the powers of Congress under the Confederation no doubt were recalculating. It would take the Convention three and a half months to complete the deliberations that had finally begun, months characterized by strident debate and flaring tempers during an unusually warm summer.

The debate over the Virginia Plan went on for the next two weeks, and it helped to precipitate one of three major crises that the convention would experience. In presenting the plan, Randolph urged boldness upon the delegates. The Virginians recommended a three-tiered structure of government, including a bicameral legislature and a national executive. The lower house was "to be elected by the people of the several states," while the upper house was "to be elected by those of the first, out of a proper number of persons nominated by the individual [state] Legislatures." In turn, the national executive was to be selected by a full session of the new national legislature. The plan also called for a national judiciary, which, besides regular judicial assignments, would have the power, in conjunction with the executive, to veto legislation. Not only would the national legislature "enjoy the . . . Rights vested in Congress by the Confederation"; it could also "legislate in all cases to which the separate States are incompetent, or in which the harmony of the United

States may be interrupted by the exercise of individual Legislation." The Virginia Plan left no doubt that its proposed new national government would be sovereign over the states. It did not enumerate specific powers, but the national legislature was to have the authority "to negative all laws passed by the several States, contravening in the opinion of the National Legislature the articles of Union."[12]

Governor Randolph, while detailing the plan, entreated the delegates "not to suffer the present opportunity of establishing general peace, harmony, happiness and liberty in the U.S. to pass away unimproved."[13] By and large, the convention reacted favorably. It resolved itself into a committee of the whole to discuss the plan in more detail. James Madison's preconvention strategy was succeeding. The delegates were contemplating much more than putting new wine into an old constitutional bottle.

Madison and his supporters carried the day only because a clear majority of the delegates believed that drastic action was necessary. Indeed, a compelling consensus in purpose kept the delegates working together through the many snares and traps that lay ahead during a steamy summer. The nationalists had enough in common (shared experiences and frustrations and common attitudes about what was wrong and what needed to be changed) to push toward the creation of a second Revolutionary settlement. In fact, the broad consensus on fundamental issues kept the "Founding Fathers" from splitting apart over special concerns, some of which had divisive sectional flavoring.

In the formulation of the Articles of Confederation, one of the hottest debates had centered on the question of whether each state would enjoy equal voting power in Congress, as opposed to the notion of representation according to population. Equality for the states had been the clear choice in 1777. Now, ten years later, the Virginia Plan called for proportional representation for the lower house. The fear among delegates from the "small" states (Connecticut, New Jersey, and Delaware for example) was that the "large" states (such as Massachusetts, Pennsylvania, and Virginia) would use superior voting strength to undermine and destroy the interests of the small states. The Virginia Plan made it possible for the more populous states—it has often been referred to as the large states plan—not only to dominate the lower house, but also to control the elections to the upper house. Moreover, the large states would be virtually assured that one of their leaders would always control the executive branch. Thus the small states could be submerged if not buried on all levels. The benefits of the new government, especially in the final allocation of federal resources, theoretically could always be at the expense of the less populous states. That prospect frightened nationalists from the small states.

On June 15, William Paterson of New Jersey rallied the delegates from the less populous states. He laid before the convention what has since been called the "New Jersey Plan." Some delegates no doubt quipped among themselves that Paterson, the shortest man at the convention at four feet, eleven inches, seemed suited for his role as the small states' spokesman. But the issue of appropriate representation was no laughing matter to the diminutive Paterson, an astute thinker who was not going to let the less populous states be swallowed up.

The New Jersey Plan countered the Virginia Plan on several fronts. It called for a unicameral national legislature in which each state enjoyed equal voting strength. There was also to be an executive elected by that body which had broad appointive powers, including the naming of national judges. The executive would also direct military operations when necessary and execute all national laws. Beyond that, the New Jersey Plan specified a number of powers to be vested in the reconstituted national government, including the authority of taxation (a modified stamp act of all things appeared in the list) and the regulation of interstate and foreign commerce. All national laws and treaties, furthermore, were to be "the supreme law of the respective States, . . . anything in the respective laws of the Individual States to the contrary notwithstanding."[14] The New Jersey Plan, known as the "small states plan," was certainly not a states rights document.

Paterson's presentation unleashed a wicked round of debate, not over the distribution of powers between state and nation, but over the question of representation. The New Jerseyite made his position clear time and again. He thought that the convention was erring in pushing the assumptions of the Virginia Plan so boldly. His proposal was more in the spirit of the original convention charge. More important, it did not sacrifice the small states. "Destroy this balance of equality," exhorted Paterson, "and you endanger the rights of *lesser* societies by the danger of usurpation in the greater."[15] Squint-eyed James Wilson responded with as much vigor. "Despotism comes on mankind in different shapes," cautioned the Pennsylvanian. "Is there no danger of a Legislative despotism? Theory and practice both proclaim it. If the Legislative authority be not restrained, there can be neither liberty nor stability; and it can only be restrained by dividing it within itself, into distinct and independent branches." "In a single house," Wilson concluded, "there is no check, but the inadequate one, of the virtue and good sense of those who compose it."[16]

As these comments suggest, the delegates had begun to talk past one another. Paterson wanted protection for the small states, but Wilson fretted about structural balance and how it would check the abuse of power by individuals. Debating quickly gave way to day-by-day picking and haggling. A few members made vague noises about leaving. To make matters worse, Luther Martin gained the floor and harangued the assemblage for two days running. Near the end of June, Benjamin Franklin made one of his rare speeches. He reproved his colleagues sharply. "Our different sentiments on almost every question . . . is methinks a melancholy proof of the imperfection of the Human Understanding," the octogenerian said. He fervently urged that the bickering stop at once, that "our little partial local interests" be set aside, and that differences be resolved so that future generations will not "despair of establishing Governments by Human Wisdom and leave it to chance, war and conquest." In closing he proposed opening daily prayers in the hope of divine guidance. He was heartily seconded.[17]

The delegates, tired and worn down by the extremely humid weather, finally sorted out the issues and labored toward what is known as the "Great Compromise." They at last focused on complementary points in the Virginia and New Jersey Plans and fused them together. First, they settled on a three-tiered structure of government, harking back to Britain's balanced model as essential for the protection of the liberties of all groups. Second, they agreed that the central government was to be supreme over the states. Now the new national government could serve as the ultimate check upon democratic licentiousness when the state governments could no longer contain popular pressures from below. Third, the new national government was to have a vast increase in specified powers. Fourth, representation in the lower house was to be proportional to population, while the states would retain equal voting strength in the upper house, called the Senate. The less populous states thus could protect their interests at the senatorial level. Indeed, what the Great Compromise did was to fuse the competing plans into a coherent whole. The convention had cleared one of its highest hurdles by the middle of July.

Differences over the mode of representation set off the second major controversy. Questions about representation inexorably provoked questions about how the expanded powers of the national government were to affect particular interests. The debates did not follow the localist-nationalist split; rather, they proceeded along North-South lines. (Sectional tensions plagued the deliberations of the convention throughout, much as they had caused turmoil for the new nation during the Jay-Gardoqui negotiations. Sectional ill will had led to threats to dissolve the union in 1786.) The delegates at Philadelphia never spoke openly in such extreme terms, but they certainly poured large quantities of vituperation upon one another. Yet by the end of August, the haggard proponents of a variety of sectional interests put the final touches on the "North-South Compromise."

The South was particularly sensitive about the subject of slavery. Throughout all the debates, there was the unspoken assumption that slavery and its possible abolition was an untouchable subject. For convenience, the delegates presumed that slavery was a matter of local concern and, therefore, not to be affected by any national constitutional arrangements. For harmony, many Northerners agreed with one in their number who rationalized that "as population increases, poor laborers will be so plenty as to render slavery useless." "Slavery in time will not be a speck on our country," he concluded.[18] Such statements may have comforted the men assembled before the altar of liberty. The reality, however, was that a frontal assault on slavery would have driven the southern delegates from the convention and probably from the union. This would have destroyed all prospects for achieving social and political stability and national longevity through constitutional change. Clearly, the latter had the highest priority on the nationalist agenda.

Similar attitudes did not prevail about the slave trade. It was a touchy and rancorous issue, but it could be discussed. The Lower South took a rigid position. "If the Convention thinks that North Carolina, South Carolina, and Georgia will ever agree to the plan, unless their right to import slaves be untouched," threatened John Rutledge, "the expectation is vain."[19] The Upper South was more flexible. Slave labor had become an economic burden in some areas there, particularly in the face of the long-term decline in the productivity of the tobacco plantations. Upper South delegates thus were susceptible to compromise because of the economic woes burdening debt-ridden planters. Limiting the supply would also enhance the market value of slaves, all to the benefit of planters who might seek to sell off their "excess property" to planters in the Deep South.

The men from the South had many other concerns. They specifically disliked export duties, which would add to the prices of their cash crops in foreign markets and reduce their ability to compete in international trade. The Southerners also sought a two-thirds voting requirement for congressional approval of import duties and commercial treaties. They produced few manufactures and imported finished products heavily from abroad. Thus import duties would raise the prices that they paid. The desire for a two-thirds majority for the approval of commercial treaties reflected recent southern memories of the Jay-Gardoqui negotiations, when the majority of eastern states had been willing to sell out the South and the West.

All told, southern delegates were intensely aware of their minority status in the union. They wanted special protection through explicit constitutional provisions, but without emasculating the thrust toward the centralization of authority. Furthermore, they demanded a decennial census. In the 1780s everyone assumed, because of the undeveloped state of the territory north of the Ohio River and the southwestern course of population movement into Kentucky and Tennessee, that the southern frontier would be the most likely spawning ground of new states—states accepting the institution of slavery and thereby identifying with southern interests. Some observers went so far as to predict an absolute decline of population in the overcrowded Northeast. A census would take these projected population shifts into account, assure the South of greater representation in the years ahead, and redress the current imbalance between northern and southern interests. In time, the minority region would achieve majority status. Without a census, as one southern delegate summarized, even if "the Southern States . . . should have three-fourths of the people of America within their limits, the Northern will hold fast the majority of Representatives. . . . The Southern states will complain: but they may complain from generation to generation without redress."[20]

What it boiled down to was that northern and southern interests, as one slaveholding South Carolinian blurted out, were "as different as the interests of Russia and Turkey."[21] And at another juncture Gouverneur Morris, a leader of the group trying to minimize northern concessions, heatedly objected: "A distinction had been set up and urged, between the Northern and Southern States. . . . If it be real, instead of attempting to blend incompatible things, let us at once take a friendly leave of each other."[22] High nationalist that he was, Morris probably spoke in anger. Morris may also have been trying to frighten strong southern nationalists into making concessions.

In the end, both sides conceded points in a series of piecemeal agreements. The North won on import duties, the adoption of which would require only majority votes in Congress. That effectively appeased middle states commercial leaders who had persistently advocated permanent revenue sources for the national government. The South carried the day on commercial treaties; the Senate was to have exclusive jurisdiction over treaties of all kinds, with a two-thirds vote necessary for ratification. In effect, the South had gained *de facto* veto control over formal commercial arrangements with other nations. The real losers were the states, not the sectional interests involved.

The South also gained the decennial census and the counting of a slave as three-fifths of a white person—this was originally a part of the Great Compromise—for purposes of calculating representation in the lower house. Yet, in what may have been a coordinated action involving the Confederation Congress in New York, the Ordinance of 1787 specifically barred slavery in the Old Northwest. The North, too, would have a future source of states to counterbalance the spread of the southern system.[23] Whether or not it was an integral part of the convention compromise package, the Ordinance gave northern delegates some hope of keeping up with the South.

At the same time, the South conceded that slaves would not only count for representation but also for purposes of direct taxation. It perhaps is not ironic that southern delegates, insisting that slaves were inviolate property, should have been so willing to award them three-fifths human status. It was more a matter of pure sectional self-interest within the context of the compromise package. It was, likewise, the kind of self-interest which was of little value when the drift of an expanding population did not produce majority status for the southern section. Though no one could have predicted it in 1787, the North forged ahead of the South in the development of new states after 1819–1820. Admitting in the Constitution that slaves were at least partial human beings did have its ironic effects in this context. The South never achieved expected majority status, and some Northerners became more resistant to the continuing spread of slavery westward as the nineteenth century unfolded, all of which ultimately shattered the carefully drawn compromise of the Constitutional Convention.

In 1787, however, nationalist feelings were clearly paramount over sectional concerns. Cooperation and consensus in the face of recent crises represented the spirit of the moment, even to the point that the Deep South delegates reluctantly conceded to Congress the right to prohibit the importation of slaves after twenty years. Moreover, their delegates accepted the point that newly imported slaves could be taxed at a modest rate. Limiting potential slave population was tied to the three-fifths clause. It helped to ease northern fears about being overwhelmed by southern representatives in national councils. At the same time, the concession on the slave trade was a prime factor in getting a fugitive slave clause into the final document as a *quid pro quo*. The "supreme law of the land" thus mandated the return of all runaway slaves to their plantation owners.

The North-South Compromise demonstrated that few of the constitution makers were radical Revolutionaries or social reformers, even by the standards of their own time. Rather, the compromise signified that leaders with vast amounts of commercial, landed, manufacturing, and slaveholding property wanted to protect such holdings through the proposed structure of government. An alliance of citizens of propertied wealth had been a central tenet of the nationalist creed since the days when Robert Morris had been Superintendent of Finance. The compromise, in temporarily muting sectional ill will, helped to solidify that alliance in the short run, just as the whole new edifice further secured property by providing additional checks against the popular fury associated with so-called democratic licentiousness.

Having come this far, the delegates were not about to run aground on the third area of disagreement—the national presidency. In postconvention commentary, Madison confided to Jefferson that questions surrounding the executive were "peculiarly embarrassing." He elaborated: "On the question whether it should consist of a single person, or a plurality of co-ordinate members, on the mode of appointment, on the duration of office, on the degree of power, on the re-eligibility, tedious and reiterated discussions took place."[24] Each delegate had his point of view. Hamilton, Dickinson, and Wilson were particularly strident in demanding a powerful executive. They presumed that such a person would always be of enlightened nationalist temperament. Hamilton even went so far as to draft a plan of limited constitutional monarchy. He could not have been serious in proposing it, as its embodiment in the Constitution would have ruined all chances for ratification. The great majority of the delegates preferred a limited term (four years with the opportunity for reelection). Also, the President was made commander in chief and given exclusive control over the conduct of foreign relations. He could also propose and veto legislation, but vetoes could be overturned by two-thirds majorities in both houses of Congress. To guard against executives who might abuse power, the delegates also included provisions for impeachment and removal from office.

Even more vexing than defining the powers of the President was the problem of procedures for electing the chief executive. The nationalists were not advocates of direct popular elections. Too much electioneering could lead the President to bow to public opinion and favor unwise legislation or, perhaps worse yet, to manipulate public opinion and the public will for demagogic purposes. Likewise, direct popular election would always favor candidates from the more populous states. The awkward scheme of an electoral college thus seemed the best solution to both problems. First of all, the states would determine whether state electors (each was to have a minimum of three electors regardless of population, effectively overweighing the less populous states in the college) would be chosen by popular ballot or by state legislatures. The presumption was that no one (except for George Washington) would have sufficient reputation to carry a majority of votes in the electoral college. In that case, choosing the winner would fall to the House of Representatives, where each state delegation, regardless of size, would have one vote. Thus each state would have an equal voice in selecting the President from among the wise and the talented. None of the delegates imagined how different the process would actually work, largely because they did not think in terms of the formation of national political parties.

It was early September before these issues had been settled. The delegates were tired and worn down by their own interminable nit-picking. Eager to go home, they gave up on the matter of designing a full-blown national judiciary. They simply provided for a Supreme Court and left to the first Congress the task of creating a network of inferior federal courts. Washington named a committee on style on September 8. Gouverneur Morris, who was most influential in refining the Constitution's language, saw to it that national powers were not weakened because of clumsy prose. The members also agreed that ratification should be obtained through popularly elected state ratifying bodies. They saw little prospect for approval by parochialist state legislatures. Moreover, they decided that the new government should go into operation once two-thirds of the states had ratified. They were not going to let one willful state stand in the way as Maryland had done with the Articles of Confederation.

Thirty-nine delegates (actually a colleague from Delaware affixed John Dickinson's signature) signed the completed document on Monday, September 17. A few still in attendance begged off. Edmund Randolph was one, indicating that he wanted to keep his options open—a polite way of saying that he did not want formal association with the Constitution if it failed of ratification. The implication was that it might hurt his burgeoning political career back home. Elbridge Gerry, feeling remorse, indicated that the document was too centralist in its intent for him. For some reason, the memory of Shays's Rebellion was no longer so vivid in his mind. The delegates, he believed, had reacted too strongly to democratic licentiousness and had written a Constitution that was inimical to a healthy balance in powers between the states and the nation.

Each delegate had his reasons for signing or not signing. On the last day, Benjamin Franklin urged them all to join with him in affixing signatures. The aging Philadelphian noted that "there are several parts of this constitution which I do not at present approve." Still the whole was better than the parts. "For when you assemble a number of men to have the advantage of their joint wisdom, you inevitably assemble with those men," he observed, "all their prejudices, their passions, their errors of opinion, their local interests, and their selfish views." Rhetorically the old man asked: "From such an Assembly can a perfect production be expected? It therefore astonishes me, Sir, to find this system approaching so near to perfection as it does." As delegates stepped forward and added their names, Franklin noted to those around him that, often during the deliberations, he had studied the carving on the back of the president's chair. He had thought that the "painters had found it difficult to distinguish in their art a rising from a setting sun," and had wondered more than once which way the "vicissitudes" were taking the nation. Then he concluded the parable: "But now at length I have the happiness to know that it is a rising and not a setting Sun."[25]

Franklin's view was optimistic. He believed that the Constitution would save the republic from its perils. During the convention, John Dickinson had reminded the delegates: "Experience must be our only guide. Reason may mislead us."[26] Dickinson had urged the assemblage to consider the history of the rise and fall of governments so that they could appreciate what had worked in the annals of nations and why. He also had encouraged the delegates not to forget recent events. Both Dickinson and Franklin believed that the delegates had framed the safest constitutional document, given the finite limitations of humanity. For them, the Constitution would provide for a buoyant future because it would encourage social and political stability. It would serve to control the democracy of citizens, yet it had not repudiated republicanism by going to some monarchical extreme. Moreover, the Constitution even guaranteed to support and to maintain republican governments in the various states. It was a happy combination of provisions for men of nationalist persuasion.

One key to a less anxious future, the delegates reasoned, was the proposed concentration of decision-making authority in the central government. Powers that had been in the jurisdiction of the states under the Articles now were to be exercised in the common interest on the national level, including those of taxation, the regulation of interstate and foreign commerce, the making of foreign treaties, the coining of money and the regulation of its value, the funding of the public debt, and the raising and maintenance of armies and navies. Moreover, Congress could legislate whatever was "necessary and proper" to assure the creation of a strong new nation. From this perspective, the Constitution resolved nationalist frustrations over the diffuseness and even utter absence of decision making in the Confederation era.

Yet the Constitution of 1787 represented something more than a mere regrouping of specific and implied powers under central auspices. It went much deeper than that for the nationalists. The Constitution, as they viewed it, could rebalance a social and political system that had leaned dangerously toward direct, popular rule as a result of the first Revolutionary settlement. Putting it more starkly, the Constitution could save the people from themselves, but in republican terms, by providing for enlightened leadership during the years ahead.

James Madison, as active as any person in determining the document's final contents, explained this broader character of the new frame of government in *Federalist Number 10*. This was one of a series of essays written by Hamilton, Jay, and Madison to counteract rather overwhelming postconvention sentiment against ratification in New York. The Virginian put forth what has come to be considered the classic characterization of the Constitution. It can be argued that *Federalist Number 10* represented the culmination of theoretical maxims about politics and proposed constitutional change which the studious Madison had been developing well before the convention.[27] It also summarized important aspects of the nationalist point of view because it explained as no other source of the time did how the Founding Fathers of 1787 reconciled republicanism with their antipopular attitudes.

Madison launched his explanation of the "numerous advantages" of the Constitution by stressing that it would work "to break and control the violence of faction." A faction could be a majority or a minority interest, although in all cases factions were "united and actuated by some common impulse of passion, or of interest, adverse to the rights of other citizens, or to the permanent and aggregate interests of the community." Groups like the Shaysites, the Rhode Island paper money men, and the Maryland land speculators were representative of factions. They were self-willed, lacking in public virtue and inimical both to liberty and republicanism.

Factions, the Virginian stressed, were also endemic to humanity. "The diversity in the faculties of men from which the rights of property originate" was "the most common and durable source of factions." Since people had varying abilities and talents, some would be more successful in amassing property than others. Thus factions grew up in societies from "the various and unequal distribution of property," which resulted in combinations among "those who are creditors, and those who are debtors, . . . a landed interest, a manufacturing interest, a mercantile interest, a monied interest, with many lesser interests . . . divide[d] . . . into different classes, actuated by different sentiments and views." Factions, self-seeking to the core, somehow had to be controlled. This, Madison insisted, was "the principal task of modern legislation."

In his discussion of the origins and nature of factions, Madison was discoursing in a way that has since warmed the hearts of economic determinists. Yet his central point was that governments had to be designed to cope with "the spirit of party and faction in the necessary and ordinary operations of government," while at the same time they had to be capable of providing enlightened legislation beneficial to the whole political community.[28] What made the problem particularly vexing was that factions could be majorities capable of destroying "both the public good and the rights of other citizens," the very liberties which well-constructed governments invariably protected. The key to successful governance, then, was a matter of designing a system which factions, either as minorities or majorities, could neither dominate nor control.

For that reason alone, pure democracy as a political system was unacceptable. Democracies had poor historical records. Madison defined a "pure democracy" as "a society, consisting of a small number of citizens, who assemble and administer the government in person." Yet even in democracies there would be factions "incompatible with personal security, or the rights of property." Since democratic political arrangements had normally characterized smaller territories with a greater homogeneity of popular interests, it had been easier for "a common passion or interest" to "be felt by a majority of the whole" population. But with no governmental restraints "to check the inducements to sacrifice the weaker party," particularly propertied interests, "democracies have ever been spectacles of turbulence and contention."

Madison strongly urged the adoption of the Constitution because it countered the insidious influence of competing factions while avoiding the pitfalls of uninhibited governmental structures like democracies. Indeed, he observed, the proposed Constitution enshrined the principle of republicanism, "by which I mean a government in which the scheme of representation takes place," as compared to the direct, popularly based, and open-field decision making of ancient democracies.

Despite accepted thinking, Madison said, republics did not function best with representatives too close to the people in interests or concerns. In building upon the writings of Scottish theorist David Hume, Madison challenged the traditional axiom that republics operated most effectively when election districts were small and popular interests were homogeneous. Smaller election districts had all of the pitfalls of democracies, because representatives were as likely as not to be "men of factious tempers, of local prejudices, or of sinister designs, [who] may by intrigue, by corruption, or by other means, first obtain the suffrages, and then betray the interests of the people." Republics constructed of small election districts were just as likely as pure democracies to result in self-interested leadership and unstable governance.

To this point, Madison's analysis had certain faint similarities to Elbridge Gerry's. But, unlike Gerry, Madison dismissed the concept of citizen virtue. Moreover, he made it clear that demagogic leaders more easily emerged from small than from large election districts, in effect more easily despoiling decision making. The solution to the problem, as embodied in the Constitution, had been the expansion of the size of the election districts: "Extend the sphere [of territory], and you take in a greater variety of parties and interests; you make it less probable that a majority of the whole will have a common motive to invade the rights of other citizens; or if a common motive exists, it will be more difficult for all who feel it to discover their own strength, and to act in unison with each other." The most effective means for checking insidious and factious behavior, then, even when majoritarian in character, was to have large election districts. Through the House of Representatives, the Constitution provided for those large spheres by spreading election districts across the land. Even if "the influence of factious leaders may kindle a flame within their particular states" through "a rage for paper money, for an abolition of debts, for an equal division of property, or for any other improper or wicked project," there was very little likelihood that any such group could come to control the small number of large federal election districts across the national landscape.

The Constitution thus assured that no one interest group would dominate the national legislative process. On the contrary, it assured something else that was dear to the hearts of all nationalists—and the key was the larger election sphere. "In the next place," Madison explained, "as each representative will be chosen by a greater number of citizens in the large than in the small republic, it will be more difficult for unworthy candidates to practice with success the vicious arts, by which elections are too often carried." Since there would be so many competing interests and candidates, it would lessen the likelihood of one demagogue being charismatic enough to influence a majority of the people; rather "the suffrages of the people being more free, will be more likely to center on men who possess the most attractive merit, and the most diffusive and established characters."

There it was! The "proportion of fit characters"—those individuals of wealth, of established community standing, of proved wisdom, who would not succumb to particular factious interests, but who had the breadth of character and vision to rise above public opinion and work for enlightened legislation—the numbers of such individuals would be greater "in the large than the small republic." They would "present a greater option, and consequently a greater probability of a fit choice" for republican leadership in national government.

If one remembers that Madison prepared these arguments to support and defend the Constitution of 1787, what he said to readers of the *Federalist Papers* becomes all the more striking. He emphasized that the nationalists had not repudiated the principle of republicanism but had fully endorsed it through the plan honoring popular representation—at least directly in one branch. Nor had they fallen into the snare of monarchism in attempting to check convulsions from below. Indeed, the Founding Fathers had designed a system which would assure the ascendancy of fit characters who would act as stewards of the people, in turn providing enlightened public policy through the legislative process. Appropriate stewards—Madison never explained why such individuals would be above self-serving behavior when he claimed that it was a trait of human nature—would be elected to office and rule wisely on behalf of the people, despite the self-interested temperament of minority and majority interests. These gentlemanly stewards would legislate by disinterested consensus in determining the best course for the whole citizenry. At the same time, because of the distribution of different types of powers (executive, legislative, and judicial) through the several branches of government (the subject of other *Federalist* numbers on the concept of checks and balances), no one leader, even if mistakenly deemed fit for office, could seize all authority for himself and become a demagogic tyrant.

The nationalists of 1787 were more concerned about licentious behavior from below than about the abuse of power from above. Political experiences from the previous decade molded their thought, as did their reading in ancient and modern history and their views about deference and hierarchy. Equally important was their placement in the postwar socioeconomic and political structures. The nationalists considered themselves to be the very kinds of individuals (men of wealth, standing, talent, and wisdom) who should have been ruling in government and society all along, especially after the collapse of imperial authority. They viewed themselves as the very individuals who would not abuse power but who could come together at the federal level to design and to execute appropriate public policies. They looked at themselves as men who had been shoved aside by the first Revolutionary settlement. Leadership had fallen into the wrong hands. Now, as Madison set it forth, the new structural edifice of government, based on the republican principle, guaranteed through enlarged election districts that the people would choose those characters fit to wield centralized power. For those nationalists who intended to reclaim a lost heritage, it all added up to a bright and vigorous future for the new American nation.

Madison, in *Federalist Number 10,* was redefining political reality and adjusting it to the American experience. He was no longer repeating axioms about the need for a three-tiered structure of government representing the traditional orders of monarchy, aristocracy, and democracy. Rather, he declared that the reality of American politics was the struggle between socioeconomic and political interest groups. He was stating that concepts like monarchy and aristocracy had long since lost any validity and meaning. Yet he also insisted that the democracy of citizens still needed the restraints of representative republicanism to ensure stability. While he presumed the worst in human behavior, he expected the best from those "natural aristocrats" of his own class. Plainly, he still accepted the doctrine of an indivisible relationship between the leaders and the led in state and society, as was demonstrated in the way in which he differentiated among human natures. Madison thus clung to hierarchical assumptions while verbalizing the reality of competing interest groups. The Virginian kept a locked grip on the past while breaking with many of

Battle of Bunker's Hill, 1775, by John Trumbull. (Courtesy of Yale University Art Gallery.)

Thomas Jefferson, by John Trumbull.
*(Courtesy of the Metropolitan Museum of Art,
bequest of Cornelia Cruger, 1923.)*

State House in Philadelphia, 1778, by Charles Willson Peale. *(Courtesy of
the American Philosophical Society.)*

The Declaration of Independence, 1786–1797, by John Trumbull.
(*Courtesy of the Yale University Art Gallery.*)

Lord George Germain, by Sir
Joshua Reynolds. *(Courtesy of the
William L. Clements Library,
University of Michigan.)*

Sir William Howe, by J. Chapman.
*(Courtesy of the William L. Clements
Library, University of Michigan.)*

John Burgoyne, portrait engraving
by A. H. Ritchie. *(Courtesy of the
William L. Clements Library,
University of Michigan.)*

Sir Henry Clinton, portrait
engraving by A. H. Ritchie.
*(Courtesy of The New-York Historical
Society, New York City.)*

George Washington at the Battle of Princeton, by Charles Willson Peale.
(Courtesy of The Art Museum, Princeton University.)

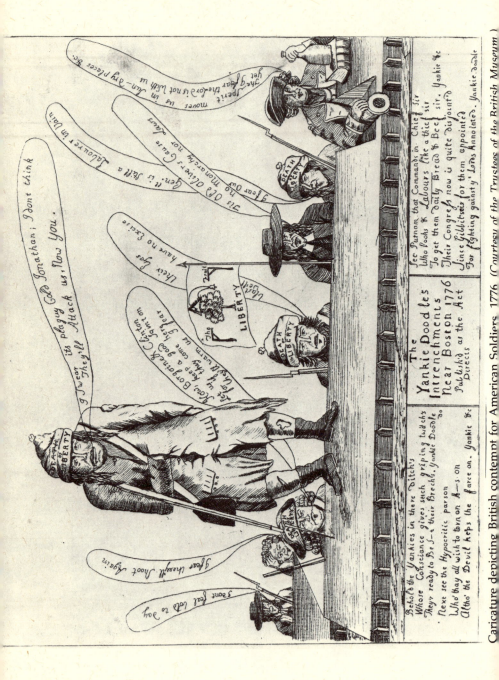

Caricature depicting British contempt for American Soldiers 1776 (Courtesy of the Trustees of the British Museum)

The Generals in America doing nothing, or worse than nothing.

British cartoon of 1779 showing
General Howe dozing while
Burgoyne falls at Saratoga.
(*Courtesy of The New-York Historical
Society, New York City.*)

Horatio Gates, by Charles Willson Peale. *(Courtesy of the Independence National Historical Park.)*

Benedict Arnold, engraving by B. L. Prévost, after a drawing by Pierre Eugène du Simitier. *(Courtesy of The New-York Historical Society, New York City.)*

Nathanael Greene, by Charles Willson Peale. *(Courtesy of the Independence National Historical Park.)*

Daniel Morgan, by Charles Willson Peale. *(Courtesy of the Independence National Historical Park.)*

JOHN BULL TRIUMPHANT.

John Bull Triumphant, a British caricature by James Gillray, London, 1780.
(Courtesy of The Historical Society of Pennsylvania.)

Yorktown in the Eighteenth
Century, by a British Naval
Officer. *(Courtesy of the Mariners
Museum, Newport News, Virginia.)*

Charles, Lord Cornwallis.
*(Courtesy of the William L. Clements
Library, University of Michigan.)*

Opposite Page
Legendary "Molly Pitcher" at the
Battle of Monmouth. *(Courtesy of
Culver Pictures.)*

Benjamin Franklin, by Charles Nicolas Cochin. *(Courtesy of the American Philosophical Society.)*

American Commissioners of the Preliminary Peace Negotiations with Great Britain, c.1783, by Benjamin West. From left to right: J. Jay, J. Adams, B. Franklin, H. Laurens, and W. T. Franklin. *(Courtesy of The Henry Francis du Pont Winterthur Museum.)*

Gouverneur Morris and Robert
Morris, by Charles Willson Peale.
*(Courtesy of The Pennsylvania
Academy of the Fine Arts.)*

Henry Knox, by Charles Willson
Peale. *(Courtesy of the Independence
National Historical Park.)*

James Madison, by Charles
Willson Peale. *(Courtesy of The
Thomas Gilcrease Institute of
American History and Art, Tulsa,
Oklahoma.)*

Alexander Hamilton, by Charles
Willson Peale. *(Courtesy of The
New-York Historical Society, New
York City.)*

The Maryland State House, site of the Annapolis Convention. *(Courtesy of
the New York Public Library, Emmet Collection 9324.)*

Elbridge Gerry, engraving by J. B. Longacre after a drawing by John Vanderlyn. *(Courtesy of the Library Company of Philadelphia.)*

Edmund Randolph, by F. J. Fisher after an original portrait no longer extant. *(Courtesy of the Virginia State Library.)*

William Paterson, by Edward Ludlow Mooney. *(Courtesy of The Art Museum, Princeton University.)*

Luther Martin. *(Courtesy of the Evergreen House Foundation, Baltimore, Maryland.)*

Pro-Constitution Celebrants in New York, 1788. (Courtesy of the Library Company of Philadelphia.)

its assumptions, all of which made the concept of representative republicanism possible for the nationalist mind.[29]

Other nationalists stated the proposition similarly. Dr. Benjamin Rush of Philadelphia, very much a person of the Enlightenment, who put great faith in scientific human reasoning but less so in human behavior, observed in a preconvention oration that, even though the war was over, "this is far from being the case with the American revolution." "On the contrary," Rush expostulated, "nothing but the first act of the great drama is closed." Then he offered his most telling point: "It remains yet to establish and perfect our new forms of government; and to prepare the principles, morals, and manners of our citizens, for these forms of government, after they are established and brought to perfection."[30] Rush's sequence is critically important. The people were not as yet "prepared" for the trust that had befallen them. New governments had to be perfected, and the people had to learn their republican responsibilities. Even as a reasoning optimist, Rush believed that the people would be qualified to assume leadership positions, but only in time and after extensive formal education. Many extreme nationalists never even imagined that possibility.

That was exactly what was wrong with the Constitution, according to its most vociferous critics. It concentrated power; worse still, it did not reveal any faith in the people, or much concern about human rights, for that matter. "Centinel" blasted the plan because it was "devoid of all responsibility or accountability to the great body of the people, and that so far from being a regular balanced government, it would be in practice a *permanent* ARISTOCRACY."[31] "Philadelphiensis" suspected "a conspiracy against the liberties of his country, concerted by a few *tyrants*, whose views are to lord it over the rest of their fellow citizens, to trample the poorer part of the people under their feet, that they may be rendered their servants and slaves."[32] George Mason, who had attended the Philadelphia Convention but had refused to sign the finished document, warned that the new government would "commence in a moderate aristocracy." In the long run he could not "foresee whether it will, in its operation, produce a monarchy, or a corrupt oppressive aristocracy." Mason held out no hope for representative republicanism, pessimistically concluding: "It will most probably vibrate some years between the two, and then terminate in the one or the other."[33]

The opposition was widespread and grew stronger during the debates over ratification. The nationalists had their hands full, yet they triumphed. Through hard work and perseverance, they refused to be defeated, more than anything else because they were so close to their goal of submerging the first Revolutionary settlement in their own second one. In achieving their goal, the nationalists employed a number of successful tactics, including that of confusing the populace by referring to themselves as "federalists" while shrewdly labeling localist critics as "antifederalists." Actually, the Antifederalists were the real federalists, because they favored a continuation of the loose confederation of sovereign states. No doubt the switch in terminology abetted the nationalist cause, gaining a few extra votes here and there in state convention elections. On the whole, enfranchised voters showed only mild interest in the controversy. It has been estimated that no more than 20 to 25 percent of the eligible voters bothered to go to the polls and cast ballots for candidates to the state ratification conventions.

The Antifederalists fought back desperately against what was to them a dangerous new attack upon liberty—and again from above. They warned the people to be wary of leaders who had no concern for basic human rights. They chided the nationalists for not including provisions for such fundamental liberties as free speech, assembly, trial by jury, religious freedom, or "due process" of law in the Constitution. The Antifederalists also pleaded for a second constitutional convention, to be charged with reviewing and modifying the recommendations of the first while preparing a national bill of rights. (The nationalists described the omission of a statement detailing human rights as a correctible oversight.) But the nationalists, taking full advantage of their momentum, swept their localist, "anarchy-loving" opponents before them.

Six state conventions had ratified by the spring of 1788, including the key states of Pennsylvania and Massachusetts. (Everyone knew that the new government could really not begin to function before New York and Virginia also ratified. Physical size and location as well as population dictated their importance.) In Delaware, New Jersey, and Georgia—among the first to ratify—localist forces were still too disorganized to prevent unanimous votes. Overwhelming victories in Pennsylvania and Connecticut were the result of superb planning by the Federalists.

Only in Massachusetts was the final tally close (187 for to 168 against). A number of factors produced positive results in a convention that should have voted Antifederalist. Samuel Adams, firmly opposed to the new plan, lost the support of street artisans and mechanics, who hoped that the Constitution would bring sustained economic prosperity. Reluctantly, Adams caved in. Many convention delegates demanded that ratification be made conditional upon amendments guaranteeing basic human rights. The nationalists agreed, promising that they would be written and sent out for state approval by the first Congress. The Federalist organizers also played it safe by appealing to Governor John Hancock's well-known vanity. Hancock had enough political followers to swing the final vote either way. There were intimations to Hancock that he deserved high office in the new government, perhaps even the presidency. It was whispered that he could even be the first President should Virginia refuse ratification and, thereby, exclude George Washington from election. Miraculously, Hancock recovered from a debilitating case of the gout which had kept him confined at home. He went before the convention and spoke warmly for ratification.

Maryland, South Carolina, and New Hampshire were the next states to fall in line, only the latter recording a close vote (57 to 46) in favor of ratification. Thus the required nine states had approved the Constitution. But New York and Virginia, already meeting in conventions, were still undecided. In Virginia, Patrick Henry, who still smelled a rat, launched into one tirade after another. No doubt his fellow delegates thought that his long-winded speeches were beginning to take on an odorous quality, as the aging defender of liberty rolled on and on. Henry's oratory may have done as much to break apart the opposition as to cement it. Even more important, promises of high office to Governor Edmund Randolph—he became successively attorney general and secretary of state in Washington's administration—had the desired effects. At last, Randolph spoke out in favor of the Constitution. Everything now seemed much clearer in his mind. Still more promises about a bill of rights also worked to finish off Henry and the other Antifederalists, this time by a vote of 89 yeas to 79 nays on June 26, 1788.

New York, the "eleventh pillar," ratified a month later in what can only be described as a bizarre struggle. Antifederalists substantially outnumbered nationalists in the state convention. Promises of a bill of rights, hints about the possibility of a second convention, and the fact that more than two-thirds of the states had already ratified led some Antifederalists to abstain in the final vote. In late July 1788, the Constitution thus gained the weakest endorsement (30 for to 27 against) that it would get. The first North Carolina convention voted resoundingly against ratification. A second convention in that state ratified in November 1789, while tiny Rhode Island finally surrendered in May 1790, a year after the new government was in full operation. By that time, no one in the nationalist leadership cadre seemed to care much one way or the other about what Rhode Island did. Perhaps that epitomized the startling turn of events that had taken place.[34]

As the summer of 1788 gave way to the autumn, Americans found themselves preparing to launch a second experiment in republicanism, one quite different from the first. The first Revolutionary settlement had emphasized life, liberty, and happiness. Its great goal had been to remove unbridled power from distant hands and to vest it securely in the people of the sovereign states. It revealed a faith in the people as the proper guardians of liberty, and it cast down those from above who abused power and seemed to be hopelessly corrupt. If some of the events that produced that settlement were parochial and grew out of the frustrations and ambitions which characterized pre-revolutionary politics in the provinces, the results were magnificently broad in scope. The struggle achieved the liberation of a dawning American republican civilization from Old World monarchism, aristocracy, and the rotten spoilage of the human condition which seemed to be inevitable when the few ruled the many.

For its time, Thomas Jefferson's affirmation of the rights of humanity and the right of revolution was breathtakingly bold and comprehensive. Reluctant Revolutionaries, many of whom became nationalists, never shared or accepted Jefferson's deep faith in a virtuous citizenry. In their view, the proper balance in political and social relationships had been needlessly shattered by the liberating temper of the times. The events of the immediate postwar years gave all the evidence that they needed for proof. Thus in 1787, they wrote a Constitution designed to restore the balance through a redistribution of power and authority upward in the new order—from the many to a few enlightened stewards. They had no intention, once they had the power, of permitting the Revolutionary ferment to end in fully egalitarian relationships or in the possible destruction of property rights. In the Constitution of 1787, the nationalists finally achieved what they had been working for, what Madison referred to as a plan of representative republicanism, or what less enamored critics called aristocratic despotism. Either way, the Constitution embodied the second Revolutionary settlement, one less favorably disposed toward the people.[35]

The all-important fact is that the nationalists, now called Federalists, had not fully renounced the first Revolutionary settlement. Even if they placed more emphasis upon structure, hierarchy, balance, deference, and property, they argued their case on republican grounds. They viewed themselves as saving the republican experiment from ruin by popular excesses, certainly not as overturning it.

Even the handful of extreme nationalists who would have relished another dosage of constitutional monarchy understood that the times had changed and might, perish the thought, keep changing. There was no turning back the clock to the world before 1776. Their major hope after 1787 was that they could dominate the councils of the new government, garner the offices for themselves, and enact enlightened public policies through gentlemanly consensus about appropriate solutions.

If the majority of nationalists were politically astute enough to accept the changing world, they were also determined to discover the formula that would protect the things dearest to them—their property, their personal standing, and the renewed stability of their society. They believed in the future of the new nation, but they trusted themselves rather than the people to see the republic through to the full realization of its potential. Thus they tried to bottle up the "leveling spirit," as they so often encapsulated the reasons for the problems of their age. For a time after 1787 it looked as if they would succeed.

The nationalists obviously were not social reformers. They showed little concern for the plight of the poor, certainly as numerous in the 1780s and 1790s as in the 1760s. In their land speculation, they were uninterested in the legitimate rights of the Indian nations (giving them something in common with the whole population), and in the years ahead they would keep shoving aside the "barbarian hordes" blocking the path of "human progress." They did not advocate awarding human rights to women (giving them something else in common with their white male political opponents). Few in their generation advocated full freedom for the enslaved population of blacks. In these and other ways, the nationalists reflected commonly held social attitudes. Above all else, their concerns focused on the abuse of power by corrupted influences. After 1776 they fretted endlessly about the convulsions from below being released by excessive Revolutionary fervor. That thought bothered them more than any other, which undoubtedly further circumscribed their full range of social concerns.

Yet all the talk about human rights, liberty, and the rule of law as superior to the rule of men could not be denied once it had been unleashed—not by the nationalists or anyone else. When Jefferson penned his eloquent phrases about equality and unalienable rights, he specifically wanted to humble the king and his minions. It did not take long to broaden and enshrine the meaning of his words through particular acts. The Massachusetts constitution of 1780, for example, was typical in acknowledging in its preamble that all men were born free and equal. The next year, Quok Walker, a slave in Worcester County, fled from his master, took up residence with another family in the vicinity, and began working for regular wages. Walker had declared himself a free man, but his former master sued in the courts for his return. In 1783 the state supreme court ruled that Walker was entitled to his full human freedom on the ground that holding him in bondage was inconsistent with the intent of the constitution. Slavery as an institution in Massachusetts thus succumbed to the broadening concern for human rights.

The institution already had been dealt a death blow in Pennsylvania during 1780 by a law stipulating that any person born into slavery after that date would become free upon reaching the age of twenty-eight. By the end of the decade, Rhode Island, Connecticut, New York, and New Jersey had passed similar acts gradually abolishing slavery; and all of these laws acknowledged the inconsistency between liberty and human bondage in a republican society. Despite the North-South Compromise embodied in the Constitution of 1787, the momentum of freedom, once set in motion, could not be stopped, no matter how hard some persons tried to do so in later generations.[36]

The beginning of the end of institutionalized repression affected other groups less noticeably. The poor, rather than experiencing relief and prosperity, simply continued their struggle for survival. Communities became more concerned about the mounting costs of supporting the downtrodden; as a consequence, more and more people found themselves being driven from towns or thrown into poorhouses. The Revolution may have left a legacy of hope, but it certainly did not result in widespread shifts toward a more equal distribution of property, despite all of the promises made to Continental soldiers, all of the sales of loyalist property, and all of the virgin western land waiting for tillage. The Constitution of 1787, with its concern about property rights, confirmed what had been reality in eighteenth-century America.[37]

Nor did the Revolution give women the opportunity to break down debilitating cultural stereotypes. In the spring of 1776, for example, Abigail Adams chided her husband concerning the inconsistency of his talk about tyranny. Back in Massachusetts running the family farm and caring for the Adams children, she exhorted John, then in Philadelphia working for independence to "Remember the Ladies, and be more generous and favorable to them than your ancestors. Do not put such unlimited power into the hands of the Husbands."

Abigail further admonished him: "Remember all Men would be tyrants if they could. If particular care and attention is not paid to the Ladies we are determined to foment a Rebellion, and will not hold ourselves bound by any Laws in which we have no voice, or Representation." Replying in mock serious tone, John wrote: "We know better than to repeal our Masculine system. . . . We dare not exert our Power in its full Latitude. . . . We have only the Name of Masters." Then he made light of Abigail's presumptuousness by relating her plea to the issues of the times: "I begin to think the Ministry as deep as they are wicked. After stirring up Tories, Landjobbers, Trimmers, Bigots, Canadians, Indians, Negroes, Hanoverians, Hessians, Russians, Irish Roman Catholics, Scotch Renegades, at last they have stimulated [the women] to demand new Privileges and threaten to rebel." For some reason, the male Adams did not fill in the word and specifically accuse women of joining in the ministerial conspiracy against liberty. Perhaps he recognized the hypocrisy of his era for what it was.[38]

The rebellion against British authority did raise social questions of revolutionary proportions, but in most cases the results were very mixed. For northern blacks, there was an end to slavery, although the process took years to complete and had its roots as much in the evangelical Christianity of the times as in Revolutionary ideology. The institution may have been struck down in certain quarters, yet racial prejudice against freed blacks lingered and was strong. All of the reasoned arguments about the stigmatizing environmental impact of slavery on black lives did not persuade the vast majority of whites that manumitted slaves were equal instead of inferior beings.

For women, the Revolution seemed to harden traditionally prescribed social roles. The theme of "republican motherhood" clearly emerged, encouraging women to think that their highest function was to raise for the republic dutiful sons who understood that personal sacrifice for the good of the community was essential for the new political order. Writers did not worry very much about providing for republican daughters.[39]

Within its temporal and chronological limits, the Revolution opened up a whole new range of human possibilities. Yet it would take generations to realize the full potential that had been so clearly expressed. To fault the Revolutionaries for focusing mainly on the issues of power and liberty and the abuse of the latter by the former, whether from above or below, would be nothing more than historical second guessing. As liberators in their times, the Revolutionaries were also constrained by the social conventions, attitudes, and cultural/racial stereotypes of their day. To ask for everything from one generation would be to insist upon too much. It would deny finite limits and human fallibilities. In sum, the Revolution, with its concern about liberty, the rule of law and, however abstractly, human equality and dignity, bequeathed a permanent, irreversible legacy from which future generations could not escape.

Such sweeping change, however, was far from the thoughts of those who had led the way to the Constitution of 1787 and its ratification. When the Federalist governing officials assembled in New York City during April 1789 and watched George Washington take the oath of office as the first President of the United States, they were pleased with the favorable turn of events. They saw themselves standing among "fit characters" eager to legislate in the national interest. At first, everything seemed to go well. There was little disagreement over providing for a cabinet, formulating a bill of rights as constitutional amendments, creating a national judiciary, or placing import and tonnage duties on foreign commerce as an initial permanent source of federal revenue. Government by consensus of the elite was functioning smoothly.

But then the trouble started. Alexander Hamilton, as Washington's secretary of the treasury, began presenting his plans for the full-scale development of the American economy. First, in January 1790 he recommended complete funding of the national debt at face value, as well as national assumption of state debts. James Madison, lodged in the House of Representatives, objected vigorously to windfall profits for those who happened to be holding wartime securities at that moment. He insisted upon compensation for those patriots who had been the original holders and who had felt the full burden of rapid market depreciation. Madison lost. There were too many speculators in Congress among those fit characters ruling the new nation.

Hamilton kept going. After pushing through a plan for a national bank, the Secretary in December 1791 urged upon Congress an extensive program to nurture nascent American manufacturing, including plans for high protective tariffs and government bounties as stimulants for the production of selected goods. Madison was appalled. Thomas Jefferson, the first secretary of state, was apoplectic. Hamilton's plans clearly favored business over agriculture. Not only was it an attack on southern interests; it also challenged Jefferson's physiocratic vision of a republic of uncorrupted freehold farmers working the soil and living simply and honestly in harmony with nature while supporting the good of the whole community.

And so the gentlemen-politicians—the men of wisdom and talent—fell to fighting among themselves. Consensus turned out to be a mirage, as Hamiltonians pursued their programs of economic nationalism and Jeffersonians tried to hold them back with accusations that their opponents were exceeding the powers of Congress under the "necessary and proper" clause. Jefferson, Madison, and their congressional followers had only one sure solution: Turn directly to the people and encourage them to oppose such abuse of power. Organize the people and get them to the polls to vote Hamilton's supporters out of office. Tell them that the "opposition" was defying the best interests of the general populace. And encourage them to elect candidates who would vote correctly on the issues once they were in Congress. By 1792, the Jeffersonians were going to the people and beginning to build a popularly based alliance. They were in the first stages of organizing a national political party, one dependent upon the people as the final arbiters in governmental decision making. Before long, the Federalists had to follow suit. Within a few years the first American party system had come to full flower.[40]

The development of that national party system effectively undermined the second Revolutionary settlement. The days were now numbered when the Constitution and the government it established would be viewed as a device for checking and controlling the people. Out of political expediency—a source of many principled ideological innovations—arose the full-blown practice that the people should be the fountainhead of enlightened legislation and the ultimate arbiters in government. The Jeffersonians buried Federalist concepts of the rule of an enlightened elite on behalf of the people and established the full national institutionalization of links between leaders and constituents. It was a bold stroke, one that continued to appall many Federalists as the eighteenth century ended. It was also revolutionary when compared to the intentions of the Founding Fathers in national constitution making.[41]

What the diehard Federalists did not understand was that the Revolution, in completing its cycle, had altered habits and practices, assumptions and attitudes, words and deeds. They fell back desperately on old arguments that political parties of any kind were nothing more than corrupting, self-serving factional combinations, which would destroy the liberties of the few for the benefit of the many, and the liberties of the many for the benefit of the few. They pointed out that the intent of the Constitution had been to circumscribe, not exalt, party influences. But fewer and fewer people, including Madison himself, paid any attention to their warnings.

The aging Federalists apparently could not grapple with the notion that the new national political parties, with all of their attendant evils, could be just as stabilizing and productive of enlightened legislation as any other source—including a favored elite of fit persons. More important, what they failed to perceive was that the forces of revolution, once put in motion, could not be easily stopped, and that the American Revolution, by happenstance and circumstance as much as by anything else, had altered the traditional definitions controlling human existence. The people of the new American republic were no longer just the democracy of citizens, trapped as they had been by that older definition. By the 1790s the people were becoming full participants in the *democratic* experiment in republicanism. A rebellion of humble beginnings had metamorphosed into something far broader—a revolution permanently altering the course of human events.

Notes

1. May 31, 1787 (Madison Notes), *The Records of the Federal Convention of 1787* (rev. ed., 4 vols., ed. Max Farrand, New Haven, Conn., 1937), I, 48. See also George Athan Billias, *Elbridge Gerry: Founding Father and Republican Statesman* (New York, 1976), 153–205.

2. Stanley Elkins and Eric McKitrick, "The Founding Fathers: Young Men of the Revolution," *Political Science Quarterly*, 76 (1961), 181–216, emphasize the national political experiences of those attending the Convention, as well as their youth. Actually, men in the middle-age category and beyond were certainly as prominent and influential as the younger delegates.

3. Charles A. Beard, *An Economic Interpretation of the Constitution of the United States* (New York, 1913), stresses the importance of public securities and personalty interests as economic influences affecting the writing of the Constitution. Critical reactions have been legion in the past two decades. See in particular Robert E. Brown, *Charles Beard and the Constitution* (Princeton, N.J., 1956); Forrest McDonald, *We the People: The Economic Origins of the Constitution* (Chicago, 1958); and Lee Benson, *Turner and Beard: American Historical Writing Reconsidered* (Glencoe, Ill., 1960).

4. Consult the list of reasons presented to the Convention by Edmund Randolph, May 29, 1787 (Madison Notes), Farrand, ed., *Convention Records*, I, 18–19.

5. To Charles Carroll, May 25, 1789, Smyth, ed., *Writings of Franklin*, X, 7.

6. To John Jay, August 15, 1786, Johnston, ed., *Correspondence of Jay*, III, 208.

7. To George Washington, June 27, 1786, *ibid.*, III, 204–205.

8. "An Oration on the Advantages of American Independence, spoken before a Public Assembly of the Inhabitants of Charleston, in South Carolina, on July 4, 1778," Niles, *Principles and Acts*, 375. (Italics mine)

9. James Hogg to James Iredell, May 17, 1783, Griffith J. McRee, *Life and Correspondence of James Iredell*, II (New York, 1858), 46.

10. "Letters of Fabius," V, 1788, Ford, ed., *Pamphlets on the Constitution*, 188.

11. To Thomas Jefferson, October 27, 1786, Johnston, ed., *Correspondence of Jay*, III, 213. The importance of the theme of tyrannical rule resulting from anarchy in the states may be traced in William M. Wiecek, *The Guarantee Clause of the U.S. Constitution* (Ithaca, N.Y., 1972), 1–77.

12. May 29 (Madison Notes), Farrand, ed., *Convention Records*, I, 20–22.

13. May 29 (Madison Notes), *ibid.*, I, 23.

14. June 15 (Madison Notes), *ibid.*, I, 242–245.

15. June 16 (Yates Notes), *ibid.*, I, 259.

16. June 16 (Madison Notes), *ibid.*, I, 254.

17. June 28 (Madison Notes), *ibid.*, I, 451–452. There have been a number of explanations about the key personalities involved in working out the compromise. See McDonald, *E Pluribus Unum*, 170–184.

18. Oliver Ellsworth, August 22 (Madison Notes), Farrand, ed., *Convention Records*, II, 371. See also Donald L. Robinson, *Slavery in the Structure of American Politics, 1765–1820* (New York, 1971), 168–247; Merrill Jensen, *The Making of the American Constitution* (Princeton, N.J., 1964), 56–66; Jordan, *White Over Black*, 269–311; David Brion Davis, *The Problem of Slavery in the Age of Revolution, 1770–1823* (Ithaca, N.Y., 1975), 255–342; William Cohen, "Thomas Jefferson and the Problem of Slavery," *Journal of American History*, 56 (1969), 503–526; and William W. Freehling, "The Founding Fathers and Slavery," *American Historical Review*, 77 (1972), 81–93.

19. August 22 (Madison Notes), Farrand, ed., *Convention Records*, II, 373.

20. George Mason, July 11 (Madison Notes), *ibid.*, I, 578.

21. Pierce Butler, August 29 (Madison Notes), *ibid.*, II, 451.

22. July 13 (Madison Notes), *ibid.*, I, 604.

23. Lynd, "The Compromise of 1787," *Class Conflict*, 185–213.

24. October 24, 1787, *The Papers of James Madison* (ed. W. T. Hutchinson *et al.*, Chicago, 1962 to date), X, 208.

25. September 17 (Madison Notes), Farrand, ed., *Convention Records*, II, 641–642, 648.

26. August 13 (Madison Notes), *ibid.*, II, 278.

27. For the full text, signed "Publius" and dated November 22, 1787, consult Hutchinson, ed., *Papers of Madison*, X, 263–270. The ideas contained in this celebrated *Federalist* number did not represent mere postconvention analysis, rather an attempt to explain what the other delegates, as prodded by Madison, had been groping toward all along. See Madison's preconvention "Vices of the Political System of the United States," dated April 1787, *ibid.*, IX, 348–358; his comments at the Convention, June 6, Farrand, ed., *Convention Records*, I, 134–136; and his letter to Jefferson, October 24, 1787, Hutchinson, ed., *Papers of Madison*, X, 212–214. See also Douglass Adair, " 'That Politics May Be Reduced to a Science': David Hume, James Madison, and the Tenth Federalist," *Huntington Library Quarterly*, 20 (1957), 343–360, which should be supplemented by other important essays by Adair, *Fame and the Founding Fathers* (ed. H. T. Colbourn, New York, 1974), *passim*.

28. Beard, *An Economic Interpretation*, 14–16, 152–188, emphasizes the apparent economic determinism of Madison's logic, rather than the Virginian's

concern with representative republicanism in large territories. Consult also Beard's *The Economic Basis of Politics* (New York, 1922), *passim.*

29. Gordon S. Wood captures Madison's broad vision of a redefinition of American politics in terms of the reality of interest groups as opposed to the traditional social orders. See *Creation of the American Republic*, 506–564, 593–615.

30. "To the People of the United States—by Dr. Benjamin Rush, Philadelphia, 1787," Niles, *Principles and Acts*, 234.

31. George Bryan, "Centinel," I, October 5, 1787, *The Antifederalists* (ed. C. M. Kenyon, Indianapolis, Ind., 1966), 12–13.

32. Number IX, February 7, 1788, *ibid.*, 71.

33. "The Objections of the Hon. George Mason, to the Proposed Federal Constitution," October 1787, *ibid.*, 195. For further commentary on the Antifederalists and their concerns, consult Cecelia M. Kenyon, "Men of Little Faith: The Anti-Federalists on the Nature of Representative Government," *William and Mary Quarterly*, 3rd Ser., 12 (1955), 3–43; Jackson Turner Main, *The Antifederalists: Critics of the Constitution* (Chapel Hill, N.C., 1961); and Wood, *Creation of the American Republic*, 483–518.

34. On ratification, see the overview study of Robert A. Rutland, *The Ordeal of the Constitution: The Antifederalists and the Ratification Struggle of 1787–1788* (Norman, Okla., 1966). For antinationalist attempts to organize in one state, consult Steven R. Boyd, "The Impact of the Constitution on State Politics: New York as a Test Case," Martin, ed., *The Human Dimensions of Nation Making*, 270–303. Valuable primary materials include *The Debates in the Several State Conventions on the Adoption of the Federal Constitution* (5 vols., ed. Jonathan Elliot, Philadelphia, 1876), now being expanded and updated in *The Documentary History of the Ratification of the Constitution* (ed. Merrill Jensen *et al.*, Madison, Wisc., 1976 to date).

35. Beard, *An Economic Interpretation*, 52–63, implies that the act of constitution making had counterrevolutionary dimensions. More recently Merrill Jensen, *The American Revolution Within America* (New York, 1974), 167–220, has employed the phrase "The Revolution of 1787." Either way, the participants themselves generally considered the settlement as forward-looking or backward-looking, depending upon their support or opposition of the document.

36. Quarles, *Negro in the American Revolution*, 33–50. J. Franklin Jameson, *The American Revolution Considered as a Social Movement* (Princeton, N.J., 1926), 21–26. See also the secondary sources listed in note eighteen above.

37. Allan Kulikoff, "The Progress of Inequality in Revolutionary Boston," *William and Mary Quarterly*, 3rd Ser., 28 (1971), 375–412, and Douglas Lamar Jones, "The Strolling Poor: Transiency in Eighteenth-Century Massachusetts," *Journal of Social History*, 8 (1975), 28–54, are important case studies. See also the materials cited in Chapter II, note two.

38. Abigail to John Adams, March 31, 1776, Butterfield, ed., *Adams Family Correspondence*, I, 369–371; John to Abigail, April 14, 1776, *ibid.*, I, 381–383.

39. Arthur Zilversmit, *The First Emancipation: The Abolition of Slavery in the North* (Chicago, 1967); Linda Kerber, "Daughters of Columbia: Educating Women for the Republic, 1787–1805," *The Hofstadter Aegis: A Memorial* (ed. Stanley Elkins and Eric McKitrick, New York, 1974), 36–59; and Mary Beth Norton, "Eighteenth-Century American Women in Peace and War: The Case of the Loyalists," *William and Mary Quarterly*, 3rd Ser., 33 (1976), 386–409.

40. On party formation, see in particular William N. Chambers, *Political Parties in a New Nation: The American Experience, 1776–1809* (New York, 1963); Richard Hofstadter, *The Idea of a Party System: The Rise of Legitimate Opposition in the United States, 1780–1840* (Berkeley, Cal., 1969); Joseph Charles, *The Origins of the American Party System: Three Essays* (Chapel Hill, N.C., 1956); Carl E. Prince, *The Federalists and the Origins of the U.S. Civil Service* (New York, 1978); and Richard Buel, Jr., *Securing the Revolution: Ideology in American Politics, 1789–1815* (Ithaca, N.Y., 1972).

41. David Hackett Fischer, *The Revolution of American Conservatism: The Federalist Party in the Era of Jeffersonian Democracy* (New York, 1965), *passim*.

BIBLIOGRAPHICAL NOTE

In the twentieth century, the task of understanding the American Revolution has become largely the assignment of professional historians, most often associated with academic institutions. But that has not always been the case. In fact, the quest to comprehend the Revolution dates back to those who actually lived during those years of resistance, rebellion, and nation making. Among the best contemporary histories are those by David Ramsay, *The History of the American Revolution* (2 vols., Philadelphia, 1789), and Mercy Otis Warren, *History of the Rise, Progress, and Termination of the American Revolution* (3 vols., Boston 1805). Ramsay and Warren represent many contemporaries who, through personal histories and memoirs, applauded the American struggle to preserve and expand liberty. Two well-known loyalists, Thomas Hutchinson and Peter Oliver, took the opposite viewpoint. Hutchinson maintained a scholar's detachment in the third volume of *The History of the Colony and Province of Massachusetts-Bay* (ed. L. S. Mayo, Cambridge, Mass., 1936), which covers the years 1749–1774. But Peter Oliver, in his *Origin & Progress of the American Rebellion* (ed. Douglass Adair and J. A. Schutz, San Marino, Cal., 1961), perceived the coming of the Revolution as the work of bedeviled popular leaders, mainly out for their own personal gain. Oliver's volume is an important key to unraveling the perceptions of those who did not support the Revolution.

By and large, the histories written by the loyalists have had little influence on later interpretations. During much of the nineteenth century, the dominant view was that the Revolution resulted from a united people in search of freedom from political repression. Most of the best history was written by gentleman practitioners, such as George Bancroft. Bancroft saw the establishment of liberty in the New World through the Revolution as part of God's "grand design" for redeeming the earth. His magisterial *History of the United States of America from the Discovery of the American Continent* (10 vols., Boston, 1834–1874), although bombastic in tone, is a storehouse of useful information.

The "grand design" explanation, although retaining some popularity among lay audiences, has not had much influence upon twentieth-century professional historians. Early in the century, a group commonly referred to in historiographical literature as the "conflict" school was particularly concerned about the role of the people. A young professional academician, Carl Lotus Becker, gave initial form to the school when he saw the developing Revolution in two-fold fashion. In *The History of Political Parties in the Province of New York, 1760–1776* (Madison, Wisc., 1909), Becker emphasized the rising tide of political feeling among the unenfranchised and underprivileged groups. It was not just widespread opposition to British policy per se, but also the drive of the awakened masses against local provincial aristocrats that turned the Revolution into a radicalizing quest for democracy. Building upon Becker, Arthur Schlesinger, Sr., described the uneasiness felt by wealthy commercial interests vis-à-vis a rising commonalty in *The Colonial Merchants and the American Revolution, 1763–1776* (New York, 1918). Charles A. Beard, in *An Economic Interpretation of the Constitution of the United States* (New York, 1913), portrayed the constitution makers of 1787 as men with vested property interests to protect, interests that could be threatened by a radicalized populace. To Beard and other conflict historians, then, the Founding Fathers of the 1780s were not necessarily liberty-loving saints, as had earlier been claimed by Bancroft or the widely read John Fiske in his *The Critical Period of American History, 1783–1789* (New York, 1888).

During the 1920s, J. Franklin Jameson brought together many of the conflict school's themes in *The American Revolution Considered as a Social Movement* (Princeton, N.J., 1926). Interpretations emphasizing formative internal conflict between the people and their traditional "stewards" have been carried forward in the writings of Merrill Jensen, including his *The Articles of Confederation: An Interpretation of the Social-Constitutional History of the American Revolution, 1774–1781* (Madison, Wisc., 1940), and *The New Nation: A History of the United States during the Confederation, 1781–1789* (New York, 1950). Jensen later argued in "Democracy and the American Revolution," *Huntington Library Quarterly*, 20 (1957), 321–341, that the Revolution had somewhat inadvertently moved America toward greater political democracy, even though that had not been a clearly enunciated goal. Books in a similar vein include Elisha P. Douglass, *Rebels and Democrats: The Struggle for Equal Political Rights and Majority Rule during the American Revolution* (Chapel Hill, N.C., 1955), and Jensen's most recent presentation, *The American Revolution Within America* (New York, 1974).

Following the Second World War, the emphasis in scholarly interpretations shifted dramatically. Overall, the new mood was more conservative. Those writing within the framework of what has since been labeled the "consensus" school had much more in common with historians like Bancroft, although their work has been less fileopietistic. Consensus writers deemphasized internal tensions among socioeconomic groups and internal class conflict. For example, Clinton Rossiter's *Seedtime of the Republic* (New York, 1953), and Daniel J. Boorstin's *The Genius of American Politics* (Chicago, 1953), stressed the underlying unity of the American people on the eve of conflict and saw them moving pragmatically toward the full establishment of uncorrupted British ideals and institutions in America. In *The Liberal Tradition in America* (New York, 1955), Louis Hartz said that the Revolution's main goal was saving what was then the world's freest society, one untainted by Europe's feudalism and corruption.

One reason for the sharp turn in historiographical emphasis was that scholars believed that they had found overwhelming evidence that voting rights were extremely widespread in the thirteen provinces. If so many adult white males could vote, in comparison to England and Europe, then it seemed logical that property holding was widespread, since only property ensured franchise rights. In *Middle-Class Democracy and the Revolution in Massachusetts, 1691–1780* (Ithaca, N.Y., 1955), Robert E. Brown insisted that conflict historians had abused the evidence. If property ownership and voting rights were widespread, there could be no reason for the commonalty to want a more democratic order. Indeed, the Revolution was really a struggle by united middle-class freeholding Americans to preserve the putative democratic order that they had created during the colonial years, a democratic order now being threatened by ministerial tyranny.

Robert E. Brown carried forward his influential interpretation with his wife B. Katherine Brown in *Virginia, 1705–1786: Democracy or Aristocracy?* (East Lansing, Mich., 1964). Many of the ideas presented in the studies by the Browns, Rossiter, Boorstin, and Hartz have been thoughtfully synthesized in Edmund S. Morgan, *The Birth of the Republic, 1763–1789* (Chicago, 1956, rev. ed., 1977), and in Bernard Bailyn, "Political Experience and Enlightenment Ideals in Eighteenth-Century America," *American Historical Review*, 67 (1962), 339–351. Other important summaries are Frederick B. Tolles, "The American Revolution Considered as a Social Movement: A Re-evaluation," *American Historical Review*, 60 (1954), 1–12, and Richard B. Morris, "Class Struggle and the American Revolution," *William and Mary Quarterly*, 3rd Ser., 19 (1962), 3–29.

The consensus school seemed to have carried the day. It was in this context that Bernard Bailyn carried out a full-scale analysis of the world view which he claimed he propelled a united American community into and through the Revolution. In his introduction to *Pamphlets of the American Revolution, 1750–1776*, Vol. I (Cambridge, Mass., 1965), later expanded and republished as *The Ideological Origins of the American Revolution* (Cambridge, Mass., 1967), Bailyn described the common perceptions of provincial Americans concerning a conspiracy to destroy liberty. He also examined the antecedents of such thinking in British opposition Whig writings and analyzed the colonists' acceptance of the radical Whig tradition in *The Origins of American Politics* (New York, 1968). These volumes should be consulted in conjunction with Caroline Robbins's *The Eighteenth-Century Commonwealthman* (Cambridge, Mass., 1959), J. G. A. Pocock's *The Machiavellian Moment: Florentine Political Thought and the Atlantic Republican Tradition* (Princeton, N.J., 1975), and Joyce Appleby's "The Social Origins of American Revolutionary Ideology," *Journal of American History*, 64 (1978), 935–958.

The influence of Bailyn's studies was widespread. A number of key volumes have analyzed the impact of English opposition Whig thought upon the Revolution. Most notable is Gordon S. Wood, *The Creation of the American Republic, 1776–1787* (Chapel Hill, N.C., 1969), which focuses much more than Bailyn does on the years following the Declaration of Independence. Also important are Pauline Maier, *From Resistance to Revolution: Colonial Radicals and the Development of American Opposition to Britain, 1765–1776* (New York, 1972), Richard D. Brown, *Revolutionary Politics in Massachusetts: The Boston Committee of Correspondence and the Towns, 1772–1774* (Cambridge, Mass., 1970), and Mary Beth Norton, *The British-Americans: The Loyalist Exiles in England, 1774–1789* (Boston, 1972). Maier assesses patterns of crowd violence within the context of Whiggism. Brown and Norton, likewise, employ the same framework to look respectively at the structures of local committees of opposition in Massachusetts and at the loyalists who left America forever for England. Jack P. Greene, however, in *The Quest for Power: The Lower Houses of Assembly in the Southern Royal Colonies, 1689–1776* (Chapel Hill, N.C., 1963), has placed greater emphasis upon the prerogative tradition as a source of American defiance. Greene and Bailyn debated the issue as part of Greene's "Political Mimesis: A Consideration of the Historical and Cultural Roots of Legislative Behavior in the British Colonies in the Eighteenth Century," *American Historical Review*, 75 (1969), 337–367.

Recent scholarship has not consistently followed either one of the well-established historiographical schools. Rather, most scholars have attempted to move beyond the conflict or consensus interpretations, even though almost all recent interpretive efforts owe their underpinnings to these two schools. For instance, the "New Left" school has some roots in the conflict tradition. Its thrust is toward a better understanding of specific groups of poorer people in early America, as well as toward a more carefully drawn economic interpretation of historical causation. Essays by Staughton Lynd, collected in *Class Conflict, Slavery, and the United States Constitution* (Indianapolis, Ind., 1967), and by Jesse Lemisch, including "The American Revolution Seen from the Bottom up," *Towards a New Past: Dissenting Essays in American History* (ed. B. J. Bernstein, New York, 1968), 3–45, and "Jack Tar in the Streets: Merchant Seamen in the Politics of Revolutionary America," *William and Mary Quarterly*, 3rd Ser., 25 (1968), 371–407, set the tone. Along with Bernard Friedman, "The Shaping of the Radical Consciousness in Provincial New York," *Journal of American History*, 56 (1970), 781–801, these historians, working within a quasi-Marxist framework, underscored the point that lumping all of the people of the Revolution together in one pile could seriously distort the reality of change and the reasons for it. In this context, it is also important to look at the anticonsensus presentations of Marc Egnal and Joseph A. Ernst, "An Economic Interpretation of the American Revolution," *William and Mary Quarterly*, 3rd Ser., 29 (1972), 3–32; Joseph A. Ernst, *Money and Politics in America, 1755–1775: A Study in the Currency Act of 1764 and the Political Economy of Revolution* (Chapel Hill, N.C., 1973); Eric Foner, *Tom Paine and Revolutionary America* (New York, 1976); the collected essays in *The American Revolution: Explorations in the History of American Radicalism* (ed. A. F. Young, De Kalb, Ill., 1976); and Philip S. Foner, *Labor and the American Revolution* (Westport, Conn., 1976).

No agreement, in noting the differences between consensus and anticonsensus writings, has yet been reached about the goals and motivations of the people who participated in mob activities. Earlier thinking, as reflected in R. S. Longley's "Mob Activities in Revolutionary Massachusetts," *New England Quarterly*, 6 (1933), 98–130, relied upon the interpretive framework of the French social psychologist, Gustave Le Bon, as presented in *The Crowd: A Study of the Popular Mind* (London, 1909). Le Bon's mobs were mindless, irrational collections of people easily manipulated by willful, scheming leaders. Modern scholars of crowd behavior have reached diametrically opposed conclusions. For instance, in George Rudé's *The Crowd in History, 1730–1848* (New York, 1964), or in E. P. Thompson's "The Moral Economy of the English Crowd in the Eighteenth Century," *Past & Present*, 50 (1971), 76–136, preindustrial crowds appear to be purposeful in organization, protective of vital group interests, discriminating in their selection of targets, and not unnecessarily destructive in the defense of group grievances.

Since the mid 1960s, those scholars who have written about violence in the Revolution have worked largely within the Rudé-Thompson framework. However, the composition of American crowds, as well as the focus of their aims and goals, have been described in two fundamentally different ways. Gordon S. Wood, following up on Rudé, in "A Note On Mobs in the American Revolution," *William and Mary Quarterly*, 3rd Ser., 23 (1966), 635–642, described prerevolutionary crowds as interested primarily in defending constitutional interests against arbitrary power. The specific implication that mob participants were fully in the economic mainstream and were defending liberty was developed more fully by Pauline Maier in "Popular Uprisings and Civil Authority in Eighteenth-Century America," *William and Mary Quarterly*, 3rd Ser., 27 (1970), 3–35, and *From Resistance to Revolution*, cited above. John Phillip Reid's *In a Defiant Stance: The Conditions of Law in Massachusetts Bay, the Irish Comparison, and the Coming of the American Revolution* (University Park, Pa., 1977), carried forward central consensus themes within a much needed comparative dimension.

Scholars in the New Left tradition have disagreed. Building upon Jesse Lemisch's "Jack Tar in the Streets," cited above, these historians have emphasized the conditions producing potential class conflict, and they argue that the crowds consisted largely of poor people who were protesting against an absence of economic opportunity and political liberty in their own lives as much as anything else. See in particular Edward Countryman, "The Problem of the Early American Crowd," *Journal of American Studies*, 7 (1973), 77–90; John K. Alexander, "The Fort Wilson Incident of 1779: A Case Study of the Revolutionary Crowd," *William and Mary Quarterly*, 3rd Ser., 31 (1974), 589–612; Gary B. Nash, "Social Change and the Growth of Prerevolutionary Urban Radicalism," A. F. Young, ed., *The American Revolution*, cited above, 5–36; Dirk Hoerder, "Boston Leaders and Boston Crowds, 1765–1776," *ibid.*, 235–271; Hoerder, *Crowd Action in Revolutionary Massachusetts, 1765–1780* (New York, 1977); and Alfred F. Young, *The Crowd and the Coming of the American Revolution: From Ritual to Rebellion in America, 1745–1776* (New York, forthcoming).

Over the years, a number of important monographs have appeared dealing with specific topics touching upon Revolutionary crowds and violence. Although they do not necessarily fall into any one historiographical camp, the following should be examined: Irving Mark, *Agrarian Conflicts in Colonial New York* (New York, 1940); Richard Walsh, *Charleston's Sons of Liberty: A Study of the Artisans, 1763–1789* (Columbia, S.C., 1959); Edmund S. and Helen M. Morgan, *The Stamp Act Crisis: Prologue to Revolution* (rev. ed., New York, 1962); Richard Maxwell Brown, *The South Carolina Regulators* (Cambridge, Mass., 1963); Benjamin Woods Labaree, *The Boston Tea Party* (New York, 1964); Hiller B. Zobel, *The Boston Massacre* (New York, 1970); Patricia U.

Bonomi, *A Factious People: Politics and Society in Colonial New York* (New York, 1971); Charles S. Olton, *Artisans for Independence: Philadelphia Mechanics and the American Revolution* (Syracuse, N.Y., 1975); Roger J. Champagne, *Alexander McDougall and the American Revolution in New York* (Schenectady, N.Y., 1975); and Richard Maxwell Brown, *Strain of Violence: Historical Studies of American Violence and Vigilantism* (New York, 1975), 37–90.

Beyond the explorations of New Left historians, a second major scholarly thrust since the mid 1960s has been the efforts of social and political historians who have searched through such nontraditional but quantifiable sources as tax lists, wills, deeds, and church and town records in attempting to reconstruct the actual conditions of life of the denizens of early America. Most newer studies have concluded that property was becoming less evenly distributed as the Revolution approached. Jackson Turner Main, in *The Social Structure of Revolutionary America* (Princeton, N.J., 1965), maintained that the Revolution arrested the trend toward extremes in wealth and poverty, extremes that had been described as virtually nonexistent by Robert E. and B. Katherine Brown (cited above) in their formulation of a prerevolutionary democratic utopia, as well as by Richard Hofstadter in *America at 1750: A Social Portrait* (New York, 1971).

Quantitative studies, however, have by and large demonstrated that there was little movement toward a more equalitarian pattern of wealth distribution, even during the Revolutionary period itself. On this critical point, the following studies are among the most essential: Aubrey C. Land, "Economic Base and Social Structure: The Northern Chesapeake in the Eighteenth Century," *Journal of Economic History*, 25 (1965), 639–654; James A. Henretta, "Economic Development and Social Structure in Colonial Boston," *William and Mary Quarterly*, 3rd Ser., 22 (1965), 75–92; James T. Lemon and Gary B. Nash, "The Distribution of Wealth in Eighteenth-Century America: A Century of Change in Chester County, Pennsylvania, 1693–1802," *Journal of Social History*, 2 (1968), 1–24; Allan Kulikoff, "The Progress of Inequality in Revolutionary Boston," *William and Mary Quarterly*, 3rd Ser., 28 (1971), 375–412; Douglas Lamar Jones, "The Strolling Poor: Transiency in Eighteenth-Century Massachusetts," *Journal of Social History*, 8 (1975), 28–54; Gary B. Nash, "Urban Wealth and Poverty in Pre-Revolutionary America," *Journal of Interdisciplinary History*, 6 (1976), 545–584; Nash, "Poverty and Poor Relief in Pre-Revolutionary Philadelphia," *William and Mary Quarterly*, 3rd Ser., 33 (1976), 3–30; and Gregory A. Stiverson, *Poverty in a Land of Plenty: Tenancy in Eighteenth-Century Maryland* (Baltimore, Md., 1978).

Not all scholars employing quantitative methods have concluded that the poor were getting poorer while the wealthy were becoming wealthier. In particular, G. B. Warden has questioned the findings of Nash and Henretta in two essays, "Inequality and Instability in Eighteenth-Century Boston: A

Reappraisal," *Journal of Interdisciplinary History*, 6 (1976), 585–620, and "The Distribution of Property in Boston, 1692–1775," *Perspectives in American History*, 10 (1976), 81–128. Also important is the work by Sung Bok Kim, *Landlord and Tenant in Colonial New York: Manorial Society, 1664–1775* (Chapel Hill, N.C., 1978). Depending upon the locale, the age of settlements, and the rate of urbanization, the poor (whose numbers were far more substantial than consensus historians have conceded) at best had a difficult time of it—before, during, and after the Revolution. Regional variations in rates of wealth is one analytical factor in Kenneth A. Lockridge's "Social Change and the Meaning of the American Revolution," *Journal of Social History*, 6 (1973), 403–439, a synthesis of important quantitative studies.

The weight of recent scholarship demonstrates there were severe limits to socioeconomic opportunity in prerevolutionary America (as the conflict historians asserted but never specifically proved); nor did the Revolution dramatically change that pattern. Unlike Becker, Jameson, and others, who saw a linear relationship between the unfolding of the Revolution and the rise of the masses, some recent historians have not been so certain that the Revolution immediately generated new levels of socioeconomic, political, or legal opportunities for the masses. In *Men in Rebellion: Higher Governmental Leaders and the Coming of the American Revolution* (New Brunswick, N.J., 1973), James Kirby Martin concluded that the transfer of power at the highest levels of government occurred within the political elite, a process from which the people eventually benefited, but not necessarily because many Revolutionary leaders wanted it that way. As this volume describes it, increasing opportunities for everyday citizens came about as much from inadvertence and historical chance as from a deep commitment to an enlargement of the rights of mankind. Particularly important in this vein are Jackson Turner Main's two studies, "Government by the People: The American Revolution and the Democratization of the Legislatures," *William and Mary Quarterly*, 3rd Ser., 23 (1966), 391–407, and *The Upper House in Revolutionary America, 1763–1788* (Madison, Wisc., 1967), and Merrill Jensen's "The American People and the American Revolution," *Journal of American History*, 57 (1970), 5–35.

In regard to opportunity in Revolutionary America, recent scholarship has also been careful to relate that concept to specific groups in the population. As a third trend, there has been an intensification of the study of such groups as black slaves, women, and the poor. In "Land of the Unfree: Legal Limitations on Liberty in Pre-Revolutionary America," *Maryland Historical Magazine*, 68 (1973), 355–368, Linda Grant De Pauw argues that the Revolution produced few gains in legal or human rights for any of these groups. By comparison, Benjamin Quarles, *The Negro in the American Revolution* (Chapel Hill, N.C., 1961), stresses improvements for the black community, even if more in terms of potential rather than real advances. Similarly, many other studies have shown linkages between Enlightenment ideals, the Revolution's concern about political liberty, and the beginnings of antislavery sentiment, which resulted in successful statewide emancipation efforts in the North. Of particular importance in exploring these themes are the following: Winthrop D. Jordan, *White Over Black: American Attitudes Toward the Negro, 1550–1812* (Chapel Hill, N.C., 1968); Duncan J. MacLeod, *Slavery, Race, and the American Revolution* (New York, 1974); and David Brion Davis, *The Problem of Slavery in the Age of Revolution, 1770–1823* (Ithaca, N.Y., 1975). Jordan and MacLeod suggest that the Revolution and its ideals had the potential to overwhelm slavery, but many other scholars disagree, including not only David Brion Davis, but also Robert M. McColley, *Slavery and Jeffersonian Virginia,* (Urbana, Ill., 1964); Donald L. Robinson, *Slavery in the Structure of American Politics, 1765–1820* (New York, 1971); and Gerald W. Mullin, *Flight and Rebellion: Slave Resistance in Eighteenth-Century Virginia* (New York, 1972). Fredrika T. Schmidt and Barbara R. Wilhelm, "Early Proslavery Petitions in Virginia," *William and Mary Quarterly*, 3rd Ser., 30 (1973), 133–146, show that many Virginians remained deeply committed to slavery during the Revolution, even to the point of petitioning against a state law of 1782 permitting private acts of manumission.

Similar scholarly concern has been shown in the words and deeds of the Founding Fathers with regard to slavery. The debate has focused primarily on Thomas Jefferson, but it has also spilled over into an analysis of the intentions of the authors of the Constitution. William Cohen, in "Thomas Jefferson and the Problem of Slavery," *Journal of American History*, 56 (1969), 503–526, argues that Jefferson had deep-seated racial prejudices which undermined his push for emancipation. By comparison, William W. Freehling, in "The Founding Fathers and Slavery," *American Historical Review*, 77 (1972), 81–93, claims that the constitution makers of 1787 attacked slavery where they could, such as by providing for the taxation of imported Africans and for the eventual termination of the slave trade to the United States. The Founding Fathers also hoped that time and other circumstances would produce the eventual destruction of the peculiar institution. Edmund S. Morgan, in *American Slavery—American Freedom: The Ordeal of Colonial Virginia* (New York, 1975), searches for a resolution of the haunting paradox of why slavery and freedom developed simultaneously in the early American experience.

Until recently, the literature on American women in the early period has been quite limited in quantity, if not in scope. During the nineteenth and early twentieth centuries those who wrote about provincial women cast their subjects as genteel, "ladylike" figures. Typical are Elizabeth F. Ellet, *The Women of the American Revolution* (3 vols., New York, 1853–1854); Elisabeth Anthony Dexter, *Colonial Women of Affairs* (2nd ed., Boston, 1931); Elizabeth Cometti, "Women in the American Revolution," *New England Quarterly*, 20

(1947), 329–346; and Walter Hart Blumenthal, *Women Camp Followers of the American Revolution* (Philadelphia, 1952). Exceptions are Mary Sumner Benson, *Women in Eighteenth-Century America: A Study of Opinion and Social Usage* (New York, 1935); and Julia C. Spruill, *Women's Life and Work in the Southern Colonies* (Chapel Hill, N.C., 1938).

Recent studies have rejected the tradition of gentility and have tried to get at the roles of various groupings of women in the Revolution. Noteworthy are John Todd White's "The Truth About Molly Pitcher," *The American Revolution: Whose Revolution?* (ed. J. K. Martin and K. R. Stubaus, New York, 1977), 99–105; Mary Beth Norton's "Eighteenth-Century American Women in Peace and War: The Case of the Loyalists," *William and Mary Quarterly*, 3rd Ser., 33 (1976), 386–409; and Linda Kerber's "Daughters of Columbia: Educating Women for the Republic, 1787–1805," *The Hofstadter Aegis: A Memorial* (ed. Stanley Elkins and Eric McKitrick, New York, 1974), 36–59. The latter is quite important with respect to exploring the concept of "republican motherhood," or women serving as the bearers of sons trained faithfully to serve the republican order.

Other studies have looked at patterns beginning in the early days of settlement and extending into the nineteenth century and have questioned, among other issues, the standard notion that some women, especially widows, had unusual freedom in colonial America. On this and other key points, important investigations are Carol R. Berkin, *Within the Conjurer's Circle: Women in Colonial America* (Morristown, N.J., 1974); Alexander Keyssar, "Widowhood in Eighteenth-Century Massachusetts: A Problem in the History of the Family," *Perspectives in American History*, 8 (1974), 83–119; the first three chapters in Mary P. Ryan, *Womanhood in America: From Colonial Times to the Present* (New York, 1975); and Joan Hoff Wilson, "The Illusion of Change: Women and the American Revolution," A. F. Young, ed., *The American Revolution*, 385–444. In these studies, the changing status of women has been explained more as a function of social, demographic, and familial patterns in preindustrial America than in terms of factors related to the Revolution.

This point reflects the doubts of some scholars about the presumed radicalizing nature of the Revolution. Such doubts relate to a fourth recent trend in historiography—a mounting interest in exploring the psychological nature of the Revolution. A number of historians have suggested the possibility that colonial Americans were caught up in a serious identity crisis on the eve of independence. While provincial society was becoming more anglicized during the eighteenth century, and while Americans were ever more eager to ape English styles, habits, and ideals, they found themselves being increasingly treated as rude bumpkins by the leaders of British government and society. In various ways, the following essays explore this phenomenon, which may have been critical to a rejection of the parent state:

Jack P. Greene, "Search for Identity: An Interpretation of the Meaning of Selected Patterns of Social Response in Eighteenth-Century America," *Journal of Social History*, 3 (1970), 189–220; John M. Murrin, "The Legal Transformation: The Bench and Bar of Eighteenth-Century Massachusetts," *Essays in Politics and Social Development: Colonial America* (ed. S. N. Katz, Boston, 1971), 415–449; Jack P. Greene, "An Uneasy Connection: An Analysis of the Preconditions of the American Revolution," *Essays on the American Revolution* (ed. S. G. Kurtz and J. H. Hutson, Chapel Hill, N.C., 1973), 32–80; Rowland Berthoff and John M. Murrin, "Feudalism, Communalism, and the Yeoman Freeholder: The American Revolution Considered as a Social Accident," *ibid.*, 256–288; and Robert M. Weir, "Who Shall Rule at Home: The American Revolution as a Crisis of Legitimacy for the Colonial Elite," *Journal of Interdisciplinary History* 6 (1976), 679–700.

A second trend in social-psychological analysis has been to explore relationships within a Freudian context, which involve the elements of a mother country, the king as a father figure, and provincial citizens as maturing adolescents locked in oedipal turmoil. This theme has been explored in Winthrop D. Jordan, "Familial Politics: Thomas Paine and the Killing of the King, 1776, "*Journal of American History*, 60 (1973), 294–308, which should be supplemented by Edwin G. Burroughs and Michael Wallace, "The American Revolution: The Ideology and Psychology of National Liberation," *Perspectives in American History*, 6 (1972), 167–306, and Bruce Mazlich, "Leadership in the American Revolution: The Psychological Dimension," *Leadership in the American Revolution* (comp. E. H. Kegan, Washington, 1974), 113–133. Others have looked at individual lives, hoping to establish linkages between child-rearing patterns and adult behavior, on a scale from prerevolutionary to loyalist. Among the more venturesome studies are Fawn M. Brodie, *Thomas Jefferson: An Intimate History* (New York, 1974), Kenneth S. Lynn, *A Divided People* (Westport, Conn., 1977), and Philip Greven, *The Protestant Temperament: Patterns of Child-Rearing, Religious Experience, and the Self in Early America* (New York, 1977). In turn, these studies should be compared to the approach in analysis found in William B. Willcox and Frederick Wyatt, "Sir Henry Clinton: A Psychological Exploration in History," *William and Mary Quarterly*, 3rd Ser., 16 (1959), 3–26, as well as the full biographical version by Willcox, *Portrait of a General: Sir Henry Clinton in the War of Independence* (New York, 1964).

Particular emphases, whether social, political, psychological, or demographic, come and go as the scholarly literature on the Revolution continues to grow. As a fifth important pattern, then, a great number of studies have not emphasized particular methodologies or historiographical schools, but have certainly deepened and enriched our comprehension of many aspects of the

Revolutionary epoch. On the British side, the work of Sir Lewis Namier on the realities of British politics in the eighteenth century has profoundly influenced a host of studies, which have not only detailed the British world of power, influence, and corruption, but have also shown how American interests fared in such a setting. Besides Namier's two classics, *The Structure of Politics at the Accession of George III* (2nd ed., London, 1957), and *England in the Age of the American Revolution* (2nd ed., London, 1961), the following are quite important: Richard Pares, *King George III and the Politicians* (London, 1953); G. H. Guttridge, *English Whiggism and the American Revolution* (Berkeley, Cal., 1942); I. R. Christie, *Crisis of Empire: Great Britain and the American Colonies, 1754–1783* (New York, 1966); John Derry, *English Politics and the American Revolution* (London, 1976); Franklin B. Wickwire, *British Subministers and Colonial America, 1763–1783* (Princeton, N.J., 1966); P. D. G. Thomas, *British Politics and the Stamp Act Crisis: The First Phase of the American Revolution, 1763–1767* (New York, 1975); John Brooke and Lewis Namier, *Charles Townshend* (London, 1964); B. D. Bargar, *Lord Dartmouth and the American Revolution* (Columbia, S.C., 1965); Bernard Donoughue, *British Politics and the American Revolution: The Path to War, 1773–1775* (London, 1964); Colin Bonwick, *English Radicals and the American Revolution* (Chapel Hill, N.C., 1977); Alan Valentine, *Lord North* (2 vols., Norman, Okla., 1967); and Ian R. Christie, *The End of North's Ministry, 1780–1782* (London, 1958).

An unusually rich investigation of the turbulence of British politics, factional differences in the American provinces, and the relationship between political instability in England and tension in America is found in Merrill Jensen's *The Founding of a Nation: A History of the American Revolution, 1763–1776* (New York, 1968). Besides several other volumes cited already, the following are particularly helpful in assessing aspects of the dawning Revolution: Bernhard Knollenberg, *Origin of the American Revolution, 1759–1766* (rev. ed., New York, 1965); Knollenberg, *Growth of the American Revolution, 1766–1775* (New York, 1975); Ian R. Christie and Benjamin W. Labaree, *Empire or Independence, 1760–1776: A British-American Dialogue on the Coming of the American Revolution* (New York, 1976); John A. Neuenschwander, *The Middle Colonies and the Coming of the American Revolution* (Port Washington, N.Y., 1974); Michael G. Kammen, *A Rope of Sand: The Colonial Agents, British Politics, and the American Revolution* (Ithaca, N.Y., 1968); H. Trevor Colbourn, *The Lamp of Experience: Whig History and the Intellectual Origins of the American Revolution* (Chapel Hill, N.C., 1965); J. R. Pole, *Political Representation in England and the Origins of the American Revolution* (New York, 1966); Arthur M. Schlesinger, Sr., *Prelude to Independence: The Newspaper War on Britain, 1764–1776* (New York, 1958); Carl Ubbelohde, *The Vice-Admiralty Courts and the American Revolution* (Chapel Hill, N.C., 1960); David Ammerman, *In the Common Cause:*

American Response to the Coercive Acts of 1774 (Charlottesville, Va., 1974); and Neil R. Stout, *The Perfect Crisis: The Beginning of the Revolutionary War* (New York, 1976).

Several valuable state and local studies have appeared in recent years, all of which have added substantially to our knowledge about the causes of the Revolution. Particularly significant are Jere R. Daniell, *Experiment in Republicanism: New Hampshire Politics and the American Revolution, 1741–1794* (Cambridge, Mass., 1970); Stephen E. Patterson, *Political Parties in Revolutionary Massachusetts* (Madison, Wisc., 1973); Robert A. Gross, *The Minutemen and Their World* (New York, 1976); David S. Lovejoy, *Rhode Island Politics and the American Revolution, 1760–1776* (Providence, R.I., 1958); Oscar Zeichner, *Connecticut's Years of Controversy, 1750–1776* (Chapel Hill, N.C., 1949); Christopher Collier, *Roger Sherman's Connecticut: Yankee Politics and the American Revolution* (Middletown, Conn., 1971); Alfred F. Young, *The Democratic Republicans of New York: The Origins, 1763–1797* (Chapel Hill, N.C., 1967); Bernard Mason, *The Road to Independence: The Revolutionary Movement in New York, 1773–1777* (Lexington, Ky., 1966); Larry R. Gerlach, *Prologue to Independence: New Jersey in the Coming of the American Revolution* (New Brunswick, N.J., 1976); James T. Lemon, *The Best Poor Man's Country: A Geographical Study of Early Southeastern Pennsylvania* (Baltimore, Md., 1972); David Hawke, *In the Midst of a Revolution* (Philadelphia, 1962); Stephen E. Lucas, *Portents of Rebellion: Rhetoric and Revolution in Philadelphia, 1765–1776* (Philadelphia, 1976); Richard A. Ryerson, *The Revolution is Now Begun: The Radical Committees of Philadelphia, 1765–1776* (Philadelphia, 1978); David Curtis Skaggs, *Roots of Maryland Democracy, 1753–1776* (Westport, Conn., 1973); Ronald Hoffman, *A Spirit of Dissension: Economics, Politics, and the Revolution in Maryland* (Baltimore, Md., 1974); Jack P. Greene, *et al.*, *Society, Freedom, and Conscience: The American Revolution in Virginia, Massachusetts, and New York* (ed. R. M. Jellison, New York, 1976); George M. Curtis, III, "The Role of the Courts in the Making of the Revolution in Virginia," *The Human Dimensions of Nation Making: Essays on Colonial and Revolutionary America* (ed. J. K. Martin, Madison, Wisc., 1976), 121–146; H. Roy Merrens, *Colonial North Carolina in the Eighteenth Century: A Study in Historical Geography* (Chapel Hill, N.C., 1964); M. Eugene Sirmans, *Colonial South Carolina: A Political History, 1663–1763* (Chapel Hill, N.C., 1966); Robert M. Weir, " 'The Harmony We Were Famous For': An Interpretation of Pre-Revolutionary South Carolina Politics," *William and Mary Quarterly*, 3rd Ser., 26 (1969), 473–501; W. W. Abbot, *The Royal Governors of Georgia, 1754–1775* (Chapel Hill, N.C., 1959); and Kenneth Coleman, *The American Revolution in Georgia* (Athens, Ga., 1958).

With respect to military aspects of the Revolution, there are primarily two kinds of literature. The first has focused largely on the ebb and flow of battles and campaigns. Particularly good works are John R. Alden, *The American*

Revolution, 1775–1783 (New York, 1954); John S. Pancake, *1777, The Year of the Hangman* (University, Ala., 1977); Howard H. Peckham, *The War for Independence: A Military History* (Chicago, 1958); Marshall Smelser, *The Winning of Independence* (Chicago, 1972); and Willard M. Wallace, *Appeal to Arms: A Military History of the American Revolution* (New York, 1951). The second type has looked at the war in terms of the goals, ideals, aspirations, and institutions of eighteenth-century British and American society. Essential writings include the collected essays of John Shy in *A People Numerous and Armed: Reflections on the Military Struggle for American Independence* (New York, 1976), as well as his *Toward Lexington: The Role of the British Army in the Coming of the American Revolution* (Princeton, N.J., 1965). From the British side, basic volumes include Eric Robson, *The American Revolution in Its Political and Military Aspects, 1763–1783* (New York, 1955); *George Washington's Opponents: British Generals and Admirals in the American Revolution* (ed. G. A. Billias, New York, 1969); Piers Mackesy, *The War for America, 1775–1783,* (Cambridge, Mass., 1965); David Syrett, *Shipping and the American War, 1775–1783: A Study of British Transport Organization* (London, 1970); R. Arthur Bowler, *Logistics and the Failure of the British Army in America, 1775–1783* (Princeton, N.J., 1975); Ira D. Gruber, *The Howe Brothers and the American Revolution* (New York, 1972); and R. Ernest Dupuy *et al., The American Revolution: A Global War* (New York, 1977). From the American side, seminal studies include Don Higginbotham, *The War of American Independence: Military Attitudes, Policies, and Practice, 1763–1789* (New York, 1971); *George Washington's Generals* (ed. G. A. Billias, New York, 1964); Jonathan G. Rossie, *The Politics of Command in the American Revolution* (Syracuse, N.Y., 1975); and Richard H. Kohn, *Eagle and Sword: The Federalists and the Creation of the Military Establishment in America, 1783–1802* (New York, 1975).

Very much related to the war effort were the diplomatic thrusts undertaken in Europe as well as relations with western Indian tribes. On the former subject, the standard treatments are Samuel Flagg Bemis, *The Diplomacy of the American Revolution* (New York, 1935); Richard B. Morris, *The Peacemakers: The Great Powers and American Independence* (New York, 1965); William C. Stinchcombe, *The American Revolution and the French Alliance* (Syracuse, N.Y., 1969); and Jonathan R. Dull, *The French Navy and American Independence: A Study of Arms and Diplomacy, 1774–1787* (Princeton, N.J., 1975). On the latter subject, Barbara Graymont, *The Iroquois in the American Revolution* (Syracuse, N.Y., 1972), and James H. O'Donnell, III, *Southern Indians in the American Revolution* (Knoxville, Tenn., 1973), represent basic starting points.

One aspect of the military problem was the role of the loyalists. Historians have had much trouble in trying to conclude why some persons joined and led a rebellion, when so many others remained neutral or loyal to the Empire. The most revealing volumes in the modern literature are William H. Nelson's

The American Tory (New York, 1961); Wallace Brown's two volumes, *The King's Friends: The Composition and Motives of the American Loyalist Claimants* (Providence, R.I., 1965), and *The Good Americans: The Loyalists in the American Revolution* (New York, 1969); Paul H. Smith's *Loyalists and Redcoats: A Study in British Revolutionary Policy* (Chapel Hill, N.C., 1964); William A. Benton's *Whig-Loyalism: An Aspect of Political Ideology in the American Revolutionary Era* (Rutherford, N.J., 1969); Mary Beth Norton's *The British-Americans,* cited above; Bernard Bailyn's *The Ordeal of Thomas Hutchinson* (Cambridge, Mass., 1974); and Robert McCluer Calhoon's *The Loyalists in Revolutionary America, 1760–1781* (New York, 1973).

If the loyalists have proved to be an enigmatic group, the decade of the 1780s has perhaps been even more difficult to comprehend. So much of the literature on the Confederation period draws in one way or another on Charles A. Beard's *An Economic Interpretation of the Constitution of the United States,* cited above. Beard saw in the process of national constitution making a greater concern for protection of certain kinds of property than anything else. Likewise, he suggested that the Constitution of 1787 acted as a counterweight to the seeming spread of human rights often associated with the flowering of the Revolution. In *The Articles of Confederation* and *The New Nation,* cited above, Merrill Jensen argued that the Articles represented an institutionalized expression of faith in the principles of the Declaration of Independence, whereas the Constitution of 1787 came from a sophisticated nationalist drive against localist forces.

During the 1950s a number of volumes in the consensus mold boldly sought to negate these conclusions, including Robert E. Brown, *Charles Beard and the Constitution* (Princeton, N.J., 1956), Forrest McDonald, *We the People: The Economic Origins of the Constitution* (Chicago, 1958), and Lee Benson, *Turner and Beard: American Historical Writing Reconsidered* (Glencoe, Ill., 1960). Simultaneously, this group was challenged by Jackson Turner Main, whose *The Antifederalists: Critics of the Constitution, 1781–1788* (Chapel Hill, N.C., 1961), explored the relationship between the degree of an individual's market orientation and the likelihood of supporting or condemning the Constitution. Also, E. James Ferguson, in *The Power of the Purse: A History of American Public Finance, 1776–1790* (Chapel Hill, N.C., 1961), found a positive relationship between holding certain kinds of securities and political behavior during the Confederation period.

Since the 1960s, the trend has been toward understanding the Constitution of 1787 as a fulfillment, rather than a rejection, of the ideals of the Revolution. This trend represents a return to a non-Beardian focus and demonstrates greater concern with the distribution of power and authority between state and nation than with the issue of property interests. Pioneering studies of lasting value include Andrew C. McLaughlin, *The Confederation and the Constitution, 1783–1789* (New York, 1905); Max Farrand, *The Framing of the Constitution of the United States* (New Haven, Conn., 1913); and Charles Warren, *The Making of the Constitution* (Boston, 1928). Recent publications which emphasize other factors besides property holdings are Robert A. Rutland, *The Birth of the Bill of Rights, 1776–1791* (Chapel Hill, N.C., 1955); Cecelia M. Kenyon, "Men of Little Faith: The Anti-Federalists on the Nature of Representative Government," *William and Mary Quarterly*, 3rd Ser., 12 (1955), 3–43; John P. Roche, "The Founding Fathers: A Reform Caucus in Action," *American Political Science Review*, 55 (1961), 799–816; Stanley M. Elkins and Eric McKitrick, "The Founding Fathers: Young Men of the Revolution," *Political Science Quarterly*, 76 (1961), 181–216; Forrest McDonald, *E Pluribus Unum: The Formation of the American Republic, 1776–1790* (Boston, 1965); Clinton Rossiter, *1787: The Grand Convention* (New York, 1966); Gordon S. Wood, *The Creation of the American Republic*, cited above; and the essays by Douglass Adair, collected in *Fame and the Founding Fathers* (ed. H. T. Colbourn, New York, 1974).

Others have pushed toward a fuller analysis of the Confederation period, but no interpretive synthesis has yet been achieved. Some studies reflect more directly the theme of conflict, such as Jackson Turner Main's two books, *The Sovereign States, 1775–1783* (New York, 1973), and *Political Parties before the Constitution* (Chapel Hill, N.C., 1973); Joseph L. Davis's *Sectionalism in American Politics, 1774–1787* (Madison, Wisc., 1977); Van Beck Hall's *Politics Without Parties: Massachusetts, 1780–1791* (Pittsburgh, Pa., 1972); and John P. Kaminski's "Democracy Run Rampant: Rhode Island in the Confederation," J. K. Martin, ed., *The Human Dimensions of Nation Making*, cited above. Those adhering more closely to the consensus approach are H. James Henderson, *Party Politics in the Continental Congress* (New York, 1974); Frederick W. Marks, III, *Independence on Trial: Foreign Affairs and the Making of the Constitution* (Baton Rouge, La., 1973); and Irwin H. Polishook, *Rhode Island and the Union, 1774–1795* (Evanston, Ill., 1969).

The transition from the Confederation to the early national period and its consequences with respect to the emergence of a democratic ethos in the United States has normally been treated as an aspect of national party formation. On the first party system, recent studies of consequence include Joseph Charles, *The Origins of the American Party System: Three Essays* (Chapel Hill, N.C., 1956); Noble E. Cunningham, Jr., *The Jeffersonian Republicans: The Formation of Party Organization, 1789–1801* (Chapel Hill, N.C., 1957); William N. Chambers, *Political Parties in a New Nation: The American Experience, 1776–1809* (New York, 1963); David Hackett Fischer, *The Revolution of American Conservatism: The Federalist Party in the Era of Jeffersonian Democracy* (New York, 1965); Richard Hofstadter, *The Idea of a Party System: The Rise of Legitimate Opposition in the United States, 1780–1840* (Berkeley, Cal., 1969); James M. Banner, Jr., *To the Hartford Convention: The Federalists and the Origins of Party Politics in Massachusetts, 1789–1815* (New York, 1970); Richard Buel, Jr., *Securing the Revolution: Ideology in American Politics, 1789–1815* (Ithaca, N.Y., 1972); Lance Banning, "Republican Ideology and the Triumph of the Constitution, 1789 to 1793," *William and Mary Quarterly*, 3rd Ser., 31 (1974), 167–188; and Carl E. Prince, *The Federalists and the Origins of the U. S. Civil Service* (New York, 1978).

There are literally hundreds of excellent biographies of the leaders of the Revolutionary period. The length of this bibliography might easily be doubled if all the biographies were listed. To keep within more modest proportions, a distinction may be drawn between seminal multi-volume works and influential one-volume studies. In the former category are such books as Page Smith, *John Adams* (2 vols., Garden City, N.Y., 1962); Broadus Mitchell, *Alexander Hamilton* (3 vols., New York, 1957–1970); Dumas Malone, *Jefferson and His Time* (5 vols., Boston, 1948–1974); Irving Brant, *James Madison* (6 vols., Indianapolis, Ind., 1941–1961); James Thomas Flexner, *George Washington* (4 vols., Boston, 1965–1972); and Douglas Southall Freeman *et al.*, *George Washington: A Biography* (7 vols., New York, 1948–1958).

Among the most revealing one-volume biographies are Peter Shaw, *The Character of John Adams* (Chapel Hill, N.C., 1976); John C. Miller, *Sam Adams: Pioneer in Propaganda* (Boston, 1936); Carl Van Doren, *Benjamin Franklin: A Biography* (New York, 1938); George Athan Billias, *Elbridge Gerry: Founding Father and Republican Statesman* (New York, 1976); James Thomas Flexner, *The Young Hamilton: A Biography* (Boston, 1978); John C. Miller, *Alexander Hamilton: Portrait in Paradox* (New York, 1959); Richard R. Beeman, *Patrick Henry: A Biography* (New York, 1974); Bernard Bailyn, *The Ordeal of Thomas Hutchinson*, cited above; Fawn M. Brodie, *Thomas Jefferson: An Intimate History*, cited above; Merrill D. Peterson, *Thomas Jefferson and the New Nation: A Biography* (New York, 1970); Clarence L. Ver Steeg, *Robert Morris: Revolutionary Financier* (Philadelphia, 1954); David Freeman Hawke, *Paine* (New York, 1974); Don R. Gerlach, *Philip Schuyler and the American Revolution in New York, 1733–1777* (Lincoln, Neb., 1964); John H. Cary, *Joseph Warren: Physician, Politician, Patriot* (Urbana, Ill., 1961); Marcus Cunliffe, *George Washington: Man and Monument* (Boston, 1958); Bernhard Knollenberg, *George Washington: The Virginia Period, 1732–1775* (Durham, N.C., 1964); and Charles Page Smith, *James Wilson: Founding Father, 1742–1798* (Chapel Hill, N.C., 1956).

No historian stands alone. All of the studies listed in this bibliographical note and many more beyond have influenced the development of this volume.

INDEX

Academy of Sciences (France), 127
accommodationists, 83–87
Adams, Abigail, 92, 234–35
Adams (the Deacon), 45
Adams, John
  and Boston Massacre, 64
  and Boston Tea Party, 78
  and Constitutional Convention, 209
  and Continental Congresses, 83, 91,
    93–94, 99
  and independence committee, 100
  as minister to Britain, 192–94
  as minister to France, 128, 149, 151,
    153, 178
  as revolutionary, 47, 154–55, 160, 161
  quoted, 79, 92, 156, 158, 162, 234–35
Adams, Samuel
  and Battle of Lexington, 89
  and Boston Tea Party, 77, 78
  and Circular Letter, 55
  and Constitutional Convention, 209
  and Continental Congresses, 91
  and General Court, 64
  and Hutchinson, 45–46, 76
  and Port Act, 82
  as radical Revolutionary, 5, 46, 83, 158
  reactions of, 6, 58, 132, 204, 230–31
Administration of Justice Act, 80
Alamance Creek, Battle of, 160
Albany, New York, 123
Africa, 87–88
American army. *See* Continental army
American merchants, 192–93
  and committees of observation and
    inspection, 94
  and Constitutional Convention, 210,
    220
  and Impost Plan, 183–84
  and national debt, 181
  and nonimportation, 58, 82
  and regionalism, 149–52
  and Shays's Rebellion, 198–99
  and Tea Act, 75
American national debt, 187, 210, 224
  and Hamilton, 236
  and Robert Morris, 178, 181–83
American trade, 73, 127, 193, 194, 224
anarchy, 48, 202, 210, 213. *See also*
    hierarchies, opportunities,
    declining; political hierarchies;
    social poor, the; stewardship of
    the elite; wealth, concentration of
ancien régime, 125
Anglican clergy, 27
Anglicization, 20–21, 156
Annapolis Convention, 203–205
Annapolis, Maryland, 188, 203
Antifederalists, 204, 210, 230
antinationalists, 204, 210, 230
Appalachian Mountains, 12, 22, 190
Aranjuez, Convention of, 152
Aristotle, 19
Army. *See* British army, Continental
    army, French army, Prussian
    army
Arnold, Benedict, 99, 140, 142

259